AF573996

Unitarian Radicalism

Also by Stuart Andrews

EIGHTEENTH-CENTURY EUROPE

ENLIGHTENED DESPOTISM

METHODISM AND SOCIETY

THE BRITISH PERIODICAL PRESS AND THE FRENCH REVOLUTION, 1789–99

THE REDISCOVERY OF AMERICA

Unitarian Radicalism

Political Rhetoric, 1770–1814

Stuart Andrews

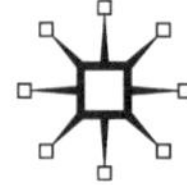

First published 2003 by
PALGRAVE MACMILLAN
Houndmills, Basingstoke, Hampshire RG21 6XS and
175 Fifth Avenue, New York, N.Y. 10010
Companies and representatives throughout the world

PALGRAVE MACMILLAN is the global academic imprint of the Palgrave Macmillan division of St. Martin's Press, LLC and of Palgrave Macmillan Ltd. Macmillan® is a registered trademark in the United States, United Kingdom and other countries. Palgrave is a registered trademark in the European Union and other countries.

ISBN 0–333–96925–1

This book is printed on paper suitable for recycling and made from fully managed and sustained forest sources.

A catalogue record for this book is available from the British Library.

Library of Congress Cataloging-in-Publication Data
Andrews, Stuart.
Unitarian radicalism : political rhetoric, 1770–1814 / Stuart Andrews.
p. cm.
Includes bibliographical references and index.
ISBN 0–333–96925–1
1. Unitarian churches—Great Britain—History—18th century.
2. Unitarians—Great Britain—Political activity—History—18th century. 3. Unitarian churches—Great Britain—History—19th century. 4. Unitarians—Great Britain—Political activity—History—19th century. I. Title.

BX9834 .A53 2002
289.1′41′09033—dc21

2002026758

10 9 8 7 6 5 4 3 2 1
12 11 10 09 08 07 06 05 04 03

Printed and bound in Great Britain by
Antony Rowe Ltd, Chippenham and Eastbourne

To the memory of Reggie Watters

The present silent propagation of truth may be likened to those causes in nature, which lie dormant for a time, but which, in proper circumstances, act with the greatest violence. We are, as it were, laying gunpowder, grain by grain, under the old building of error and superstition, which a single spark may inflame, so as to produce an instantaneous explosion; in consequence of which that edifice, the erection of which has been the work of ages, may be overturned in a moment, and so effectually as that same foundation can never be built upon again.

Joseph Priestley,
Reflections on the Present State of Free Enquiry in this country (1785)

Let not the King, let not the Prince of Wales, be surprised in this manner. Let not both Houses of Parliament be led in triumph along with him, and have law dictated to them by the Constitutional, Revolution and Unitarian Societies. These insect reptiles, whilst they go on caballing and toasting, only fill us with disgust; if they go above their natural size, and increase the quantity, whilst they keep the quality, of their venom, they become objects of the greatest terror. A spider in his natural size is only a spider, ugly and loathsome; and his flimsy net is only fit for catching flies. But, good God! Suppose a spider as large as an ox, and that he spread cables about us; all the wilds of Africa would not procure anything so dreadful.

Edmund Burke,
Speech on the Petition of the Unitarians (1792)

Contents

Preface

Edmund Burke famously dismissed Richard Price and his fellow-Dissenters as 'half a dozen grasshoppers under a fern'. Yet within a year of Price's death, Burke spoke in Parliament denouncing the Unitarians as a threat to the constitution. *Was* Unitarian Radicalism significant as a potentially destabilizing force? This study tries to answer that question by examining the confrontational rhetoric of Unitarians and the political establishment, as reflected in pamphlets, published sermons and parliamentary debates.

William Godwin's diary records ten Dissenting 'revolutionists' (apart from Price) who attended the London Revolution Society's celebratory dinner on 4 November 1789. All ten were antitrinitarians: Thomas Brand Hollis, Thomas Belsham, John Disney, Andrew Kippis, Theophilus Lindsey, Capel Lofft, Abraham Rees, Robert Robinson, Samuel Rogers and Joseph Towers. The list hardly amounts to a revolutionary army, or even a fifth column. But it is a reminder of the powerful team of 'Rational Christian' polemicists who would challenge Burke and harass Pitt throughout the 1790s and beyond.

Godwin's list of antitrinitarians excludes, besides Priestley himself, the Cambridge ex-Anglicans (Frend, Garnham and Wakefield), the Unitarian poets (Coleridge, Dyer and Anna Laetitia Barbauld) together with the Aikins (father and sons), Thomas Christie, Joseph Johnson and Richard Phillips, all of whom were active Unitarian publicists. And Godwin's list leaves out the local leaders of provincial Unitarian congregations, linked to London by something approaching a national network centred on Lindsey's Essex Street Chapel.

This well-educated, close-knit and highly articulate opposition was all the more formidable for being prolific producers of pamphlets and political sermons, and for wielding editorial control over the *New Annual Register* and many of the literary reviews. Marginalized they may have been in direct parliamentary influence, and unable to rival the political contacts enjoyed by eighteenth-century commonwealth-men like Thomas Hollis. Yet they shaped the public discourse in ways that are not always recognized.

Standing firmly within the Protestant biblical tradition, the Unitarians' outspoken hostility to the church establishment – inflamed by government refusal to ease their civil disabilities – reignited earlier anticlerical debates and was more politically significant than all the compliments that Price and Priestley heaped on the French Revolution. To claim that Pitt and Burke 'played the patriotic card' against Unitarian publicists whom they feared for other reasons, is perhaps to claim too much. Priestley's millennialist rhetoric could be seen as potentially subversive, as could his incautious use of Guy Fawkes imagery. But the effect of much of my analysis is to show how wildly inappropriate the smear of 'Jacobin' is, when applied to men whose arguments were rooted in Scripture, and who were primarily concerned with questions of Christology and eschatology.

Apart from the early scene-setting chapters, I have tried not to cover already well-worked ground. I have not retraced James Bradley's steps in his patient tracking of politically motivated Dissent in the 1770s, notably in his *Religion, Revolution and English Radicalism* (1990). I have perhaps been less successful in avoiding overlap with James Cookson's *The Friends of Peace* (1982). I have certainly leant heavily on the published and unpublished work of Grayson Ditchfield, especially on the role of Essex Street. My debt to other authorities is acknowledged in the endnotes, but I have been particularly motivated by Jonathan Clark's groundbreaking work in de-secularizing the so-called Age of Reason. Tom Paine's work of that title so alarmed Priestley that he published his response within weeks of setting foot in America.

The American thread runs through this story, which starts and ends with an American war. By extending my account to encompass the War of 1812 and the final passing of the Unitarian Relief Bill (1813), I have sought to show that the Unitarians' distinctive Christian anticlericalism (and the political opposition to which it gave rise) did not evaporate when Priestley and many of his coreligionists emigrated to the United States. The patriotic demands of defeating the 'imperial Jacobin' meant that Unitarian criticism became more muted, but there was nevertheless a continuity of anti-government rhetoric between Price of the 1770s and Belsham of the early 1800s.

There has been no full-length study of the political impact of the Unitarians since Anthony Lincoln's Prince Consort Dissertation of 1938 (*Some Political and Social Ideas of English Dissent 1763–1800*), though Knud Haakonssen has edited an important collection of essays (*Enlightenment and Religion*, 1996). Lincoln wrote: 'Perhaps England never witnessed so prominent a minority.... Priestley, Price and Robinson were quoted by indignant orators in Parliament; and every government poet strove to immortalize their damnation.' Marxist historians have tended to write them out of history, but 30 years after E. P. Thompson's best-selling *Making of the English Working Class* came the posthumous publication of his *Witness against the Beast*. Despite his antipathy to Unitarianism and to his own Methodist tradition, Thompson documents the political impact of theology in the subterranean strata of Protestant Dissent.

I must record my personal thanks for the assistance I received from the resources of Dr Williams's Library, and from the longsuffering staff of Bristol Reference Library; and also for the interest shown by Ronald Wendling of St Joseph's University, Philadelphia. But I owe a particular debt to John Walsh for his friendly encouragement over almost 50 years, for his shrewd suggestions for improving the present work and for his readiness to believe that this was a story worth telling.

Stuart Andrews

Acknowledgements

The jacket illustration of Priestley as Dr Phlogiston is reproduced by permission of the British Museum. I am grateful to Dr G. R. Ditchfield for permission to reproduce extracts from his 1968 Cambridge PhD thesis, 'Some Aspects of Unitarianism and Radicalism, 1760–1810'. Quotations from other copyright material are fully acknowledged in the endnotes, but Jenny Graham's *The Nation, The Law and The King: Reform Politics in England 1789–1799* (University Press of America: 2000) was a particular help in tracing connections between radical reformers, not least through her excellent index.

Introduction: Unequal Toleration

The Toleration Act of 1689 did not extend to Unitarians. Protestant Dissenters were required to subscribe not only to an oath of allegiance and to a newly worded oath of supremacy, but also to 35 of the Thirty-nine Articles. In the 1740s it had seemed possible that the Articles might be amended. The liberal English Presbyterian, Samuel Chandler, was then exploring a possible reunion with the Anglican establishment on the basis of abandoning the Athanasian creed, changing the Articles into 'scripture words', and perhaps even discarding the Nicene Creed, kneeling at Communion and the sign of the cross in baptism. The then Archbishop of Canterbury, Thomas Herring, seems to have responded positively, acknowledging that it was 'the impertinence of men thrusting their words into articles instead of the words of God'.[1] Hopes for such an accommodation were misplaced even in the 1750s, when perhaps one-third of the bishops could be classified as liberal in politics or latitudinarian in religion. But in the 1760s, with the Hanoverian succession secure under a young and conscientious king, the Anglican episcopate proved increasingly assertive in defending of the establishment. Thomas Secker, George III's first Archbishop of Canterbury, had been educated at a Dissenting Academy, and was influenced 'for some time' by Samuel Clarke's claim that the Trinitarian doctrine was unscriptural. But, while wishing that 'such things as we think indifferent' could be 'altered or left free in such a manner that we might all unite', Secker concluded, 'still I see no prospect of it'.[2]

Clarke's *Scripture-Doctrine of the Trinity* (1712) had precipitated a split in Dissenting ranks. In 1719, when London's Dissenting ministers met at Salters' Hall, a proposal to declare denial of the Trinity 'contrary to Scripture' was narrowly defeated. Most of the Presbyterians and General Baptists present voted against the declaration, while most Independents and Particular Baptists voted for continued insistence on Trinitarian belief.[3] But the prime concern of English Presbyterians in the first half of the century was to challenge Calvinistic teaching that only the elect could be saved. The opposing Arminian view was that predestination was conditional not absolute, and that all mankind might be saved. The issue divided Wesley from Whitefield, and in 1777 Wesley would call his new periodical the *Arminian Magazine*. Wesley remained uncompromisingly evangelical in his preaching, and uncompromisingly Tory in his politics. Yet Arminian teaching challenged not only the orthodoxy of Calvinistic Presbyterianism, but also the Anglican Articles of Religion – in particular the long Article XVII 'Of Predestination and Election'.

Unitarians offended against the very first Article, which not only asserts belief in 'one living and true God everlasting', but also affirms that 'in unity of this Godhead there be three Persons, of one substance, power and eternity; the Father, the Son and the Holy Ghost'. And the 1689 Toleration Act itself explicitly provided that its concessions did not extend to 'any person that shall deny in his Preaching or Writing the Doctrines of the Blessed Trinity as it is declared in the aforesaid Articles of Religion'.[4] The relief given to Dissenters who held to belief in the Trinity was admittedly only partial. As William Blackstone later argued, the Toleration Act did not abolish, but only suspended the penalties: 'Nonconformity is still a crime by the Laws of England and has heavy penalties annexed to it notwithstanding the Act of Toleration.' According to Blackstone, the Act expressly kept in force penalties against

> All papists, oppugners of the Trinity, and persons of no religion, and only exempts from their rigour such serious, sober-minded Dissenters as shall have taken the oaths and subscribed the declaration at the Sessions, and shall regularly repair to some licensed place of worship.[5]

The exemption did not apply if the Dissenters assembled for worship 'with the doors locked, barred or bolted', or in a meetinghouse not licensed by the bishop, archdeacon or magistrate; nor were Dissenters freed from payment of tithes or poor rates, or from serving as churchwardens and constables. Subscription to the Articles was required for any Dissenting minister or schoolmaster, as well as for those Dissenters who sought municipal or public office.[6]

The Dissenters' campaign against subscription for their ministers and schoolmasters was conducted during the 1770s, in parallel with the Cambridge campaign to release graduates and Anglican ordinands from the need to subscribe to the Articles (see Chapter 2). The Anglican campaign failed, but in 1779 Dissenting ministers and schoolmasters were allowed to substitute, in place of subscription, a solemn declaration that they believed that 'the Scriptures of the Old and New Testaments, as commonly received among Protestant Churches, do contain the revealed will of God'. This form of words, proposed by Lord North, was specifically intended to exclude antitrinitarians.[7] It left Unitarian teachers and ministers still subject to the penal statutes that had been suspended for other Dissenters; and Unitarians were also theoretically subject to the so-called Blasphemy Act of 1698, which imposed penalties on those who 'deny any one of the persons of the Holy Trinity to be God'.[8]

Though Unitarian theology became increasingly prevalent among English Presbyterians, Unitarianism did not become a separate denomination until the nineteenth century. In the 1770s, it was still merely a theological tendency, in one of its main variant forms of Socinianism or Arianism. Socinians, though acknowledging Jesus as Messiah, denied his divinity – which they could not find attested in Scripture. Arians (like Samuel Clarke) thought Christ's divinity inferior to that of the Father, while holding to the Incarnation doctrine that Jesus was both God and man. Many Unitarians made their theological progress to Socinianism through Arianism, as did Priestley himself. But others, like Price, retained their Arian beliefs until the 1790s, when they were sidelined by the Socinians' exclusive claim to the Unitarian label.[9] In the 1770s and 1780s, it was Unitarian theology in its loosest sense, rather than denominational affiliation, that drove both clergy and laymen into active political opposition. In terms of church polity, Presbyterians stood between Anglicanism and the more congregationalist assumptions of Baptists and Independents. Presbyterians thus tended to take the lead in Dissenting protest – which made their drift into Unitarianism politically significant. But Dissenters of the 1780s jointly opposed the Test and Corporation Acts, thus challenging the Anglican establishment, before events in France provided a continental cue for reform.

The closest Dissenters came to securing repeal of the Test and Corporation Acts was in 1789 when Henry Beaufoy, MP for Great Yarmouth, made his second attempt to introduce a bill for repeal, and was defeated in the Commons by a mere 20 votes. Beaufoy had first tried in 1787, when he argued that Dissenters not only had 'a right as *men* to think for themselves in matters of religion', but also 'a right as *citizens* to a common chance with their fellow subjects for offices of civil and military trust, if their sovereign shall deem them worthy of his confidence'.[10] The French *Declaration of Rights of Man and Citizen* had not yet been drafted, but a pamphlet in favour of repeal had already invoked the example of France, where 'all the enlightened sentiments of refined liberality' were at last prevailing, and where, with the Assembly of Notables in session, Protestants were 'being restored to equal privileges and opportunities with their fellow citizens'.[11] The Dissenters' committee, formed to promote repeal, similarly claimed that the times were propitious. The committee's chairman, Edward Jeffries, had not expected success at the first attempt, but he was confident that 'after a full and fair discussion of the question', public opinion in 'this enlightened and liberal age' would ensure the Dissenters' success, for '*magna est veritas et praevalebit*'. Ironically the same Latin tag would supply the caption to Gillray's *Cave of Jacobinism* as frontpiece to the first bound volume of the *Antijacobin Review*.[12]

A more immediate omen was the *Gentleman's Magazine*'s notice of Priestley's *Letter to Pitt* (1787). The reviewer claimed that Priestley's programme would purge the established church of 'all New Testament Christianity', and substitute 'that of the author of *The History of the Corruptions of Christianity* by letting Unitarians avow their principles'.[13] In the 1787 Commons debate on the Test and Corporation Acts, Pitt took the same line: 'To exclude the violent, the bulwark must be kept up against all. I am endeavouring to take every prudent and proper precaution.' The motion was lost by 176 votes to 98.[14] Beaufoy's more successful attempt in 1789 was made when the centenary celebrations of the Glorious Revolution briefly coalesced with public euphoria over the reforming mood of the French. In his centennial sermon William Enfield, Unitarian minister of the Octagon Chapel in Norwich, spoke of the political developments in France 'for the event of which all Europe is waiting with impatient expectation'. He continued mildly:

> If our progress be at present retarded by a timid policy which represents all innovations as dangerous, it may be confidently expected that time and further experience will soon correct this mistake and convince those who are intrusted with the administration of public affairs that they cannot execute their trust more faithfully than by listening to and, upon mature consideration, adopting plans of improvement.

And speaking of the surviving penal statutes against heterodox religious beliefs, he had little doubt that 'very soon these disgraceful relics of intolerance will be cleared away'.[15]

The 1789 debates on the second motion for repeal of the Test and Corporation Acts exposed the divide between the government and Dissenters that was to run throughout the 1790s. Fox, speaking in favour of repeal, argued that 'men are the best judges of the consequences of their own opinions and how far they are likely to influence their actions'. It was 'most unnatural and tyrannical to say, "because you *think* so, you must *act* so. I will collect the evidence of your future conduct from what I know of your opinions."' The contrary was true: 'Men ought to be judged by their actions and not by their thoughts.'[16] Pitt argued in reply that, although Fox might be right in general terms, the government had a duty to take note of opinions that might result in a 'civil inconvenience', and was right to 'guard against the probability of civil inconvenience being produced', rather than waiting 'till, by being carried into action, the inconvenience has actually arisen'. He continued: 'It is not on the ground that they *would* do anything to affect the civil government of the country that they have been excluded from holding civil office, but that if they had any additional degree of power in their hands they *might*.'[17]

By the time Fox moved to bring in a third repeal bill in March 1790, Price had preached his Old Jewry sermon to the London Revolution Society, and Burke had started to write his *Reflections* in reply. Yet Fox denied any connection between the Dissenters' campaign and events in France, reminding the House that a similar motion for repeal had been presented three years before 'when no person could have predicted the singular events which have occurred on the continent'. He had no wish to damage the established church, nor did he hold a brief for any particular denomination. He was speaking on behalf of those who believed in the rights of mankind:

> Of what consequence is it to the State whether a man is a Unitarian or a Trinitarian; a believer in transubstantiation or the real presence; an advocate for infant baptism or for adult baptism? To abandon general principles upon the ground of partiality is a procedure which cannot be defended...[18]

Pitt objected in reply that Fox's proposal would 'throw open a door for the entrance of *some* individuals who might consider it a point of *conscience* to shake our Establishment to its foundations'.[19]

Burke objected in turn to the abstract principles invoked by Fox and appealed to by Dissenters. Of all abstract principles, 'abstract principles of natural right (which the Dissenters rely upon as their stronghold) are the most idle because the most useless, and the most dangerous to resort to'.[20] Burke's targets included not only Price and Priestley, but Robert Robinson, whose *Political Catechism* (1782) he characterized as 'containing no one precept of religion, but consisting of one continued invective against King and Bishops'. Burke represented the *Catechism* as designed 'to lisp out censures in condemnation of the Church Establishment, while, possibly, the Dissenting teachers are preaching up robbery and plunder as in France'.[21] This imputation drew a furious riposte from the Unitarian MP William Smith, who reminded the House that Burke had 'attacked a nation abroad while in the very act of struggling for their liberties', and calling them 'an irrational, unprincipled, confiscating, plundering, ferocious, bloody and tyrannical democracy'. Now he had chosen to 'libel a respectable body of men at home who have by no part of their conduct deserved to be treated with so much asperity'.[22]

The *Gentleman's Magazine* for May 1790 devotes eight double-column pages to reporting the debate. It notes that Pitt distinguished 'with great accuracy' between a 'discreet, liberal and fair toleration, and the new-fangled toleration which levelled all distinction'. It cites Burke's reminder that Priestley 'hated all religious establishments', and thought them 'sinful and idolatrous', and that Priestley 'talked of a train of gunpowder being laid to the Church Establishment'. The *Gentleman's Magazine* reports that Burke pointed to Price's 'famous Sermon, and commented on it with great severity', and that Burke offered to meet the Dissenters to give them a fair chance 'to refute the proofs he had adduced'. He is nevertheless recorded as reminding the House of 'Lord George Gordon's mob, which had nearly levelled the Constitution in Church and State, by surrounding that House and attacking their Bank'.[23]

The Gordon Riots of 1780 had resulted from a Protestant campaign against the granting of moderate relief to Catholics, by repealing various laws relating to Catholic worship, Catholic schoolmasters and the right of Catholics to own real estate. The Catholic Relief Bill (1778) had been followed in 1779 by the bill relieving Dissenting ministers and schoolmasters of the need to subscribe to the Thirty-nine Articles. Following their 1790 failure to repeal the Test and Corporation Acts, some Dissenters now lent their support to the campaign for Parliament to grant further relief to Catholics. Michael Dodson, chairman of the Standing Committee of Protestant Dissenters, was a member of Theophilus Lindsey's Essex Street congregation. In a letter to William Tayleur of Shrewsbury, Lindsey records the Catholics' grateful if somewhat surprised reply to the committee's expression of support, and refers to the rumour that Pitt 'will try to put a stop to the business, foreseeing that it will involve him in difficulties respecting the Dissenters'.[24] It was again Fox who supported the bill, and Lindsey reported enthusiastically to Tayleur that Fox had 'declared his intention of bringing in a bill on better and more extensive principles for the relief of Protestant as well as Catholic Dissenters if the Ministry would not undertake it'.[25]

Such misplaced optimism was perhaps understandable in view of the analogous pairing of pro-Catholic and pro-Dissenter legislation in 1778–9. But in contrast to the Gordon Riots, the violence was now directed by Church and King mobs against Dissenters – with the consequent destruction of Priestley's Birmingham meetinghouse and laboratory. In the first part of his *Appeal to the Public* following the riots, Priestley asked:

> Can it be pretended that the man who confines his adoration to *one God,* and who calls this one *the God and Father of Jesus Christ,* is a worse subject of civil government than he who, in addition to the worship of this one God, pays equal divine honours to Jesus Christ, and also to another divine person called *the Holy Ghost,* or than he who adds to all these the worship of the virgin Mary and of all the saints and angels in the Popish calandar?

Why, he asked, should Unitarian Dissenters 'be more exposed to violence, and left out of the protection of the state, than *Trinitarian* Dissenters or the Roman Catholics, to whom the favour of government has of late been very justly extended?'[26]

George III, urging Dundas to send troops to restore order in Birmingham, had added the revealing admission: 'I cannot but feel better pleased that Priestley is the sufferer for the doctrines he and his party have instilled, and that the people see them in their true light...'[27] It was evidently not an auspicious moment for a Unitarian Relief Bill. Yet the Unitarian Society for Promoting Christian Knowledge, established in 1791 and including Lindsey, Dodson, Priestley and Tayleur among its founder-members, decided to campaign for what Lindsey called 'the repeal of the laws against antitrinitarians'. A petition to Parliament would be offered for approval by 'a general meeting of the members of our Unitarian Society', and a decision would be taken whether to present it in the current parliamentary session. 'Mr Fox,' Lindsey explained, 'has very obligingly offered his services and advised this mode of application.'[28]

Fox was as good as his word, and moved for permission to bring in a Bill to repeal the penalties against Unitarians. By the time the debate took place, France and Austria were at war. Pitt opposed Fox's proposal on the grounds that it would be 'especially foolish at this time to give encouragement to avowed enemies of the Constitution'. If Fox's motion were carried, those who benefited would 'most certainly represent it as a first step to the gradual abolition of all the establishments and fundamental principles of the Constitution'.[29] Burke conjured up an even more alarming scenario. Reminding the House that 'a Statesman differs from a Professor in a University', he denounced the Unitarians as allies of the French Jacobins. He further claimed that Unitarian and other reformers sought to 'collect a multitude of sufficient force and violence to overturn the Church', adding that their 'designs against the Church are concurrent with a design to subvert the state'. Burke urged the House not to wait

> till the conspirators, met to commemorate the 14th July, shall seize on the Tower of London and the magazines it contains, murder the Governor, and the Mayor of London, seize upon the King's person, drive out the House of Lords, occupy your gallery, and thence, as from an high tribunal, dictate to you.[30]

Fox's motion was defeated by 142 votes to 63.

Even allowing for recent memories of the Gordon Riots, Burke's rhetoric seems excessive. Priestley may have earned his nickname 'Gunpowder Joe' for his talk about grains of gunpowder, but despite such rhetorical flourishes he was no Guy Fawkes. Burke's Irish roots may have made him more sympathetic towards relief for Catholics than for Unitarians. In 1778 he had supported Savile's Catholic Relief Bill, and in 1779 had pressed the government to compensate Catholics who lost property in the consequent Scottish riots. Yet that same year, in the debate on relieving Dissenting ministers and schoolmasters from subscription to the Articles, Burke had supported Lord North in substituting the declaration of Protestant faith, which effectively excluded Unitarians.[31] Historians are nevertheless probably right to suggest that, in the 1770s, Burke was sympathetic to the repeal of the Test and Corporation Acts, and that the Dissenters provoked his later hostility by combining with East India Company interests and the court to unseat the Fox–North coalition in the 1784 election.[32]

Burke did not attend the debates on Beaufoy's repeal motions of 1787 and 1789, and when Richard Bright, representing the Bristol Dissenters, pleaded for Burke's support on the second occasion, he was told (in a reference to the trial of Warren Hastings) that Bristol's former MP was

> endeavouring to relieve twenty millions of Dissenters from the Church of England, in Asia, from real grievances which God forbid any of the

> Dissenters in Europe should have more feeling of, in their persons, than any of them appear to have in any sympathy with the Sufferers.

And in less tortured syntax, Burke went on to reveal his personal animus by complaining that, in 1784, Dissenters 'seem'd to act in Corps', and have since 'held me out to public Odium, as one of a gang of Rebels and Regicides, who have conspired at one blow to subvert the Monarchy, to annihilate without cause, all the Corporate privileges in the Kingdom, and totally destroy this Constitution.'[33] Ironically, Burke's complaint comes close to the very language he would later direct at Dissenters in general, and Unitarians in particular. In December 1789, shortly after Price's Old Jewry sermon, Fox sought Burke's support in obtaining approval for Priestley to dedicate *Experiments and Observations on different kinds of Air* (1790) to the Prince of Wales. Burke replied that he could not conceive 'what objection the prince can have to be considered as an encourager of Science'. And he added: 'Besides this consideration Dr P. is a very considerable leader among a set of men powerful enough in many things, but most of all in elections; and I am quite sure that the good or ill humour of these men will be sensibly felt at the general election'.[34]

Yet in a letter to Bright in February 1790, while working on the *Reflections*, Burke accused the Dissenters' leaders of trying 'to draw us into a connection and concurrence with [France], upon the principles of its proceedings, and to lead us to an imitation of them'.[35] The Dissenters' writings attacked by Burke in the debate on the repeal of the Test and Corporation Acts in March 1790 dated from the 1770s and 1780s. Robinson's *Political Catechism* had been published in 1782, while his *Plan of Lectures on the Principles of Nonconformity* had been adopted by the Eastern Association of Baptists as early as 1778, midway through the American War of Independence. Similarly, Priestley's best-known anti-establishment and antitrinitarian works, and his expositions of his materialist philosophy, had all been published before the end of the American War – though it was Gunpowder Joe's *Present State of Free Inquiry* (1785) that Burke supposedly quoted with so much relish. Why, asked Priestley, did Burke delay his public denunciation of the dangerous tendencies of Unitarianism for so long?[36]

Whatever Burke's personal motivation, Pitt's approach seems to have been largely pragmatic. As he candidly admitted in the 1787 debate on the Test Acts:

> If I were arguing on principles of *right*, I should not talk of alarm; but I am acting upon principles of *expediency*. The Church and State are

> united upon principles of expediency, and it concerns those to whom the wellbeing of the State is entrusted to take care that the Church should not be rashly demolished.[37]

Some historians have put it more cynically, arguing that, despite their exclusion from the Toleration Act, Unitarians could preach against the Trinity so long as they did not attack the government.[38] The Commons defeat of the 1792 Unitarian Relief Bill, was followed in the same month by the royal proclamation against seditious writings, and the founding of John Reeves's Loyal Association for 'preserving Liberty and Property against Republicans and Levellers'. The disappointment of Unitarian hopes ensured the persistence of articulate Dissenting opposition to the government's war policy – an opposition (this study seeks to show) that long outlasted Priestley's emigration to America in 1794.[39]

The antijacobin press, for its part, would portray Dissenters as crypto-republicans, self-proclaimed levellers and secret traitors. By 1799, the *Antijacobin Review* was quoting approvingly Jonathan Boucher's contention in his *American Revolution* that the loss of the colonies was not the fault of His Majesty's ministers. It was rather due to 'that spirit of republicanism which overturned the constitution of Great Britain in 1648, and a large portion of which was carried over to America by the first puritan emigrants'.[40] Priestley, Price and Lindsey had been on the 'wrong' side in the American Revolution too. The fact that Burke himself had then sided with them helps to explain their new sense of betrayal.[41]

Part I
Grains of Gunpowder

1
Denying the Trinity

The term 'Rational Christian', which Priestley perhaps unjustifiably equated with 'Unitarian', must not be taken to imply thoroughgoing theological scepticism.[1] The discoverer of oxygen, and author of treatises on both electricity and optics, thought that Old Testament prophecies predicted the French Revolution. He also believed in the bodily resurrection of Jesus, in the General Resurrection at Christ's Second Coming, and in the Christian Millennium and Last Judgement.[2] As he wrote in his *Appeal to the Serious and Candid Professors of Christianity*, first published in 1770 and republished in 1791: 'Be not backward, or afraid, my brethren, to make use of your reason in matters of religion, or where the Scriptures are concerned. They both of them proceed from the same God and Father of us all, who is the giver of every good and perfect gift.' But he was careful to add: 'Do not think that, by recommending the use of reason, I am about to decry the Scriptures.'[3] And in 1778 he told a correspondent that he believed 'in a *God*, a *providence*, and a *future state*, in the *divine mission of Christ*, and *the authority of the Scriptures*.'[4] Priestley appealed to revelation as much as to reason, and his attack on the doctrine of the Trinity was firmly grounded in the New Testament. Like his orthodox Dissenting contemporaries, Priestley was heir to the Protestant tradition famously expressed by William Chillingworth, prebendary of Salisbury: 'The Bible and the Bible only is the religion of Protestants.'[5]

Priestley had written his *Appeal* while minister of Mill Hill Chapel in Leeds. During his years at Leeds (1767–73), besides publishing his *Directions for impregnating water with fixed air* and his summary of discoveries in optics (both in 1772), he published 28 new non-scientific works.[6] And it was of his Leeds ministry that he would later write:

> Here I had no unreasonable prejudices to contend with, so that I had full scope for every kind of exertion; and I can truly say that I always considered the office of a Christian minister as the most honourable of any upon earth, and in the studies proper to it I always took the greatest pleasure.[7]

It was at Leeds that he resumed what he called his 'application to speculative theology'. He explains: 'By reading with care Dr Lardner's Letter on the Logos, I became what is called a Socinian.' Until that point, Priestley tells us, 'I was still an Arian, having never turned my attention to the Socinian doctrine, and contenting myself with seeing the absurdity of the Trinitarian system.'[8]

Socinianism was derived from Socinus, the Latinized surname of the Italian Fausto Paolo Sozzini (1529–1604). Socinus denied the divinity of Christ, but nevertheless encouraged His adoration as the mediator through whom prayers to God might be addressed. Arianism had an older pedigree, dating back to the debates in the fourth-century Church and the bitter dispute between Arius and Athanasius, arising from the teaching of the Council of Nicaea (325) that Jesus was both perfect God and perfect man. Any attempt to expound the subtle theological differences that separated rival sections of the Church, from the age of Constantine onwards, necessarily risks stumbling into caricature. But in *Corruptions of Christianity*, Priestley summarizes the Arian position: 'Christ was neither of the same substance of the Father, nor formed out of the pre-existing matter, but like other things was created out of nothing'.[9] Eighteenth-century Arians held that, before he became man, Christ existed in glory 'as a divine person higher than all the angels', but below the Father.[10] Trinitarian theology, by contrast, held the Son to be 'consubstantial' and 'co-eternal' with the Father.

Priestley concedes that, wherever Unitarianism prevailed in the Roman world, it took the form of Arianism. He cannot trace what he calls 'the proper humanity of Christ' much later than the Council of Nicaea, 'the Arian doctrine having been much more prevalent for a considerable time afterwards'. What later became the Socinian doctrine was revived first among the Albigenses, then at the Reformation, and was prominent at the time of the English Civil War. Yet in the late seventeenth-century Arianism again displaced the Socinian version, until (Priestley records) 'of late years, Dr Lardner and others have written in favour of the simple humanity of Christ'.[11] Priestley looks forward to a time when all Christians will profess 'the great article of the *unity of God*', and expects that Christianity, being 'freed from other corruptions and embarrassments' will then be accepted by 'Jews and Mahometans, and become the religion of the whole world'.[12] Four years later, the preface to his *History of Early Opinions concerning Jesus Christ* (1786) records that he had hoped to have a public discussion with 'a learned Arian' before composing the work, but in default of an Arian antagonist, he had himself 'endeavoured to suggest all that I possibly can in defence of their opinion'. His attempt at impartiality does not, however, preclude Priestley from considering the Arian hypothesis to be 'equally destitute of support in the Scriptures, in reason and in history'.[13]

Priestley begins with the Scriptures. He appeals first to Old Testament texts: 'Thou shalt have no other gods before me' (Exodus 20.3), 'Hear, O Israel, the Lord our God is one Lord' (Deuteronomy 6.4) and Isaiah's prophecy regarding the Messiah's suffering and death. From the New Testament he selects Mark's reiteration of the injunction from Deuteronomy (Mark 12.29) and Paul's words from I Timothy 2.5: 'There is one God, and one Mediator between God and men, the man Christ Jesus.' And quoting the risen Christ's words to Mary Magdalene in John 20.17 ('Go to my brethren, and say unto them, I ascend unto my Father and your Father, and unto my God and your God.'), Priestley comments: 'It cannot, surely, be God that uses language such as this.'[14] The Synoptic Gospels, says Priestley, make no mention of Christ's divinity or of his pre-existence, despite the obvious importance of these topics: 'Since, therefore, the evangelists give no certain and distinct account of them, and say nothing at all of their importance, it may be safely inferred that they were unknown to them.' And he argues that it must strike everyone who looks at the language of the New Testament 'that the terms Christ and God are perpetually used in contradistinction to each other, as much as God and man'. Even the fact that Jesus was so much as Messiah 'was divulged with the greatest caution both to the apostles and to the body of Jews'.[15]

Sixteen years earlier, in his first major work to address the New Testament evidence, Priestley had defined the person of Christ in Peter's description (Acts 2.22) of 'a man approved by God – by miracles and wonders and signs, which God did by him'. Jesus, Priestley argues, had claimed no more of himself: 'No Jew expected any thing more than man for their Messiah, and our Saviour nowhere intimates that they were mistaken in that expectation.'[16] Such emphasis on the humanity of Christ challenged the Church's doctrine of the Atonement. If Jesus was mere man, his sacrifice on the cross would imply an angry and vengeful God, who had to be appeased by sin-offerings:

> How must the genuine spirit of mercy and forgiveness, which so eminently distinguish the gospel of Christ, be debased, when God himself (whose conduct in this very respect is particularly proposed to our imitation) is considered as never forgiving sin without some previous atonement, satisfaction or intercession.[17]

In an earlier essay on the Atonement in his *Theological Repository*, established and edited during his years at Leeds (1767–73), Priestley argues that Biblical texts which speak of Christ 'bearing our sins' ought to be interpreted as bearing our sins away: 'The phrase *bearing sin* is never applied under the law but to the *scape-goat* on the day of expiation, which was not sacrificed, but as the name expresses, was turned into the wilderness, a place not inhabited.'[18]

In his *History of the Christian Church* (1790) Priestley considers the connection between crucifixion and resurrection: 'The manner in which Jesus died was peculiarly favourable to the design of Providence, which was to make the most distinguished preacher of the doctrine of the resurrection, himself a proof of the fact.' Priestley has no doubt that Christ's resurrection 'was proved by the abundant evidence of those who best knew him, and who were therefore the best judges of the fact, and who had no more expectation of it than his adversaries...' As for the Ascension:

> Lastly, he met the apostles, and many others, after their return to Jerusalem; and having conversed with them at leisure, and conducted them as far as the mount of Olives, he ascended above the clouds in their sight; two angels standing by, and informing those who were present, that in the same manner in which they themselves saw Jesus going up to heaven, they would see him return again from heaven.[19]

So wrote Priestley the experimental scientist and rational theologian, with all the Biblical literalism of the orthodox Dissenting tradition.

Priestley also believed that, at Christ's Second Coming, the General Resurrection would be in bodily form – as the Apostle's Creed proclaims. He wrote in 1777: 'As a materialist and a Christian, I believe *the resurrection of the body*, that is of *the man*; and that upon this foundation only, in opposition to the opinion which places it on the *natural immortality of the soul*, I rest my belief of a future life.'[20] He was not disconcerted by his knowledge of chemical decomposition: 'Time was, when the total solution of a piece of metal in a chemical *menstruum* would seem to be as absolute a loss of it, as the dissolution of the human body by putrefaction, and the recovery of it would have been thought as hopeless.'[21] Priestley was equally committed to belief in the Last Judgement, though unsure what form it would take: 'From revelation we learn the actual certainty of a future state, and have an absolute assurance of its being a state of exact retribution, in which every man shall receive according to his works.' As evidence in support, he cites Daniel's prophecy (12.2) that those who 'sleep in the dust of the earth shall awake, some to everlasting life, and some to shame and everlasting torment'. And he quotes Paul's warning to the Corinthians (2 Cor. 5. 10, 11): 'For we must all appear before the judgement-seat of Christ, that every one may receive the things done in his body, according to that he hath done, whether it be good or bad. Knowing therefore the terror of the Lord, we persuade men.'[22]

In abandoning belief in predestination, 'Rational Christians' embraced an alternative form of determinism derived from David Hartley's influential *Observations on Man*, which Priestley met in his student days under Dr Doddridge at Daventry Academy. Hartley distinguished between the physiological action of the brain in organizing facts received through physical sensation, and the spiritual activity of the mind, which constructed ideas by a process of association. Hartley's blend of rational theology with Newtonian physics required the application of human discipline, and the prospect of divine judgement and punishment, in order to ensure benevolence in this world and happiness in the world to come.[23]

Priestley's insistence on bodily resurrection reflects his opposition to the Hellenization of New Testament faith. He points to the consequences of translating the Old Testament into Greek, which led learned Jews like Philo of Alexandria 'to find in the books of Moses, and the prophets, all the great principles of the Greek Philosophy, and especially that of Plato, which at that time was most in vogue.'[24] This, Priestley claims, led to the misapplication of the Psalmist's 'word of the Lord' (translated in the *Septuagint* as *Logos*) to Christ himself. Priestley insists that the first chapter of John's Gospel, far from identifying the *Logos* with Christ, is careful to make clear that 'the *Logos*, by which all things were made, was not a being, distinct from God, but God himself, being his attribute, wisdom and power, dwelling in Christ, speaking and acting by him'.[25]

As part of the same exposition, Priestley cites evidence from the early Christian Fathers and from Tertullian to demonstrate not only the slow adoption of belief in Christ's divinity, but also the even slower adoption of the Trinitarian view of the Holy Spirit. Tertullian (we are told) 'in one place evidently confounds the *Holy Spirit* with the *Logos*, and therefore it is plain that he had no idea of a proper third person in the Trinity'. Similarly the 160 bishops at the Council of Sardica (347) 'did not distinguish between the *Holy Spirit* and the *Logos* any more than Tertullian did'. Priestley accepts the tradition that Athanasius was 'the first who applied the word *consubstantial* to the Spirit, it having before been applied to the Son only'.[26] Since the Council of Chalcedon (451), the doctrine of 'what is called the *catholic church*' has been that 'in Christ there are two distinct *natures*, united *in one person*, but without any change, mixture or confusion'. Priestley goes on to explain how the doctrine of the two natures is supposed to answer objections to the idea of God suffering on the cross, and adds: 'To such wretched expedients, which do not deserve a serious consideration, are the advocates for Christian polytheism reduced.'[27]

The asperity of that last phrase is a reminder that Priestley was not always a gentle antagonist, but it is difficult to quarrel with his summary of the Trinitarian development over the first five Councils of the Church:

> The first general council gave the Son the same nature with the Father, the second admitted the Holy Spirit into the Trinity, the third assigned to Christ a human soul in conjunction with the *Logos*, the fourth settled the hypostatical union of the divine and human nature of Christ, and the fifth affirmed that, in consequence of this union, the two natures constituted only one person.[28]

It was Priestley's claim that the Christian Church of the first three centuries had been Unitarian, which posed the greatest theological threat to the Anglican position. For unlike most other 'reformed churches', the Church of England grounded its teaching not only on Scripture, but on the first four Councils of the Church. This was the main battleground of his pamphlet warfare with Samuel Horsley. Priestley's *Corruptions of Christianity* had been published in 1782. The following year Horsley, then Archdeacon of St Albans, published his visitation charge to the clergy of his archdeaconry. When Priestley responded with his *Letter to Dr Horsley* (1783), the future bishop declined further combat, asserting that his attack on Priestley 'was not so much upon the opinions you maintain, however much I hold them in abhorrence, as upon the credit of your Narrative'.[29] When Priestley nevertheless returned to the attack in a further *Letter* (1784), Horsley responded in his Christmas Day sermon at St Mary Newington in 1785, and with his remarks on Priestley's second *Letter* in the spring of 1786. The exchange continued until 1789, when Horsley reissued his contributions to the controversy in a single volume.[30] Although contemporaries hailed Horsley as the victor, his most recent biographer concedes that it is Priestley's account of the late appearance of the Trinitarian doctrine in the early Church which is vindicated. The debate was revived at the end of our period by Thomas Belsham, who republished Priestley's tracts, in order to combat extravagant claims made by Horsley's supporters after his death.[31]

The year 1782, which saw Priestley's first *Letter to Dr Horsley*, also saw the second edition of *Institutes of Natural and Revealed Religion*. First published during Priestley's years at Leeds, it was now prefaced with an 'Essay on the Best Method of Communicating Religious Knowledge to Members of Christian Societies'. The essay begins with a complaint about 'the superficial knowledge, or rather the general ignorance of the generality of youth in the present age, with respect to religion'. As the minds of the young have not 'been seasoned with the principles of religion, they become mere men of the world, without vice, perhaps, but also without virtue'. And Part II of the *Institutes* begins with the reminder that the author's target-readership is 'the *young*, the *ignorant*, or the *unsettled*'.[32] Part I had marshalled evidence for the existence of God, relying on the already well-rehearsed argument from design. As Priestley would later argue in his attempted refutation of Hume: 'Will any person say that an eye could have been constructed by a being who had no knowledge of optics, who did not know the nature of light or the laws of refraction?'[33] Yet only the first 60-odd pages of the *Institutes* deal with the natural religion of the Deists, or the psychology of the affections as expounded by Hartley. Three hundred pages are concerned with evidences for the Jewish and Christian revelations, and Priestley condemns contemporary writers who have 'abandoned revelation, and have pretended at least to be guided by nature only'.[34]

For Priestley and his fellow-Unitarians, Deism was no better than atheism. Indeed his introduction to Part II of the *Institutes* seems at times to echo John Wesley's sermon on 'The almost Christian'. Priestley wrote that it was 'a matter of the greatest consequence, not only that unbelievers be made converts to the Christian faith, but that the faith of the believers themselves be strengthened, and they be thereby converted from merely nominal into *real* Christians'. Those who aspire to be real Christians should 'study the evidences of their religion; they should meditate upon the life, discourses and miracles of Christ; and make familiar to their minds every thing relating 'to the history and propagation of Christianity in the world'. They should 'both frequently read the Scriptures, and also other books which tend to prove their truth and illustrate their contents'.[35]

Although the Scriptures remained for Priestley the basis of Christian faith as well of Unitarian belief, he thought the Church was mistaken to insist on 'the absolute inspiration of all the canonical books of Scripture'. He instances the unauthenticated story of the Wise Men (which appears only in Matthew) and contrasts it with 'the history of the death and resurrection of Christ [as] related by three other Evangelists, as well as by Matthew himself'.[36] He nevertheless defends participation in the Lord's Supper 'in commemoration of his death', on both Scriptural and rational grounds: 'This rite having such excellent moral uses, and the celebration of it being an express command of Christ who said, "Do this in remembrance of me", I do not see how any person, professing Christianity, can satisfy himself with refusing to join in it.'[37] The centrality of the Scriptures in Priestley's theology is perhaps nowhere better demonstrated than in his devoting the last years of his self-imposed exile in America to writing commentaries on every book of both Old and New Testaments. The *Notes* were published in America in 1804, the year of his death.[38] Concluding a section on 'The Harmony of the Four Evangelists', Priestley writes: 'The proper end of the evangelical history is to convince mankind of the divine mission or Messiahship of Jesus; and the end of this is obedience to his gospel, which will insure our immortal life and happiness.'[39]

In a dedicatory letter to Theophilus Lindsey, published more than 20 years before *Notes on the Old and New Testaments*, Priestley expressed his own optimism regarding the fate of 'Rational Christianity': 'The gross darkness of the *night* which has for many centuries obscured our holy religion, we may clearly see is past; the *morning* is opening upon us; and we cannot doubt but that the light will increase, and extend itself more and more into *the perfect day*. Happy are they who contribute to diffuse the pure light of this *everlasting gospel*.'[40] Lindsey and Priestley had first met in Richmond, Yorkshire, at the house of Lindsey's father-in-law, Archdeacon Blackburne, where

> they passed some days together in that unreserved and delightful interchange of sentiments, and in those free and amicable discussions

> which would naturally take place among persons of high intellectual attainments, in whose estimation the discoveries of divine revelation held the most honourable place, and who were all equally animated with the same ardent love of truth, and with the same generous zeal for civil and religious liberty.[41]

The *Corruptions of Christianity*, which Priestley had dedicated to Lindsey, was not only an attack on the alleged doctrinal distortions of orthodox Anglicanism. Priestley concluded the second volume with an 'Address to Advocates for the present Civil Establishment'. In the address, he disclaimed any expectation that he would personally benefit 'by any alteration that can take place in the ecclesiastical system of the country'. He explained his more modest aim:

> All I wish, as a Christian, from the powers of this world, is, that they would not intermeddle at all in the business of religion, and that they will give no countenance whatever to any mode of it, my own, or that of others, but show so much confidence in the principles of what they themselves deem to be true religion, as to think it able to guard itself.

To this unambiguous appeal for the civil equality of all religious denominations, Priestley adds a plea for the clergymen of the Established Church:

> Many excellent men among the clergy of the church of England are exceedingly distressed with the obligation to subscribe what they cannot believe, and to recite what they utterly condemn; and yet their circumstances are such, as too strongly tempt them to make the best of their situation, rather than absolutely starve; and many others are continually prevented from entering the church by the same state of things in it.[42]

Priestley's promotion of such anti-establishment principles would inevitably give a political thrust to antitrinitarian theology.

2
Opposing Subscription

The Anglican campaign against subscription to the Thirty-nine Articles, re-launched in 1772 with the so-called Feathers Tavern petitions, followed closely on the Wilkes agitation, and was itself followed by the petitions of 1775 urging conciliation with America. Petitioning of Parliament had been forbidden by Charles II's 1661 Act against Tumultuous Petitioning. The Act required the approval of three or more JPs for any petition that was signed by more than 20 persons and addressed to 'the King or both or either Houses of Parliament for the alteration of matters established by Law in Church and State'. The preamble explains that the Act was made necessary by the 'soliciting and procuring' of signatures to 'Petitions, Complaints, Remonstrances and Declarations and other Addresses' demanding 'redress of pretended grievances in Church or State or other publique Concernements'. Such petitions had been 'made use of to serve the ends of Factious and Seditious persons'.[1] The Act had never been repealed. The 1689 Bill of Rights proclaimed that 'it is the Right of Subjects to petition the King and all Commitments and Prosecutions for such Petitions are Illegal'.[2] This did not deter Parliament in 1701 from imprisoning the MPs who presented a petition from the county of Kent calling on the House of Commons to 'turn their loyal addresses into bills of supply'. The Tory Commons declared the petition 'scandalous, tending to destroy the constitution of parliaments and to subvert the established government of these realms'.[3]

Historians have tended to discount public petitioning before Wyvill's 1779 Yorkshire petition in favour of parliamentary reform. Yet the 1775 petitions for conciliation with America, addressed to the Crown rather than to Parliament, carried a total number of signatures 'roughly equivalent to the number of voters in a general election'.[4] The petitions against subscription carried hundreds rather than thousands of signatures, but throughout the 1770s Lord North's ministry evidently felt that church and state were simultaneously under attack.[5]

The campaign against subscription to the Articles was led by an Archdeacon. Francis Blackburne had subscribed on becoming Archdeacon of Cleveland in 1750. A Cambridge graduate, Blackburne had left the university in 1728, having been denied a fellowship, and had advertised his heterodox theological leanings by placing his son under Priestley at Warrington Academy. From 1739 to 1787 Blackburne was Rector of Richmond, where he wrote most of his controversial works and edited the memoirs of Thomas Hollis. It was at Richmond in the 1760s that he wrote *The Confessional*. In it he argued that the government could not assert 'a right to require assent to a certain sense of Scripture, exclusive of other senses, without an unwarrantable interference with those rights of private judgement which are clearly guaranteed to the individual by the Scriptural terms of Christian liberty'. Such an interference amounted to 'contradicting the original principles of the Protestant Reformation'. For Protestants, orthodoxy 'should mean only an agreement in opinion with the Scriptures'.[6] Blackburne was in the Cambridge Latitudinarian tradition of Benjamin Hoadly, sometime Fellow of St Catharine's, who achieved notoriety as Bishop of Bangor, and since 1734 had been Bishop of Winchester. Hoadly died in 1761 in his mid-80s. Archbishop Matthew Hutton, his junior by nearly 20 years, and former Fellow of Christ's, would move from York to Canterbury in 1757, dying in 1758. Another Fellow of Christ's, Edmund Law, born in 1703 and coming back to Cambridge in 1756 as Master of Peterhouse, represented a new generation of Latitudinarians. Law warmly supported Blackburne's campaign, both in Cambridge and (from 1768) as Bishop of Carlisle. Law's anonymous *Considerations on the Propriety of requiring Subscription to Articles of Faith* appeared in 1774. He also edited the *Works* of Locke.[7]

More immediate support for Blackburne came from Thomas Edwards, Fellow of Clare College, Cambridge, in his University Sermon of 29 June 1766, when he condemned the unnatural mixture of 'Scholastic Jargon, Popish Superstition and Calvinistic Enthusiasm' which had been allowed to adulterate 'the simplicity and purity of the principles and doctrines of Christianity'.[8] The campaign against subscription was directed not only against the requirement for ordinands to subscribe, but also against the similar requirement for students proceeding to a degree – the so-called University Tests. At Cambridge, subscription was required before graduation; at Oxford, it was required for matriculation at the start of the degree course.[9] It was an Oxford man, John Jones, Chaplain of Worcester College, who had campaigned against subscription as early as 1749 (when Vicar of Alconbury) in his *Free and Candid Disquisitions relating to the Church of England*. But the anti-subscription campaign (as Norman Sykes reminds us) was 'largely a Cambridge movement'.[10]

Apart from Thomas Edwards, Fellows of Cambridge colleges who supported the campaign included: John Jebb of Peterhouse, his pupil John Baynes of Trinity, Robert Tyrwhitt and Gilbert Wakefield of Jesus, James Lambert of St John's, Robert Plumptre and Thomas Fyshe Palmer of Queens'. Of these, Jebb, Palmer and Wakefield would later figure prominently in radical politics, together with Jebb's Peterhouse pupils, John Disney and Capel Lofft. Plumptre was twice Vice-Chancellor, and from 1769 to 1788 Professor of Moral Theology. He nevertheless signed Blackburne's petition. Even the University's Chancellor, the Duke of Grafton would write of the Feathers Tavern petitioners: 'I shall ever lament that they were not successful in their application to Parliament.' Grafton would later frequent Lindsey's Essex Street Chapel. The Duke's Socinian tendencies did not become apparent until after he left political office in 1782, when he wrote in defence of Unitarians; but soon after his installation as Chancellor in 1769, he declined an honorary doctorate rather than subscribe to the Articles.[11]

Jebb died in 1786 at the age of 50, and so did not see the French Revolution, but he took an active part in the Cambridge campaign. In *Letters on the Subject of Subscription* (1770) he wrote:

> The first article of our church professes to treat of faith in the Holy Trinity, an expression not to be found in Scripture, a doctrine not connected with the performance of a single duty in social life. A man may believe the contrary, and yet be a good christian, a good father, a good master, a good husband, a good citizen, and a good friend . . .[12]

His Unitarian views had first been revealed in the late 1760s, when he began his lectures on the Greek New Testament and was simultaneously conducting his campaign for the abolition of University Tests. In 1771 he supported Blackburne's proposal for petitioning Parliament, which led to the first Feathers Tavern petition, with its plea that petitioners 'may be restored to their undoubted rights as Protestants of interpreting Scripture for themselves without being bound by any human explanation whatever'.[13]

Blackburne's two Cambridge sons-in-law were equally active in the campaign against subscription. John Disney, undergraduate at Peterhouse under Jebb (and future editor of his works), was a leading member of the Feathers Tavern Association pledged to promote the abolition of subscription for the clergy. He defended Blackburne's *Confessional*, and signalled his own Unitarianism by omitting the Nicene Creed from his use of the Prayer Book. He would become the first secretary of the Unitarian Society for Promoting Knowledge of the Scriptures, set up in conjunction with Jebb and Lindsey in 1783, before eventually succeeding Lindsey at Essex Street ten years later.[14] Lindsey, Blackburne's other son-in-law, had been briefly a Fellow of St John's in the late 1740s, and was in the 1770s Rector of Catterick. In support of the subscription petition, he reputedly rode over 2000 miles to collect signatures, writing to William Turner of Wakefield: 'The Master of Jesus College, Cambridge, and every resident Fellow has signed the Petition. The Bishop of Carlisle highly approved.' Lindsey collected some 200 signatures from clergy, and nearly another 50 from medical men and lawyers.[15]

The petition was presented to the Commons on 6 February 1772 by Sir Henry Hoghton, MP for Preston. It was opposed by Sir Roger Newdigate, MP for Oxford: 'If you remove this institution I cannot see how the state can a moment subsist. Civil and religious establishments are so linked and incorporated together that when the latter falls, the former cannot stand.' He reminded the House that, by the Act of Union, the religious establishment in neither Scotland nor England could be altered: 'The Union, as well as Magna Carta, I hold an irreversible decree, binding at all times and in all circumstances like the laws of the Medes and the Persians.'[16] By contrast, Lord Germain appealed to the ideas of Clarke and Hoadly, Locke and Newton, and also spoke as a father against the absurdity of University Tests: 'Is it not time to remove so great a stumbling-block? For my part it appears a melancholy thought and indeed a crying grievance that my son at sixteen must subscribe upon entering the university what I cannot understand, much less explain to him, at sixty ...'.[17] Lord North, graduate of Trinity College, Oxford, knowing how hostile George III was to the measure, argued that if a bill were passed, only outright popery would exclude a man from the universities and from claiming membership of the Church of England: 'A thousand doctrines of Popery may rush in at the door the honourable gentleman would open for two or three hundred men.'[18] Burke, objecting characteristically because the petition was based on 'abstract principles', denied that the Act of Union was immutable, since Parliament was sovereign. Yet he was opposed to 'innovations in religion when the people are not in consequence of some religious abuse much aggrieved'.[19] Fox supported Burke on the general issue of subscription, though hoping for a not too distant end to University Tests. The motion was defeated by 217 votes to 71.[20]

Yet barely two months later, Hoghton's more limited bill, relieving Dissenting ministers and schoolmasters of the need to subscribe to the Articles, passed its Second Reading debate in the Commons by 70 votes to 9. Was this because there was an election in the offing? George III, writing to North on 2 April, suggested that members elected in the Dissenting interest should not be encouraged to oppose the measure, as 'you may be driving them out of those seats on a new Parliament'. He nevertheless urged North to oppose the bill 'personally through every stage which will gain you the applause of the Established Church and every real friend of the Constitution. If you should be beat, it will be in doing your duty, and the House of Lords will prevent any evil . . .'.[21] The Lords duly voted the bill out by 102 votes to 29. Yet Burke had defended the bill in the Commons on the grounds that the existing requirement led 'rather to the propagation of presbyterianism than to the establishment of the national religion'.[22]

In 1772, Lindsey was still an Anglican clergyman. Even before the defeat of the first Feathers Tavern petition, Priestley had been doubtful whether the Dissenters should follow the Blackburne petitioners in applying to Parliament for relief. As he wrote somewhat sententiously to Lindsey:

> As the disciple of a Master whose Kingdom is not of this world, I should be ashamed to ask any thing of temporal powers, except mere peace and quietness, which, being temporal blessings they may bestow; but I should be sorry to make any application to them which should imply an acknowledgment of their having any other kind of power.

He continued: 'The more I think of an application to such a House of Commons, or such a Parliament as ours, on the subject of religion, the more does the absurdity of it strike me.' Then, perhaps sensing that he had been unduly combative, he added: 'But I shall say no more on the subject, lest I should offend you. I really did not intend to say so much.' A week later he was promising Lindsey support 'in any thing for the relief of either ourselves or you'.[23]

Amid the euphoria over Commons support for the Dissenters' Relief bill in 1772, he warned Lindsey that the omens for a second Feathers Tavern petition were not good. In the debate, Priestley reported, 'all the speakers laid great stress on the difference between your case and ours, contending for a strict establishment and a large toleration'.[24] The second Feathers Tavern petition, presented at the beginning of March 1773, comfortably passed its Third Reading in the Commons, in spite of Sir William Bagot's warning that the intention behind the petition was 'to throw down the best barriers of Christianity, and open a door for the admission of infidels of every species into the pale of the Church'.[25] As in 1772, the bill was lost in the Lords by only a slightly narrower margin (86 to 28). Lindsey quickly accepted defeat, writing to Turner at Liverpool that he saw 'little hope' of further progress in Parliament, 'since Lord North is made Chancellor of Oxford and the whole bench of bishops declare themselves resolved to oppose everything we shall propose . . .'.[26]

Lindsey resigned his Lincolnshire livings in 1773. His colleagues and near contemporaries among Cambridge Unitarians mostly followed suit. Jebb resigned his Peterhouse Fellowship in 1775, having been refused permission to continue his lectures on the Greek New Testament; Wakefield (who had remained in deacon's orders) surrendered his Jesus Fellowship to become Classical Tutor at Warrington Academy; Fyshe Palmer stayed at Queens' until 1783, when he left to become a Unitarian minister, first at Montrose and (from 1785) at Dundee. Disney had held Lincolnshire livings since 1769, becoming Doctor of Divinity (Edinburgh) in 1775 and Fellow of the Royal Society in 1778, before resigning his livings in 1782 to help at Essex Street. Other Unitarians remained in Cambridge. Robert Garnham, Fellow of Trinity, vowed soon after his ordination in 1777 'never to repeat his subscription to the Thirty-nine Articles for any preferment which he might be entitled to'. He resigned his livings in 1789, the year in which he published an attack on a Trinitarian sermon preached at St Paul's before the Lord Mayor of London. Yet he was still appointed College Preacher in 1793.[27] John Symonds, Fellow of Peterhouse and protégé of Grafton, remained Professor of History until his death in 1817; Lambert was not removed as Bursar of Trinity until 1799, after Pitt had secured the appointment of William Mansel as Master.

Mansel, a Fellow of Trinity since 1775, was active in the 1793 prosecution of William Frend for blasphemy. Frend had been Fellow and Tutor of Jesus since 1781, adopting Unitarian views only in 1787, when he resigned his Cambridgeshire livings. Frend published *An Address to the Inhabitants of Cambridge*, defending his antitrinitarian views. As a result he was removed from his tutorship but continued to reside in college, where Coleridge came under his influence.[28] Jesus College, in the late 1780s and early 1790s, had a recognized Unitarian reputation. William Burdon, Fellow of Emmanuel from 1788, could write to an Oxford correspondent: 'Socinianism . . . has gained some ground here, three of the fellows of Jesus College are avowedly of the persuasion and some others are thought to have a tendency towards it.'[29] But when, in 1793, Frend published his *Peace and Union*, the University authorities indicted him before the Vice-Chancellor's Court. In his new pamphlet, he attacked not only the clergy of the established church, but also the war policy of the Pitt ministry (see Chapter 9). Henry Gunning, nineteenth-century historian of Cambridge, was clear that 'the great object in prosecuting Frend was of a political rather than of a religious character'.[30] By 1793, in the aftermath of the failure of the Unitarian petition of the previous year, antitrinitarian belief and opposition to the war were equated with republicanism. As Isaac Milner, the Evangelical Master of Queens' College wrote to Wilberforce in 1798: 'I don't believe Pitt was ever aware of how much consequence the expulsion of Frend was. It was the ruin of the Jacobinical party as a *University thing* so that the party is almost entirely confined to Trinity College.'[31]

Not all Cambridge Fellows who campaigned against subscription in the 1770s were antitrinitarians; and not all Cambridge Unitarians were heterodox Anglicans. George Dyer, who graduated from Emmanuel in 1778 and later became a close associate of Frend and Coleridge, was intended for the Church, but was converted to Unitarianism by a Cambridge Baptist minister.[32] Robert Robinson, whom Burke would attack so vehemently in the 1790 parliamentary debates on the Test and Corporation Acts, was Arian pastor of a Baptist Chapel congregation numbering 800 by the 1770s. A recent appraisal of Robert Hall, Robinson's successor at Cambridge, concludes that 'by the late 1780s, Robinson and his followers at St Andrew's Street in Cambridge had gained a reputation as one of the most theologically heterodox and politically radical Particular Baptist congregations in England'.[33] It was unusual for the Calvinistic Particular Baptists (who taught particular or predestined redemption) to embrace Arianism or Socinianism. Unitarian views were more usually exhibited by General Baptist congregations, who (Arminian in theology) believed in *general* redemption. More confusingly the General Baptists had split in 1770 into the orthodox 'New Connection' and the increasingly heterodox 'Old Connection', which would ultimately reinforce the Unitarian ranks.

Robinson was an active member of the County Association movement in 1779–80, and a founder-member of the Cambridge Constitutional Society. His *Political Catechism* (1782) takes the form of a dialogue between a father and his son 'George'. The father proposes annual parliaments, and agrees with George that 'if all the people have lives, liberties and properties, all the people have a natural right to choose the guardians of them'. Election excesses are deplored: 'Canvassing, carouzing, intoxication, bribery, perjury and all the usual attendants on a modern election, disgrace candidates and destroy all confidence in them, and at the same time deprave and debauch the morals of the whole community.' George is reminded that (according to 'the great Locke') there 'remains at all times inherent in the people, A SUPREME POWER to alter or remove the legislative'. When the legislature betrays 'the trust reposed in them, the trust is abused and forfeited, and devolves to those who gave it'.[34] Robinson died in his mid-50s, not in Cambridge but while staying with the Unitarian family of William Russell in Birmingham. Priestley preached the funeral sermon, in which he described Robinson at the time of his death as 'one of the most zealous Unitarians'. In a footnote to the published sermon, Priestley ventures the claim that Robinson's adoption of antitrinitarianism was 'in some measure occasioned by my own writings'. In his only letter to Priestley, Robinson had written: 'I am indebted to you for the little I know of rational, defensible Christianity. But for you, I should have gone from *enthusiam* to *Deism*; but a faith founded upon evidence rests on a rock.'[35]

In 1774, still writing as an Anglican priest, Disney had warned the Archbishop of Canterbury that the bishops' opposition to the subscription relief bills had caused 'a trial of spirits to be made throughout the land into the nature and extent of our religious rights ... and the times cannot help but foster a spread among the people of the idea that all religious groups have a right to teach and preach their beliefs'.[36] Disney's appeal to 'religious rights' recalled Locke's *Letters on Toleration*, and with it his political teaching on natural rights, soon to be embodied in the Virginian Bill of Rights and the new state constitutions. In 1774 Joshua Toulmin, Unitarian minister of a Baptist congregation at Taunton, used the phrase 'our full natural rights' in *Two Letters on the Late Application to Parliament by the Protestant Dissenting Ministers*. Addressing those who argued that the Dissenters enjoyed freedom of worship, and that the penal laws were either suspended or rarely enforced, Toulmin protested:

> A man who is not indifferent to the rights with which the Author of nature hath invested him, and who knows that conscience ought to be left in the enjoyment of perfect freedom and ease, will always seek something more than a partial toleration or a liberty by connivance.[37]

Toulmin did not then know that in 1779, at the third attempt, Dissenting ministers and schoolmasters would be excused subscription to the

Articles. By then he had advertised his Unitarianism by writing a life of Socinus. He was encouraged in the project by Priestley, writing from Leeds:

> Your scheme of a life of Socinus strikes me very much as peculiarly seasonable at this time; but you overrate my acquaintance with history, if you imagine I am able to direct you to any materials for it. Besides a critical life is not the thing I wish to see so much as a plain and judicious narrative calculated to give a favourable idea of his principles, and to inspire the lukewarm Freethinkers among us with a greater zeal for truth, and more serious endeavours to promote it.[38]

The failure of the Anglican campaign against subscription, and the consequent dispersal of Cambridge Unitarians, brought small but powerful reinforcements into the ranks of 'Rational Christians'. The resulting intellectual infusion would help to intensify the increasingly animated political discourse of the 1780s and 1790s.

3
Predicting the Millennium

Writing to Lindsey in the summer of 1771, Priestley explained that he had 'of late been very busy about some experiments on *air*, with respect to respiration and vegetation'. But he also confided to his correspondent that he sensed the approach of catastrophe: 'I shall be looking for the downfall of Church and State together. I am really expecting some very calamitous, but finally glorious events'.[1] It was not until the mid-1790s that millennialist expectations came to dominate Priestley's correspondence, and by then he had crossed the Atlantic to settle in Northumberland county, Pennsylvania. His Fast Sermon of 28 February 1794, published as *The Present State of Europe compared with antient Prophecies* had been his swan song before emigrating to America.[2]

The 1794 sermon, as befits a wartime fast day, dwells less on the glories of the thousand-year rule of Christ and his saints than on the calamities that must precede Christ's coming in judgement. Priestley nevertheless insists that Christ's kingdom will be a real kingdom, not a spiritual one, and appeals to the prophecy in Daniel 7.8: 'The saints of the Most High shall take the kingdom, and possess it for ever, even for ever and ever.' But he adds that Christ's kingdom, though a kingdom of truth and righteousness, 'will not be established without the greatest convulsions and the violent overthrow of other kingdoms'. He finds that 'every description, figurative or otherwise, of this great revolution, clearly implies violence, and consequently great calamity'.[3] Priestley, citing Jehovah's promise that 'I will shake all nations...and in this place will I give peace' (Haggai 2: 6–9), asks:

> What can be this *peace*, but the future peaceful and happy state of the world, under the *Messiah*? And what can be this *shaking of the*

> *nations* that is to precede it, but great convulsions, and sudden revolutions, such as we see now beginning to take place?

Priestley is satisfied that all New Testament prophecies concerning 'the fall of *Antichrist,* and the commencement of the proper kingdom of heaven, and of Christ, exactly correspond with those I have quoted from the *Old Testament'*.[4]

Turning to the Apocalypse, Priestley decides:

> The account that is given, in the Book of *Revelation* (xi. 15) of the commencement of the last great period, signified by the blowing of the seventh *trumpet,* when *the kingdoms of this world* are to become *the kingdoms of our Lord Jesus Christ,* is immediately preceded by *the third,* and probably far the greatest of the *three woes,* the first of which was occasioned by the conquests of the *Saracens,* and the second by those of the *Turks,* as the order of events described under the preceding trumpet evidently implies.

When (he asks) have we seen 'such anger and rage in nations, such violence in carrying on war, and such destruction of men, as at this very time?' He calculates that the allies' most recent campaign 'has destroyed more men than all the eight years of the *American* war, and probably more than the long war before it'; and considering 'the increased armaments of the belligerent powers, and their increasing animosity, it is probable that the approaching campaign will be more bloody than the last'.[5]

Priestley's implied censure of Pitt's war against republican France is followed by an attack on the 'antichristian and idolatrous ecclesiastical establishments of Christianity' in the western world, 'many more persons having been destroyed by *Christians,* as they have called themselves, than by *Heathens*'. The principal church establishment, the Papacy, is 'already and completely destroyed', in spite of attempts by European governments (foretold, according to Priestley, in Revelation 19. 19–20) to reverse the French Revolution: 'And I saw the beast, and the kings of the earth, and their armies gathered together, to make war against him that sat on the horse, and against his army.'[6] Yet in both the 1794 Fast Sermon, and his Fast Sermon of 1793, Priestley accepts the war as providential. 'War,' he explains, 'does not materially differ from other afflictions, by which God is pleased to instruct the world, and correct the vices of it. The discipline is, no doubt, severe, but it is calculated and salutary.' War operates 'like pestilence and other diseases, and various calamitous accidents, in rendering life precarious', and is 'the discipline of a wise and kind Providence'.[7] Similarly, in 1794, despite his condemnation of England's role in the war against France, Priestley finds God behind it all.[8]

Conscious perhaps of the visionary fatalism implicit in his assertion of the authenticity of scriptural prophecy, Priestley admitted to his Hackney congregation:

> As a believer in revelation, and consequently in prophecy, I am led by the present aspect of things, to look forward to events of the greatest magnitude and importance leading to the final happy state of the world. At every idea of this unbelievers will smile. But I am now addressing a society of Christians, believers in revelation and in prophecy, as well as myself; and I see no reason to be ashamed of this belief.[9]

It is not only eighteenth-century unbelievers who have smiled. Modern scepticism in matters of religion makes it difficult to take Priestley's millennialism seriously, and too easy to bracket his writings on prophecy with the extravagant millenarian claims of Richard Brothers, self-styled 'King of the Hebrews'. Yet Pitt's administration thought it necessary to call Brothers before the Privy Council, where he was cross-examined by the Lord Chancellor. The original charge against Brothers at the time of his arrest for 'treasonable practices' seems to have been quietly changed to 'writing, printing and publishing various fantastical prophecies, with intent to create dissensions, and other disturbances within this realm'. This enabled the government, like modern totalitarian regimes, to have him confined in a private asylum as a lunatic, rather than imprisoned for sedition.[10] Londoners certainly took Brothers seriously enough for thousands of them to leave the capital in the expectation that the world would end on 4 June 1795, George III's birthday.

The 1790s had opened with a spate of millenarian tracts. In 1790, the Unitarian bookseller Joseph Johnson published *The French Revolution foreseen in 1639*. Johnson's *Analytical Review* identified the original author as Thomas Goodwin, who had conjectured in his commentary on Revelation 11.13 'that some great and special honour is reserved for the saints and churches belonging to the kingdom of France; and that this kingdom will have the honour to have the last great stroke in the ruining of Rome'.[11] The *Analytical*, though not convinced that St John was predicting the French Revolution, nevertheless reviewed a number of Apocalyptic interpretations of current events, notably:

> *A Prophecy of the French Revolution, and the Downfall of Antichrist* (1793)
> *The Signs of the Times; or the Overthrow of the Papal Tyranny in France* (1793)
> *Antichrist in the French Convention* (1795)
> *The French Revolution exhibited in the Light of the Sacred Oracles* (1795).

Even the *Gentleman's Magazine* for March 1795 reviewed no less than seven millennialist publications in a single issue; and later that year it accorded a brief notice to *Conjectures on the Prophecies of Daniel and the Apocalypse of St John, in order to ascertain the Periods when the Vials of Wrath will finish*... In July 1798 the same journal would devote three double-column pages to Edward King's *Remarks on the Signs of the Times*.[12]

The year of King's publication saw William Blake annotating his copy of Richard Watson's *Apology for the Bible* with the words: 'To defend the Bible in this year 1798 would cost a man his life. The Beast and the Whore rule without control.'[13] Poetic imagery is not to be taken too literally, but Coleridge had written in *Religious Musings*:

> Rest awhile
> Children of Wretchedness! More groans must rise,
> More blood must steam, or ere your wrongs be full.
> Yet is the day of Retribution nigh:
> The Lamb of God hath open'd the fifth seal:
> And upward rush on swiftest wings of fire
> Th' innumerable multitude of Wrongs
> By man on man inflicted! Rest awhile
> Children of Wretchedness! The hour is nigh:
> And lo! The Great, the Rich, the Mighty Men,
> The Kings and the Chief Captains of the World,
> With all that fix'd on high like stars of Heaven
> Shot baleful influence, shall be cast to earth,
> Vile and down-trodden, as the untimely fruit
> Shook from the fig-tree by a sudden storm.
> Ev'n now the storm begins...[14]

Though not published until 1796, *Religious Musings* was written on Christmas Eve 1794, ten months after Priestley's farewell Fast Sermon.

In November 1794, having safely crossed the Atlantic, Priestley wrote to Lindsey from Northumberland: 'A new state of things is certainly about to take place, and some important prophecies, I believe, are about to be fulfilled.' He continued:

> The late events, and my continued attention to the prophecies, make me see this in a stronger light than I did when I wrote my Fast Sermon. Many more of the prophecies than I was then aware of indicate the great destruction that will be made of mankind before the restoration of the Jews . . . The destruction of kings seems to be particularly mentioned . . .[15]

A month later, in a reference to *Signs of the Times* by the Baptist, James Bicheno, Priestley wrote: 'I like Bicheno's idea of the seven thunders meaning the seven wars which have lately taken place since the conquests of the Turks, but there is little else that I admire of him.' As for Robert Garnham: 'I think he hazards a great deal in foretelling the duration and issue of the present war against the French.' Priestley explains: 'I am endeavouring to settle my opinion of the most probable interpretations of the principal prophecies in Daniel and the Revelation, and when I have done it, I shall write to you more fully on the subject. I have no satisfaction like that which attends the study of the Scriptures.'[16]

Shortly before leaving for America, Priestley spoke to Thomas Belsham, his successor at Hackney, about the imminence of the Second Coming: 'You may probably live to see it. I shall not. It cannot, I think, be more than twenty years.'[17] And when Lindsey objects to his views on the Second Coming, published in *Observations on the Increase of Infidelity* (London and Northumberland 1796), Priestley replies:

> You think my expectation of the second coming of Christ and the millennium, a little visionary, and therefore do not wish to have them brought forward. However the sentiment that offends you in this pamphlet, is in my Fast Sermon, and more enlarged upon.

His answer to the sceptics is that 'our Saviour supposed, not only that the second coming would be most unexpected, but that, at the time, there would be a general unbelief with respect to its ever taking place.' And what Christ himself predicted, Priestley sees 'no impropriety or inconvenience in saying after him'.[18]

A year later, Priestley writes to Lindsey from Philadelphia commending *Illustrations of Prophecy* (1796) by the young Unitarian, Joseph

Lomas Towers: 'I am glad to find that we have a young man among us of such ability, and whose mind is so properly and seriously impressed. I have learned much from this work, though I differ from him in respect to the Millennium.'[19] The scope of Towers's two-volume work may be gauged from its title: 'Illustrations of Prophecy, in the course of which are elucidated many Predictions which occur in Isaiah, or Daniel, in the Writings of the Evangelists, or the Book of Revelation; and which are thought to Foretell, among other Great Events, a Revolution in France, favourable to the Interests of Mankind, and the Overthrow of Papal Power, and of Ecclesiastical Tyranny, the Downfall of Civil Despotism, and the subsequent Melioration of the State of the World.'

Priestley similarly ranked Old Testament prophecies with those of the Gospels and the Apocalypse. Indeed the Christian Millennium is often indistinguishable from the Jewish predictions of the Last Times, which were seen as the closing period of the old order when the Messiah would appear, and the conflict between Good and Evil would reach its height. The scene is portrayed in the ancient prayer from the Jewish Prayerbook:

> We therefore hope in thee, O Lord our God, that we may speedily behold the glory of thy might, when thou wilt remove the abominations from the earth, and the idols will be utterly cut off, when the world will be perfected under the Kingdom of the Almighty, and all the children of flesh will call upon thy name, when thou wilt turn unto thyself all the wicked of the earth.[20]

'You need not be concerned,' Priestley wrote to Lindsey, 'about my not finding prophecies concerning the Messiah . . . I only expressed some *doubts* about the Christian interpretation of the 53rd of Isaiah, thinking that of the Jews, which I have been considering, more plausible than I used to think'.[21]

The recurrence of yellow fever in Philadelphia, killing over 3000, prompts Priestley to write to Belsham:

> *Pestilence* and *earthquakes,* as well as war, are to precede the second coming of Christ. I consider the *Millennium* as the day or season of judgment, and the coming of Christ to be visible and to precede this. But the Jews must first be restored to their own country, and there is some appearance of this great work being in agitation.[22]

And when news of Bonaparte's seizure of power reaches Priestley in America, he writes again to Belsham: 'I cannot believe that any turn of events will restore monarchy to France, or reinstate the popes in their temporalities; and if these two horns of the beast fall, the rest must follow.' He agrees with Belsham that there is a tendency to 'overrate the importance of events of our own times', but is convinced that the contemporary European upheavals 'are of peculiar magnitude compared with the preceding ones since the writings of Revelation'.[23]

Priestley, like Isaac Newton, would spend his last years trying to reconcile biblical prophecies both with contemporary events and with each other. In his *Notes* on the Old and New Testaments, Priestley painstakingly comments on the individual books one by one, and verse by verse. In some general observations on the subject of prophecy, interpolated between his commentaries on Ezekiel and Daniel, Priestley advises against too literal an interpretation of precise number. If we can see that 'the end, or general catastrophe, was foreseen and foretold, we should be satisfied'. The 1260 days, which occur in both Daniel and Revelation, 'may not correspond with exactness to just twelve hundred and sixty years'. Still less, he explains, can we expect 'such a number as *two thousand three hundred*, during which the temple is to remain polluted, to be literally true': the 2000 years may refer merely to the starting-point. Thus

> if the present commotions in *Europe* should eventually lead to those glorious times which is the subject of so many prophecies, and which is called by Daniel *the kingdom of heaven*, the time fixed for it more than two thousand years ago may now be come; though the happy conclusion be at a considerable distance.[24]

In his notes on the New Testament, besides specifically referring to Newton's millennialist writings, Priestley considers the relationship between the coming of Christ's kingdom at the Millennium and the four preceding kingdoms or empires. He thinks that Daniel's four beasts, which reappear in Revelation, represent the Babylonian, Persian, Macedonian and Roman empires. As for the Moslem empire, 'the resemblance between these *locusts* [in Revelation 9.3] and the *Saracens* under Mahomet and his successors, is so great that there cannot well be any doubt of their having been intended in this prophecy'.[25] Continuing his exposition of the Apocalypse, Priestley notes that 'these *kings of the earth* are, no doubt, those that are represented by *the ten toes* of *Nebuchadnezzar's* image, and the *ten horns of the beast*. And this account 'much resembles what we have lately seen in the combination of the kings of Europe against the French republic'; and the results to date of this confederacy of kings has been 'so much the same with the events announced, that it is hardly possible to recite the prophecy but in such language as describes the events'.[26]

In May 1798 the *Gentleman's Magazine* observed, not unreasonably:

> That Civil Governments are marked with censure in the Revelation is too notorious to be denied; but that political Tyranny, whether by Kings, Consuls, Dictators, Decemvirs, Directories or Cinqvirs, are not equally branded, none but those who are blind to the oppressive system of government which now desolates France, and stick at nothing to palliate it, can deny.[27]

Yet in England of the 1790s, the Apocalyptic emphasis on the overthrow of earthly kingdoms seemed to coalesce with republican rhetoric. Priestley's Unitarian standpoint differed significantly from the republican utopianism of the American poet, Joel Barlow. But the fact that from 1792 they shared not only much of the same imagery but also the same London publisher – and that both were elected to honorary French citizenship – strengthened the impression that their political aims converged, and posed a combined threat to the British constitution. Barlow, the only American apart from Washington and Hamilton to be honoured with French citizenship, was a friend of Thomas Christie, founder of the *Analytical Review*. Barlow had arrived in London with a letter of introduction from Thomas Jefferson, and the April 1792 issue of the *Analytical* carried notices of both Priestley's *Appeal to the Public on the Riots in Birmingham* and Barlow's *Advice to the Privileged Orders*.[28]

The *Monthly Review* had already noticed Barlow's pamphlet in March, reviewing it immediately before Paine's second part of the *Rights of Man*. Like the *Analytical*, the *Monthly* printed extracts from Barlow's work, and both journals singled out his invective against 'aristocratical tyrannies':

> The tyrannies of the world, whatever be the appellation of the government under which they are exercised, are all aristocratical tyrannies. An ordinance to plunder and murder, whether it fulminate from the Vatican, or steal silently from the Harem; whether it come clothed in the *certain science* of a Bed of Justice [the French *lit de justice*], or in the legal solemnities of a bench of lawyers; whether it be purchased by the caresses of a woman, or the treasures of a nation, – never confines its effects to the benefit of a single individual; it goes to enrich the whole combination of conspirators, whose business it is to dupe and to govern the nation.[29]

Both notices were in circulation before the May 1792 debate on the Unitarian Relief Bill. The government proscribed Barlow and seized his papers, but this did not prevent the *Analytical* for May from quoting 40 lines from his 300-line poem, *Conspiracy of Kings*. The *Analytical* reviewer notes: 'With the prophetic spirit which the subject inspires, our poet warns tyrants of the world not to flatter themselves with the imagination

> that nations, rising in the light of truth,
> Strong with new life and pure regenerate youth,
> Will shrink from toils so splendidly begun,
> Their bliss abandon or their glory shun,
> Betray the trust by Heav'n's own hand consign'd
> The great concentred stake, the interest of mankind.

More specifically, a second extract attacks the alliance of despotic powers combining to crush the French republic:

> Ye speak of kings combin'd, some league that draws
> Europe's whole force, to save your sinking cause;
> Of fancy'd hosts by myriads that advance
> To crush the untry'd power of new-born France.
> Misguided men! These idle tales despise;
> Let one bright ray of reason strike your eyes;
> Show me your kings, the sceptred horde parade,
> See their pomp vanish! See your visions fade!
> Indignant MAN resumes the shaft he gave,
> Disarms the tyrant, and unbinds the slave.

The concluding excerpt is a predictable paeon to 'Gallia's sons, so late the tyrant's sport'.[30]

Few of the *Analytical's* readers would have read Barlow's earlier poem, *The Prospect of Peace* (1778), which drew its imagery from the book of Daniel, and looked towards a scriptural millennium:

> Then love shall rule, and Innocence adore,
> Discord shall cease, and Tyrants be no more;
> 'Till yon bright orb, and those celestial spheres
> In radiant circles, mark a thousand years.[31]

It was a short step from Barlow's millennial vision of the end of discord and tyranny to his more avowedly political *Conspiracy of Kings*. While gently mocking Barlow's later poem for its 'American thunders', the *Monthly Review* for July 1792 used the *Conspiracy of Kings* as a peg on which to hang an anti-ministerial moral:

> We hope that these royal conspirators will meet with something more real and efficacious to arrest their career, than the fictions of poetry. We hope, above all, that they will find their subjects too wise to assist in forging, for other nations, chains which are afterward to be put on their own necks.[32]

In the summer of 1792, Britain was not yet at war with France. By the time Priestley preached his Fast Sermon in February 1794, it would be even harder to disentangle sedition from eschatology.

Part II
Pulpit-Politics

4
Essex Street: Lindsey, Disney, Belsham

In his public address to his parishioners at Catterick, explaining why he was leaving the Church of England, Theophilus Lindsey took as his prime target the liturgy of the Anglican prayerbook. Reminding his hearers of the campaign against subscription to the Thirty-nine Articles, he drew a distinction between 'our holy religion itself, the religion of Christ' as contained in 'the inspired writings of the New Testament', and 'the religion which men have made out of it, whether contained in the common-prayer book, or any other book'.[1] He recalled the attempts to revise the Anglican liturgy in the 1690s by 'many great and excellent men, Archbishop *Tillotson*, Bishops *Patrick*, *Burnet* and others', which 'through the violent opposition of some factious persons' came to nothing. Since then no further attempts at reform had been initiated by government 'through fear, perhaps, of creating disturbance in the state'. Yet Lindsey was convinced that 'an improved liturgy, brought nearer the standard of holy scripture, would be generally acceptable to the nation, and contribute to the public peace, as well as to the notion of true religion'.[2]

Lindsey next explains his personal difficulty with the established liturgy. Among things 'contrary to God's word, and sinful', he told his parishioners, are prayers addressed to the Trinity:

> I cannot approve, or offer up such prayers myself; or authorize them to be offered up by another for me. The case is different with regard to you, who have no authority in the church, who are only hearers, and do not lead the devotions of others. If you should disapprove of any part of the service which you hear, you can pass it over, and not join in it; but your minister, by reading it, makes it his own.[3]

And in his *Apology*, directed at a wider audience and quickly running to a second edition, Lindsey explains why he now focuses on the liturgy rather than the Articles. Since 'the devotions of the church are framed in strict agreement with the articles', he considers 'my continuing to officiate in them as a constant virtual repetition of my subscription'.[4] The *Apology* provides a history of Unitarianism since the Reformation, quoting Luther's description of the Trinity as 'a human invention', and Calvin's claim that the term itself was 'barbarous, insipid, profane; a human invention; grounded on no testimony of God's word; the *popish* God unknown to the prophets and the apostles'. Lindsey also prints the text of the 1698 Blasphemy Act, and devotes three pages to a long extract from Lardner's *Credibility of the Gospel History*.[5]

Lindsey's *Apology* accords eight pages to reprinting 'a list of exceptionable parts of the liturgy' which Samuel Clarke had deleted or amended in the revised liturgy he drew up but never used.[6] It was Clarke's liturgy that Lindsey adopted for his Essex Street Chapel, and which gave Essex Street its *raison d'être*. In defending the Essex Street liturgy, Priestley went further than Lindsey in arguing that laymen should not be required to participate in Trinitarian forms of public worship, even selectively. Luther and Calvin 'might with a better conscience have even received the mass, than you can kneel at the recitation of the Litany, or stand up at the repetition of the *Athanasian* creed'. If every 'serious, enlightened Christian', Priestley continues, had the courage 'to withdraw from the communion of a church in which he sees such sinful prevarication encouraged, the attention of the most supine statesmen would be excited by it'. Like Lindsey, Priestley believes that many silent supporters want a revised prayerbook, and that, while secretly agreeing with the Dissenters, they are 'ashamed of being seen in one of their places of worship, because their acquaintance in the fashionable world never come there'.[7]

That was hardly true of Essex Street. In 1774, John Lee (one of two Yorkshire MPs who were trustees of the Essex Street congregation) wrote to the Unitarian minister Newcome Cappe at York: 'There were about ten coaches at the door; which I was glad of, because it gave a degree of respectableness to the congregation in the eyes of people living thereabouts.' Listing people of substance who attended, including Lord Despenser and Benjamin Franklin, Lee added: 'All the rest were to all appearance persons of condition, and in the whole I think two hundred, and mostly of the establishment.' Lee ends with the hope that the venture 'will teach those who ought not to have needed such teachings, that Reformation is both safe and easy work'.[8] Among subscribers to the chapel were the Duke of Grafton, Chancellor of the University of Cambridge and former Prime Minister, Charles James Fox and several other MPs. Charles Howard, MP for Carlisle, supporter of parliamentary reform and later 11th Duke of Norfolk, had a pew, though he attended only occasionally. Lord Shelburne promised £100, but (unlike Fox) never paid. Grafton , who continued to attend Essex Street during William Frend's trial for blasphemy in Cambridge, would write to Belsham on Lindsey's death: 'His memory will be revered by us to our latest breath, as having done more then anyone to spread genuine Christianity.'[9]

Despite such parliamentary connections – and political prints depicting Lindsey and Priestley delivering violent speeches from the same pulpit – there is no sign in Lindsey's sermons of political reforming zeal. In some 50 published sermons in the 1810 edition, there are only the most meagre hints of a political agenda. In a sermon preached in April 1778 on the Pharisees, Lindsey permits himself to comment: 'So short-sighted are human politics when grounded on iniquitous principles... For the unjust attempts of these Jewish rulers against the life of Christ brought on the destruction of their country by the Romans.' And more specifically, in January 1780, preaching on Christian divisions at Corinth, Lindsey argues that uniformity of religious opinion and practice leads to the danger of becoming increasingly 'supine and negligent, and totally ignorant of the grounds of divine truth'. He continues:

> This really was the case before the Reformation in our own country, when no dissent from the established religion, which was popery, was permitted; and it is still seen in those christian countries of Europe, where it is held a mortal sin to doubt any of their established articles of faith; and likewise is still seen, I am sorry to say it – but I forbear to say more – in the present day in our own country.

In similar vein, Lindsey refers to imprisonment for religious opinions, 'our own country far from being excepted, even since the [1688] Revolution'. And 'at this very day, to the reproach of our nation, there are laws, not yet abolished, made against honest conscientious men, merely professing and maintaining religious opinions different from those publicly established'. The second volume closes with a sermon preached in April 1789, combining compliments to Locke with another reminder that 'cruel and unjust laws still remain in force against the rights of men and of conscience, though the spirit of the times forbids their execution...'[10]

Lindsey's mild criticisms of the Pitt ministry's support of the Anglican establishment were not quoted by Burke in Parliament. They were not even published in Lindsey's lifetime. It is modern historians who have pointed to the 'unequivocally hierarchical' assumptions of the Book of Common Prayer, and so given something of a political complexion to Lindsey's reformed liturgy.[11] If we turn from Lindsey's sermons to his private correspondence and non-theological publications, we do begin to glimpse a political motivation. The year that the first temporary premises opened in Essex Street saw the convening of the first Continental Congress in Philadelphia – a cause that Lindsey warmly supported. And in the previous year (1773), when he resigned his Catterick living, he attacked the despotic powers of Europe in his *Polish Partition*. The burlesque form of the pamphlet (in which Frederick, Catherine and Maria Theresa plan the impending partition, while the appalled Polish monarch eavesdrops on their conversation) does little to soften Lindsey's censure.[12] In the 1790s he never openly condemned Louis XVI's execution, while he wrote to Robert Millar that Pitt had lost the confidence of the House of Commons, and retained his majorities only 'by places and pensions and promises and the incalculable influence he has in his power'. A year later, he confided to Belsham his belief in Pitt's insanity, while Mrs Lindsey would comment harshly on Pitt's death: 'As a private man he had virtues, *which* may lessen the crimes of an arrogant and ambitious mind, the scourge of this vain and ungodly nation.'[13] Such private comments are important because of Essex Street's links with the political radicals of provincial Unitarian congregations. Communication occurred not only through private correspondence, but through the more public channel of the Unitarian Society for Promoting Christian Knowledge.[14]

John Disney, newly arrived at Essex Street, was the first secretary of that society. Grandson of the Rector of St Mary's Nottingham, Disney had Dissenters among his forebears. Yet he himself took Anglican orders, and was not only an honorary chaplain to Edmund Law, formerly Master of Peterhouse, but also (like Lindsey) a son-in-law of Archdeacon Blackburne. He was slower than Lindsey to resign his Anglican livings, remaining in the Lincolnshire parishes of Swinderby and Panton until 1782. After working alongside Lindsey at Essex Street for the next 11 years, he succeeded him in 1793 – an ominous year in which to pick up the reins. Disney was more politically motivated than either Lindsey or Belsham. In the early 1780s, he was involved in the parliamentary reform movement in Nottingham, and he later edited the works of John Jebb, who had been his Cambridge tutor. Jebb attended Essex Street until his death in 1786. Disney had literary links with the Commonwealth-men tradition of Thomas Hollis, whose biography Blackburne compiled. Disney would write a life of Thomas Brand Hollis (Thomas Hollis's adopted heir), and would be with Brand Hollis at the Revolution Society Dinner on 4 November 1789 after Price's famous sermon. Brand Hollis, a member of Essex Street for 30 years, helped Jebb set up the Society for Constitutional Information, and was deputed by Paine to take the key of the Bastille to George Washington.[15]

Explaining to his Lincolnshire parishioners in 1782 why he was resigning his livings, Disney referred to the 1772 petition against subscription, in which Blackburne and Lindsey took the lead: 'That petition had my entire concurrence. It maintained the only principle upon which any Protestant church, or society of Christians, can defend itself against the arguments urged in behalf of popery...' More revealingly, he conceded that, despite the petitioners' ostensibly limited aims, 'I presume there were few, if any, in the number of the petitioners, who did not look forward to a review and amendment of the established forms of public worship.'[16] In the 1770s, Disney was himself convinced that 'many doctrines received as true by the church of England, in her articles and liturgy, were not only in no agreement, but in direct contradiction to what appeared to me to be the word of God'.[17] He had nevertheless continued in the Anglican ministry, persuading himself that he could satisfy his conscientious objections by omitting the offending parts of the service:

> I never did read in the public service, the Creed, vulgarly called the Creed of Athanasius, considering it, to say the least, as entirely foreign to every good end of Christian edification. And it is now about ten years since I entirely omitted the litany and Nicene Creed, without giving any offence to my congregation.

But such omissions did not allow the minister to jettison the Trinity, since 'Trinitarian expressions and forms of worship, and express prayer to Jesus Christ, occur so frequently, and are so blended and united throughout the service, that there is no satisfactory relief to be had by partial omission...'[18]

As Disney turned his back on the Anglican Church, he looked forward to taking up a post where he might 'still bear my testimony to the truth and witness of the Gospel', and 'where prayer is avowedly made to the only true God, the Father of our Lord Jesus Christ'.[19] Disney's first publication after joining Lindsey at Essex Street was *Two Friendly*

Dialogues (1784). The first, reprinted in Philadelphia in 1785, takes the form of a dialogue between an Athanasian and a Unitarian. The Unitarian laments the fact that 'such a gross corruption of the pure religion of the holy Jesus' as the Trinitarian doctrine was not long ago 'banished from the church of England; which in the most solemn manner professeth the Scripture as the only rule of faith and practice'. Despite the departure of Unitarian clergy from the established church, 'while many more remain behind, groaning and oppressed by their conformity', the unreformed prayerbook continues in use 'in the midst of light and knowledge', and therefore 'common Christians are, with the highest reason, called upon to examine, judge, determine, profess and protest; to disregard all public authority when it stands in competition with the express declaration of Christ and his apostles'.[20] The political implications are obvious.

Yet in the 1780s it was still possible to believe that the Test Acts and other disabilities might soon be removed. In the preface to his 1787 edition of Jebb's works, Disney explains that his editorial labours have been undertaken 'in the ardour of friendship, and a firm zeal for the interest of truth, the civil and religious liberties of our country, and the improved education of the rising generation'; and he expresses the optimistic view that 'we may by gradual, and perhaps slow paces, advance in the ways of peace, to the perfection of our christian and constitutional privileges, until both prince and people shall enjoy the utmost practical extent of true liberty of both kinds'.[21] Three years later Disney would publish his *Arranged Catalogue* of publications (1772–89) relating to the campaign against subscription, and to demands for repeal of the Test Acts. The catalogue lists some 160 publications and republications on both sides of the question. His preface appeals to the Scots to 'unite with their fellow subjects in England' in campaigning for repeal'. And in a long footnote, Disney quotes the supportive resolutions proposed in Edinburgh's Presbyterian General Assembly on 27 May 1790, and the Assembly's decision that a committee be appointed 'to take the earliest opportunity to obtain redress of the grievances stated in the resolutions which the assembly have adopted, by every legal and constitutional mode which they shall judge to be the most effectual'.[22]

A fortnight after the Edinburgh resolutions, Parliament was dissolved. An attempt by a diocesan bishop to instruct his clergy on the way they should cast their vote, in the ensuing election, provoked Disney's *Address to the Bishops*. The bishop had written to warn his clergy against those MPs who supported the repeal of the Test Acts. Disney describes the letter as

> so dangerous in the principles which it advances; so unbecoming a christian and a protestant in the spirit in which it is written; so indecent and disrespectful to the commons of Great Britain in the matter of constitutional privilege, that I forbear to affix the signature, though from a principle of justice to the writer and myself, I have reprinted the libel.[23]

If the ecclesiastical constitution of Britain would be overthrown by the repeal of the Test and Corporation Acts, Disney argues, then 'this same ecclesiastical fabric', which had been laid as recently as Charles II's reign, 'must have been very feebly built, and cemented with untempered mortar, if now ready to fall in pieces after so short a lapse of time'.[24]

Disney concedes that the campaigners against the Acts also want a reformed liturgy, and the power of the bishops 'confined to the superintendency of the clergy'. But he insists that 'these matters are neither directly, nor indirectly aimed at by the application for the repeal of the Corporation and Test Acts'. Indeed, if Disney were an Anglican bishop, he would protest if the Acts were *not* repealed,

> because Christ never intended his religion to be the creature of the civil power, much less the engine of oppression; or that the rite instituted in commemoration of his death should be made a qualification for any public office civil or military.[25]

In opposition to 'the right reverend electioneer', Disney concludes that a clergyman's duty is to 'endeavour to promote the true liberty, as well as the true knowledge of the gospel of Jesus Christ', and that he is 'false to his own character' if he does not 'consent to the only justifiable principle of protestantism, in consistency with itself, by maintaining the sufficiency of the scriptures and the right of private judgement'.[26]

The preface to the first two volumes of Disney's published sermons (1793) contains a similar claim:

> The great principle of Christian liberty allows to others the same right of interpreting the scriptures, and of making profession of our judgment of them before the world, which each assumes to himself; and this liberty is the corner-stone and bulwark of the protestant reformation.[27]

And in the first sermon he preached at Essex Street as sole minister, after Lindsey's retirement in 1793, Disney argued that 'the gospel history does not necessarily require more than a plain understanding and an ingenuous and teachable disposition'.[28] Disney, like Lindsey, Priestley and Belsham, was ever the Christian preacher and teacher.

Thomas Belsham, Disney's successor at Essex Street, came from a different background. The son of a Dissenting minister at Bedford, he had a conventional Nonconformist education, starting under John Aikin at Knibworth, and eventually arriving at Daventry Academy in 1766.[29] At the end of his academic course, he was appointed assistant tutor, moving in 1778 to be minister of a Worcester congregation. When he returned to Daventry in 1781 as Divinity Tutor, Belsham was still orthodox in theology, remarking on the doctrine of the Atonement: 'So long as the Epistle to the Romans and that to the Hebrews stand as part of my Bible, so long I must take the liberty to differ from Dr Priestley.'[30] Belsham did not, however find his prospects at Daventry inviting, reflecting after his first term as Tutor: 'I have removed to a situation, the duties of which I cannot discharge, the temptations of which I cannot resist, and the trials of which I know not how to bear.' Yet he gave notable lectures on Hartleian philosophy, and one of his students would later claim that Belsham had 'found Daventry Academy brick and left it marble.'[31]

Priestley had been tutor at Warrington, but was a student at Daventry where the spirit of Doddridge's former Northampton Academy lived on. During his Daventry days, Priestley read a formidably formative list of books, from the Koran and Josephus to Samuel Clarke on the Trinity.[32] Daventry was the main training-ground for entrants to the Dissenting ministry. When Belsham was invited in 1785 to move to Warrington, he declined, even though he was by then abandoning Trinitarian theology. His method of instructing his students was:

> To state every system, to propose the arguments for and against it, to direct them to a critical investigation of the true meaning of the sacred oracles, to recommend candour, diligence, humility, impartiality, patience and perseverance in the pursuit of truth, and fervent prayer to God for divine illumination. I then leave them to judge for themselves, as in the presence of God, and accountable to him.[33]

According to his own account, it was by pursuing this method that he was himself convinced of the scriptural basis of the Socinian position. A 'meditation' dated 9 November 1787 had begun:

> The Son of God died. He came into the world to die; to give his life as a ransom. This was determined by the Father, and he was actually

> slain. Why was this great sacrifice offered? Why was the blood of the Son of God spilt? Was it to pacify the Father's wrath? The thought is absurd and blasphemous.[34]

Belsham saw that his theological beliefs were now incompatible with his continuance as tutor at Daventry. But he also clashed with the trustees on disciplinary matters. The students had petitioned the trustees for permission to use written rather than extempore prayers when leading their fellow-students in 'family' devotions. The trustees refused the request, and were understandably displeased by what Belsham called 'the unwise, unhandsome conduct' of the students in printing a letter on the subject and 'circulating it throughout the kingdom'. Yet he saw the issue as 'the encouragement given to freedom of enquiry'. He told the trustees:

> Young men, if allowed to inquire, will think and judge, and speak and act for themselves, and will sometimes differ from their seniors in opinion, and will carry matters to a greater length than those that are older and wiser can approve. Put a stop to freedom of inquiry, and I will engage for it that the Trustees will never be troubled with petitions and remonstrances. But would they wish to purchase peace at so dear a price?[35]

The same question would soon be put to the Pitt ministry by Unitarian publicists. But Belsham told his Daventry students in his farewell address that he was 'not one of those spiritual Quixotes who go in quest of adventures to acquire a name'.[36] He was now saved from obscurity by Dr Price's invitation to become resident tutor at the new Dissenting Academy at Hackney. After first declining the offer, Belsham wrote his letter of acceptance on 28 June 1789, less than three weeks before the Bastille fell.[37]

Writing 'in the confidence of friendship' to one of the Daventry trustees in 1785, Belsham had insisted: 'I have no spiritual knight-errantry in my constitution. I have no ambition to be ranked in the number of the Lindseys or the Disneys of the age; and am the farthest in the world from being inclined to "meddle with those who are given to change".'[38] And when in 1805 he was invited to succeed Disney at Essex Street, Belsham suggested that 'some seceding clergyman' would be a more suitable choice.[39] Thomas Madge, his assistant and eventual successor at Essex Street, later wrote that 'Mr Belsham's mind was of a much more sinewy and gigantic frame' than Lindsey's. Noting that the new minister was 'intimately and critically conversant with the Greek of the New Testament and the Septuagint', Madge claims that Belsham's translation and elucidation of the Pauline texts shows that

> Unitarianism makes no partial appeal to Scripture, but is the doctrine of the Old Testament and of the New; of Moses and of Christ; of the Evangelists and of the Apostles; of Peter and of Paul; of the historical and of the argumentative books; of the earliest and of the latest; of the sermons which were preached, and of the epistles which were written; of the plainest and simplest passages, and of those which are most fraught with difficulty and most liable to perversion.

Belsham's preaching is also described:

> He did his work by the sole agency of the understanding. He could accomplish little or nothing by means of the imagination or the affections. Dr Channing's sermons were not to his taste; nor could he have any such sympathy with Burke's orations, or the pathetic and impassioned pleadings of Erskine, or with the logical eloquence of Fox.[40]

The tally of Belsham's publications, listed by the same memorialist, comes to more than 50. Thirty-five of these titles are published sermons.

Barely a year after his arrival at Essex Street, Belsham preached a sermon commemorating the death of Fox. The preacher expected his audience to acquit him 'of frequently introducing political subjects into public discourse'. Such topics, Belsham considers, 'do not often find a suitable place among the lessons of moral and religious wisdom'. But he trusts that he may be excused for paying tribute to a politician 'who distinguished himself at all times as the patron and advocate, not only of civil but of *religious* liberty'. Indeed Dissenters 'would have been put into complete possession of their civil rights, if his wise and liberal policy had been adopted'.[41] Fox was not only the friend of reform, but was 'the advocate for peace; and had his counsels been pursued by this country, they would probably have ensured universal peace'. As for his response to the French Revolution: 'In this unprecedented crisis, a system was pursued by this country, directly the reverse of those mild, temperate and conciliatory measures' which Fox had proposed; in a pamphlet Fox had 'predicted with a precision little short of inspiration, the miserable consequences which ensued'. But 'so little regard was paid to his warning voice that the country, seduced by the fascination of a deluded eloquence, as though it were under a demoniacal infatuation, hurried into the opposite extreme'.[42]

Writing of Belsham as a controversialist, Madge conceded that 'like the Virginian troopers, he struck more heavily and cut more deeply than was necessary in order to disable the enemy'.[43] But in his sermons, Belsham more often adopted an oblique approach, drawing on his knowledge of St Paul. Thus, preaching at Hackney on the death of Priestley, Belsham was presumably speaking not only of St Paul:

> The most malignant opposition which the apostle encountered proceeded from those who professed, indeed, to believe in Christ, but who corrupted the simplicity of the gospel by a mixture of Jewish fable and pharisaic tradition, who were the determined enemies to the liberties of the gentile church, and were desirous of bowing the necks of the heathen converts to the yoke of ceremonial law.[44]

And in a Fast Day Sermon delivered at Essex Street on 5 February 1812, protesting at a threatened tighter enforcement of the restrictions of the 1689 Toleration Act, Belsham took his text from Acts 18. 12–16 ('And when Gallio was proconsul of Achaia . . .'). How much happier would it have been for the Christian world, the preacher suggests, if Christian governments had, like 'this philosophic heathen', 'limited the authority of penal laws to matters of injustice, licentiousness and wicked mischiefs, the proper objects of penal restraint, and had refused to take cognizance of speculative doctrine of religious distinctions, and of different interpretations of divine revelation'.[45]

Even when celebrating the removal of the stigma of blasphemy from Unitarians in 1813, Belsham contrasts 'the facility, the expedition, the unanimity with which this great measure has lately been carried through both Houses of Parliament' with the vote in 1792, when Fox's motion 'was instantly and indignantly opposed and crushed by all the power of government, and by the fascinating eloquence of celebrated politicians, who too frequently succeeded in making the worse appear the better part'.[46] Unitarian grievances of the 1790s had not been forgotten.

5
Old Jewry and Gravel Pit

Richard Price's famous sermon 'On the Love of Our Country', addressed to members of the London Revolution Society at the Old Jewry meeting-house on 4 November 1789, was preached 12 months late. He had been the designated preacher of the centenary sermon the year before, but had to withdraw through illness. Andrew Kippis, who stood in for Price in 1788, had been William Godwin's tutor at Hoxton Academy in the 1770s and was an active campaigner to relieve Dissenting ministers and schoolmasters from the need to subscribe to the Thirty-nine Articles.[1] When in 1779, North's ministry allowed Dissenters to make an affirmation of orthodox Protestant belief as an alternative to subscription, Kippis (as chairman of the committee of Dissenting ministers that had negotiated with the government) observed: 'The bill now passed does not come up to those ideas of complete and perfect toleration which we all think reasonable and just.'[2] Kippis left Hoxton Academy in 1784, shortly before it closed, and in 1786 became a tutor at the new Hackney College, though he remained minister of Princes Street Chapel, Westminster – a post he held for more than 40 years.

Now, in November 1788, hailing the 1688 Revolution as 'the most illustrious era in the civil history of Britain', Kippis began his centenary sermon by noting that the Revolution 'has been wisely celebrated from year to year, by several religious societies and several political associations'. Moreover: 'In the zeal of these various societies, for the sacred cause of Liberty, we sincerely rejoice; and we affectionately concur with them in the endeavour of promoting, by religious, civil and social acts, the genuine principles of Whiggism and of the English Constitution.'[3] Like Burke, he sees English freedom as stretching back far beyond the 1688 Revolution. Citing Tacitus as witness that our liberties came originally from Germany, and that 'as Montequieu observes, this beautiful system was invented first in the woods', Kippis continues: 'From Germany it was transplanted by our Saxon ancestors, who established a form of administration which limited the prince, and required that public affairs should be settled by assemblies of the chief men of the nation.'[4] Thus the Revolution Settlement, like Magna Carta, embodied both the recovery and the foundation of our rights.

Yet 1688 also 'conferred additional rights on the subject; fixed additional limitations to the crown and provided additional security for the continuation of our felicity'. It was then that toleration 'for the first time received a legal sanction', though the penalties imposed on Catholic priests 'were enormously severe (happily too severe to be carried into execution)'. And Kippis mildly notes the passing of the 1698 Act 'which under the pretext of restraining blasphemy, interdicted the full discussion of all religious topics, which should be allowed in every free and enlightened country'.[5] The preacher is prepared to praise the reign of George III for placing toleration of Dissenters 'on a foundation far more enlarged', expressing the hope that 'perhaps it may be reserved for the farther glory of this reign, to abolish all penal laws in matters of religion, and to put every man on the fair footing of being answerable to God for his conscience'.[6] Kippis concludes his celebratory sermon by urging parents in particular to 'inspire the breasts of ingenuous youth with an early regard for the Protestant religion, the rights of conscience and the sacred interests of political and civil liberty'. His audience's response to calls for patriotism should be: 'We will never suffer such inestimable benefits to be wrested from us; we will piously transmit them to our descendants.'[7]

The contrast between Kippis's Whiggish tone, and the more explicitly contractual rhetoric of Price's sermon a year later, is striking. Yet Kippis was unequivocal in his enthusiasm for the early achievements of the French Revolution. Preaching at Price's burial service in April 1791, Kippis first acknowledged Price's more robust language: 'It was only from a love to his country that he was sometimes inclined to deliver sentiments, which, though they might be offensive to the pride of the nation, were, in his judgement, important and salutary truths.'[8] Price had left the public in no doubt about 'the joy which he derived from the French Revolution' and he had 'occasioned a discussion that will only tend to the defeat of the enemies of freedom'. Kippis announced his own supporting position:

> May I never possess the head or heart of those who do not exult in the emancipation of twenty-five millions of people from a wretched tyranny and despotism, in the diffusion of equal happiness among

> such numbers of men; and in the prospect now afforded of the gradual melioration and the growing, perhaps, too, the rapid improvement of the state of the world in general.[9]

Kippis's scaling down of Price's overestimate of the French population does nothing to conceal how close he comes to the sentiments of Price's famous *Nunc dimittis*.

Kippis preached Price's funeral sermon only weeks before the French royal family's flight to Varennes. Price's 1789 Old Jewry sermon was preached barely a month after the march of the women to Versailles. Only the last two-and-a-half printed pages, of a 51-page address, focus on events in France. But they contain Price's notorious reference to 30 million Frenchmen 'demanding liberty with an irresistible voice; their king led in triumph, and an arbitrary monarch surrendering himself to his subjects'.[10] And not only did Price attach the French Declaration of Rights as an appendix to the published version, but he himself proposed sending the Revolution Society's congratulatory address to the National Assembly. The address reads:

> The Society for commemorating the Revolution in Great Britain, disdaining national partialities, and rejoicing in every triumph of liberty and justice over arbitrary power, offer to the National Assembly of France their congratulations on the Revolution in that country, and on the prospect it gives to the first two kingdoms in the world, of a common participation in the blessings of civil and religious liberty.

The London society's address goes on to express 'particular satisfaction' at the 'glorious example' which the French have given to encourage other nations to bring about 'a general reformation in the government of Europe and to make the world free and happy'.[11]

The sermon itself, based on words from Psalm 122 ('Our feet shall stand within thy gates, O Jerusalem'), commended the 'three chief blessings of human nature' as truth, virtue and liberty. Love of country was not 'a principle of the same kind with that which governs clans of *Indians* or tribes of *Arabs* and leads them to plunder and massacre'. On the contrary, 'our first concern, as lovers of our country, is to enlighten it'. After listing the imperfections remaining in the British constitution after the expulsion of James II, Price comes at last to the French Revolution – almost as a postscript. Referring to events in America, he expresses his delight at having been witness to *two* revolutions, 'both glorious', and calls on the 'oppressors of the world' to recognize that a new age has dawned: 'Restore to mankind their rights; and consent to the correction of abuses before they and you are destroyed together.'[12] The *Monthly Review* admitted that some readers might consider the preacher 'as entirely carried away by the turbulent spirit of party, and condemn him as deficient in true patriotism'. But the *Monthly* thinks such a verdict too harsh, 'and as philosophers and citizens of the world, we do not hesitate in expressing our general approbation of those sentiments of freedom and benevolence, which glow in the pages before us'. Yet even the *Monthly* doubts whether it was appropriate, in a congratulatory address, 'to inform the king in plain English that he is only the servant of the people'.[13]

Priestley, a Socinian in theology, had challenged Price's Arianism in *Letters to the Rev. Dr Price* (1787), but had conceded that 'you and I must wait for farther light till the arrival of *the great teacher Death*, and the scenes that will follow it'.[14] Despite their theological disagreement, Priestley welcomed Price's sermon before he had read it, writing to Lindsey from Birmingham at the end of November:

> I long much to see Dr Price's sermon, I hear so much of it from all quarters. I hope it will come soon. I rejoice that the cause of liberty seems to go on so well in Brabant and Flanders. I hope the Emperor will let them alone, and pursue his advantage against the Turks, in which I rejoice also.[15]

Having read the discourse, Priestley thought it 'most eloquent'. He told Lindsey: 'The court will be galled, but they will never hurt him. I hope it will be reprinted in a form, to distribute through the country. If you see him, do mention this to him. It may have as great an effect as his tract on Civil Liberty.'[16]

Price's *Observations on the Nature of Civil Liberty*, published in February 1776 in defence of the American colonists, went through a dozen London editions within two years, and was republished in Philadelphia, Boston, New York and Charleston. In Part I of the *Observations*, avowedly derived from Lockean principles, Price describes government as the 'creature of the people', and insists that it was 'conducted under their direction and has in view nothing but their happiness'. By contrast, the theory of Divine Right 'represents mankind as vassals formed to descend like cattle from one set of owners to another'.[17] (He used the same image when he preached at Hackney in November 1779, reminding his audience that 'we are men and not cattle'.)[18]

Part II of the *Observations* is an attack on the war with America. Sensing the futility of Britain's attempt to coerce the colonists, Price writes, in the authentic tones of the Dissenting minister, that Britain's blockade of American ports will do the colonists 'unspeakable good by preserving them from the evils of luxury and the temptations of wealth'. And Price pointedly asks: 'Instead of contending for a controlling power over the governments of America, should you not think of watching and reforming your own?'[19] The *Observations* sold over 60 000 copies in six months, and provoked a rash of hostile replies. John Wesley recorded in his *Journal*: 'I began an answer to that dangerous tract, Dr Price's *Observations upon Liberty*, which, if practised, would overturn all government and bring in universal anarchy'.[20] So vigorous was the critical response that Price wrote *Additional Observations* (1777), which he addressed to the Lord Mayor, Aldermen and Corporation of the City of London, who had presented him with a golden snuffbox together with the freedom of the city. While denying that he could be considered 'an advocate for a pure democracy', Price nevertheless emphasizes the contractual nature of government.[21] He pledges support for the British constitution, while making clear how far it falls short of his ideal. He predicts that the American war will shake the British political system to its foundations; and in a 'general introduction and supplement' to his first two tracts on America, he depicts the glorious future awaiting the colonists:

> A great people likely to be formed, in spite of all our efforts, into free communities under governments which have no religious tests and establishments! A new era in future annals and a new opening in human affairs beginning among the descendants of Englishmen in a new world. A rising empire extended over an immense continent without bishops, without nobles and without kings.[22]

Price resumed this theme after the 1783 Treaty of Paris, which recognized American independence. In his *Observations on the Importance of the American Revolution* (1784), he not only claims to see 'the hand of Providence in the late war working for the general good', but lists the major discoveries of what he calls 'the present age of increased light', likening the success of the Revolution to Newton's formulation of the laws of universal gravitation. Price goes further: 'Next to the introduction of Christianity among mankind, the American revolution may prove the most important step in the progressive course of human development.'[23] In 1778, Price had declined the offer of American citizenship, made by Congress to secure his 'assistance in regulating their finances'. The offer reflects his reputation as a writer on financial and economic matters, as much as his support of the colonists' cause.

It was for his work on mathematical probability that he was elected FRS, while his actuarial pamphlets and *Observations on Reversionary Payments* have since prompted the claim that he was 'the founder of national insurance, and the father of old-age pensions'.[24] Pitt consulted him about plans for a sinking fund, and the French finance ministers Turgot and Necker both sought his advice. Although he did not accept the Congressional invitation, Price was proud of his transatlantic connections. When he published his Old Jewry sermon, he recorded on the title-page that he was not only Fellow of the Royal Society, but 'Fellow of the American Philosophical Societies at Philadelphia and Boston'. In 1787, as the first stirrings of reform were seen in France, Price told Benjamin Franklin that 'this spirit originated in America'.[25] It was this linking of the English, American and French revolutions as part of a single movement of progressive amelioration that so incensed Burke.[26]

Before provoking Burke into writing his *Reflections*, Price had taken up the theme of progressive improvement in an earlier Old Jewry sermon (on 25 April 1787) in support of the newly founded Hackney College. Taking as his text the familiar words of the Lord's Prayer ('Thy kingdom come, Thy will be done on earth as it is in Heaven'), Price centred his hearers' attention on 'a kingdom of Christ still to come'. Christianity, he explained, 'will hereafter extend itself over all nations'. It was now 'dishonoured by much contention, superstition and wickedness. Hereafter it is to be cleared of these evils, and to triumph over all false religions ...'.[27] Discoveries may be made in the future 'which like the discoveries of the mechanical arts and the mathematical sciences in past time, may exalt the powers of men and improve their state to a degree, which will make future generations as much superior to the present as the present are to the past'.[28] Citing the discoveries of Bacon, Boyle and Newton, this new Fellow of the Royal Society is persuaded that 'the same preparation of ages, which is required to bring about advances in philosophical knowledge, is required also in religious knowledge'.[29] Price perceives progress towards complete toleration: 'God be thanked, the burning times are gone; and a conviction of the reasonableness of universal toleration is spreading fast.'[30]

In view of the violence of Burke's later attack on Price, the 1787 sermon makes instructive reading, when the preacher turns to constitutional questions. Price insists: 'So far am I from preferring a government purely republican, that I look upon our own constitution of government as better adapted than any other to this country, and in THEORY excellent.'[31] And in a footnote, he suggests that this is the view of *all* Dissenters:

> I know not *one* individual among them, who would not tremble at the thought of changing into a Democracy, our mixed form of government, or who has any other wish with regard to it, than to restore it to purity and vigour, by removing the defects in our representation, and establishing that independence of the three states on one another, in which its essence consists.[32]

Yet while extolling the separation of powers, Price states his objective of 'gaining an open field for discussion by excluding from it the interposition of civil power, except to keep the peace; by separating religion from civil policy, and emancipating the human mind from the chains of church-authority, and church establishments'.[33] The new college at Hackney will provide 'a succession of able and useful ministers', whose dissent from the established church derives from 'a dislike of the *creed* as well as the *ceremonies* of the church – from a regard to Christ as the only lawgiver in his kingdom, and the rejection of all human authority in religion'.[34]

In the advertisement to his published Fast Sermon of 1779, Price had explained (in the third person) that the notice the author had taken of 'public measures' arose necessarily in 'discussing the subject he had chosen, and in considering the present state of the kingdom'. He added a further disclaimer: 'This, however, is the first time in which he has entered into politics in the pulpit, and, perhaps, it may be the last.'[35] Ironically, several sentences from his sermon of 1779 apply equally to Britain's declaration of war in 1793. Commenting on the belligerent speed with which North's government responded to the Franco–American alliance of 1778, Price wrote: 'The alliance was commercial, and not exclusive. We might have consented to it and determined to withdraw our forces from the colonies.' Instead 'national safety was forced to give way to national dignity'.[36] Price did not live to see the 1793 declaration of war against France, but he lived a few months beyond the publication of Burke's *Reflections*. In his sermon at Price's interment, Kippis was presumably thinking of Burke when he observed:

> Amidst the strange eccentricities and obliquities of the human understanding, we have seen it to be possible for the Revolution in France to be attacked by all the power of genius, by all the richness of imagery, and by all the lustre of flowery and diversified language;

> but the most brilliant efforts of this kind are no more than the coruscations of the northern lights, which diverge into a thousand lines, and entertain the eye with their various appearances; but which at best present only a splendid confusion, and soon end in total darkness.[37]

As the founder of the *New Annual Register* in opposition to Burke's *Annual Register*, and as the editor who commissioned Godwin to write the annual historical summary of events, Kippis was well used to opposing Burke. But he was right to emphasize that, despite Price's political involvement, 'no one could be more faithful and zealous than he was in the discharge of the sacred office which belonged to him as a Christian Minister'.[38] A second obituary sermon was preached five days later by Priestley, who happened to be visiting preacher at the Gravel Pit meeting-house. This time Price's political contribution was given prominence. Reminding his audience that the French National Assembly – what he called 'the most august assembly in the world' – had styled Price 'the apostle of liberty', Priestley turned to the service the Arian minister had rendered his countrymen by warning of 'the danger arising from the increasing weight of the *national debt*'. Yet Price's political pamphlets were even more influential than his exhortations on financial matters: 'In the writings of Dr Price, citizens may ever see their rights, and magistrates their duty.'[39] His writings had made 'liberty appear more desirable and tyranny more detestable'. And Priestley famously suggested that Price's death amid the early triumphs of the French Revolution might be compared to 'the death of a warrior in the moment of victory'.[40] Even the *Gentleman's Magazine* which would soon make vitriolic comments on Priestley's emigration to America, chose to claim that when posterity celebrated 'the eras when men began to open their eyes to behold their own rights, and when this gave rise to the splendid Revolutions of America and France, the name of Price will be mentioned among those of Franklin, Washington, Fayette and Paine'.[41]

The year of Price's death was also the year of the Birmingham riots which destroyed Priestley's meetinghouse and laboratory, and thus unexpectedly brought him to Hackney as Price's successor. In his *Memoirs* Priestley described what he considered to be the success of his Hackney lectures which he 'opened to young persons'.[42] Preaching in Old Jewry, the day after Price was buried, Priestley commended the education provided in the Dissenting academies, and spoke disparagingly of England's universities: '*Newton* did not learn his system of the world from *Cambridge*. The metaphysical and moral system of *Locke* was so far from being any thing that he learned at our universities that it was a long time before it was received there.' And, as for 'the still greater discoveries of Hartley in the same field, it is only of late that they may have been known to any individuals either at *Oxford*, or at *Cambridge*, where he studied . . .'. If the minds of the young are inspired with a love of truth, 'they will be *ready for every good work*'. But if, instead, 'their minds be cramped by systems, and thereby habituated to servitude and disinclined to think for themselves in their early years, they will be prepared to oppose, instead of favouring, any great and noble efforts.'[43]

Priestley would record of his days at Hackney:

> On the whole, I spent my time even more happily at Hackney than ever I had done before; having every advantage for my philosophical and theological studies, in some respects superior to what I had enjoyed at Birmingham, especially from my easy access to Mr Lindsey . . .

He did not expect 'on this side of the grave' to be able to enjoy himself so much as he did 'by the fireside of Mr Lindsey, conversing with him and Mrs Lindsey on theological and other subjects, or in my frequent walks with Mr Belsham, whose views of most important matters were, like Mr Lindsey's, the same as my own'.[44] Priestley's most important publications during the three years he spent at Hackney were a new edition of his *Corruptions of Christianity* (first published in 1782), his Fast Sermon of 1794 and the first part of his *Letters to the Philosophers and Politicians of France*. While reiterating his reasons for being unable to sit in the Constituent Assembly, Priestley nevertheless accepts with gratitude the honour of French citizenship for himself and his son, and expresses his own willingness 'to do every thing in my power for the country that has so generously accepted me'. But he realizes that he may be about to forfeit the good opinion of his fellow citizens in France by addressing them on the subject of religion – 'a subject which I conceive to be of infinite importance to all mankind, though it appears to be much overlooked or grossly misrepresented, by the greatest part of the French nation'.[45]

Priestley was to be disappointed in his expectations, not only of the French, but of the young men of Hackney College. Belsham, who took Priestley's place as tutor when he and his wife left for America, would later give his own reasons for the failure of the college, which closed in 1796:

> It did not fail from any deficiency in attention or zeal, either on the part of the committee or the tutors. The spirit of the times was

> against the institution. And the mania of the French Revolution, which began so well and ended so ill, pervaded all ranks of society, and produced a general spirit of insubordination. The ferment of the times gave birth to insidious and even to daring attacks upon natural and revealed religion, which produced mischievous effects upon uninformed and undisciplined minds.[46]

Belsham was writing in 1812. Kippis had died in 1795, but his *New Annual Register* was still sufficiently supportive of the Unitarian cause for a correspondent in the *Antijacobin Review* to complain in January 1800:

> That the Socinian school has dealt as largely in impudence and excessive vanity, as their brother quacks of all denominations, Belsham and Priestley have testified, I acknowledge, in as convincing a manner as the writer in the New Annual Register: but not one of the three if *three there be* (for these three gentlemen must allow that it is no uncommon thing in the grand conspiracy for *three writers* ostensibly different to be *one person*, however they may deny the similar proposition on another occasion) is formed either by nature or education even to become an able polemic.

Condemning the '*old heads* that took advantage of the unsettled opinions of young men to lead them into error', the correspondent claims that the Unitarians' religious and political principles 'are shockingly confuted in characters of blood', and describes 'Socinian blasphemy' as calculated 'to generate a worse hell in eternity than Socinian politics have already done in Europe'.[47]

It would take more than the *Antijacobin Review* to silence the Unitarian voice. In a sermon preached at the Gravel Pit on 1 June 1802, to mark a General Thanksgiving for the signing of peace with France, Belsham paid tribute to 'our gracious sovereign, who hath removed from his councils those violent men who breathed the spirit of rancour and resentment, whose language was ever that of hostility and defiance, who haughtily rejected overtures of peace...' The ministers who left the government, when Pitt resigned as Prime Minister, 'by their late declarations plainly evince that as long as their counsels maintained an ascendancy, the horrors of war would have been perpetuated, and peace would have been banished from the world'.[48]

6
Fasts and Thanksgivings

Proclamations ordering the observance of specific days, as public fasts or thanksgivings, provided an unsolicited pretext for preaching and publishing politics. Consideration of such sermons as a separate genre, distinct from the occasional sermons of Chapters 4 and 5, and from the anti-war pamphlets of Chapter 9, does highlight some paradoxes. Apart from the inherent contradiction in opponents of an established church undertaking to preach at government behest, the very notion of Fast Days seems at odds with Unitarian perceptions of Providence. To invoke the aid of the Almighty by proclaiming a fast, suggests a belief in providential intervention more characteristic of a Wesley than a Priestley. But although 'Rational Christians' did not look for the *particular* providences recounted so frequently in Wesley's *Journal*, Priestley and Price both believed in a *general* providence working within history, and in the providential purposes of war. And as Fast Days were by definition proclaimed when things were going badly, censure was therefore expected – whether of public morality or government policy.[1]

Belsham used the Fast Day appointed for 5 February 1812 to reiterate the claim that 'the sacred and unalienable rights of conscience extend to the ADOPTION, the PROFESSION and the peaceable PROMULGATION of religious principles'. He called on 'all who are nonconformists to the established religion respectfully but firmly, to unite in application to the Legislature, for the repeal of the *whole* persecuting code'. If that repeal were carried, Belsham concludes: 'With what anxious vigilance would they unite in guarding the holy ark of the civil government, the sacred depository of their civil and religious freedom.' And with what

> heroic ardour would they bid a proud defiance to the gigantic foe, who, having laid waste the thrones and liberties of Europe, now

> menaces the peace of these fortunate islands, and places all his hopes in fomenting divisions in our councils, and in fanning the flame of civil and religious discord.[2]

Belsham's words come close to implying that Unitarian support of the government's war policy is conditional on the removal of the disabilities retained in the Toleration and Blasphemy Acts.

By the time Belsham came to preach his Thanksgiving Sermon in 1814, the government had not only made peace with Napoleon, but had removed the disabilities relating to Unitarians. So the preacher feels able to praise the British government for 'a laudable spirit of conciliation' and for 'treating with an humbled enemy on a footing of liberal equality'.[3] The former despotic aggression of the central European powers, is now portrayed as 'the heroic conduct of our great and magnanimous allies'. Nor must the heroic exploits of our own armed forces be forgotten, 'to whose energetic prowess and undaunted bravery, under divine Providence, this highly favoured country stands indebted for the great and singular privilege of being preserved from the ravages of war'.[4] Such unequivocal patriotic utterances doubtless reflect both a realization of the threat Napoleon had posed, and relief at any kind of peace after more than 20 years of hostilities.

Belsham had taken Isaiah 2.4 as his text: 'Nation shall not rise up against nation, neither shall they learn war any more.' He did not imagine that the newly concluded peace meant the end of war: 'It would be an infatuation to believe it. The pacificators themselves do not believe it. In the very articles of peace, provision is made for the renewal of the war.' Yet he expresses the 'unhesitating conviction that notwithstanding the present dark and unsettled state of human affairs, the glorious period alluded to in the text will in due season certainly arrive.' It is evident, Belsham claims, 'that the continually accelerated mode of human improvement confirms it; that the voice of prophecy has announced it; that the growing progress, the promised final and universal establishment of the Christian religion ensures it'.[5] Belsham is convinced that 'the times we live in are the childhood of the world. ... But the state of childhood will not last for ever. The world will grow up to maturity, and the follies, the sports and the quarrels of infancy will pass away'. Defensive wars 'must indeed always be lawful', but as men improve in wisdom and virtue, 'they will see that it is their interest not to have recourse even to the most just and necessary defensive wars', except after 'every expedient of negotiation, remonstrance and arbitration have been exhausted in vain'.[6] In referring to 'just and necessary' wars, Belsham was echoing the phrase Pitt used to justify Britain's entry into war with the French republic in 1793. It was perhaps an unconscious echo, but Belsham's insistence on 'negotiation, remonstrance and arbitration' recalls Fox's desperate attempt to avert Pitt's declaration of war 21 years before.

While measuring human improvement by 'the advancement of science, of good morals and of useful arts', and by 'the improvement of civil government, the establishment of personal and civil liberty, the powerful and impartial protection of law, and the diffusion of rational religion', Belsham makes clear that he finds his guarantee in Biblical prophecy. The promised period when wars shall cease 'will take place under the auspicious government of the Messiah, the Prince of Peace, the great object of the Hebrew prophecies, and of the expectation of the Jewish nation'.[7] Priestley had also used millennialist imagery in his Fast Sermons of 1793 and 1794 (see Chapter 3), but he had emphasized tribulation and judgement. In Belsham's *Thanksgiving Sermon*, the Apocalypse is no longer threatening.

Belsham's upbeat tone after so long a war, is reminiscent of a Fast Sermon preached by Price at Hackney near the end of the American war – eight months before Cornwallis capitulated at Yorktown. Price recognized that his audience might be tempted to give way to despair

> were the course of events under no wise and good direction, or were the present scene of trial and tumult the whole we are to enjoy of existence; – were the universe forlorn and fatherless; did joy and grief, defeat and success, prosperity and adversity, arise fortuitously without any superintendency from a righteous and benevolent power...

But if on the contrary 'there is a perfect order established in nature and infinite wisdom and goodness govern all things; and if also the scene will mend hereafter, and we are to sink only to rise to new heavens and a *new earth wherein dwelleth righteousness*', then 'the lot appointed to us is glorious'.[8] Yet Price is soon contrasting the heavenly kingdom with 'the disorders and troubles which take place among the kingdoms and under the corrupted governments of this world'.[9]

Warming to his theme, Price recalls that governments generally forget that they are 'trustees for the people governed', and that 'when they abuse their trust they forfeit their authority'. Too often they forget 'both the source and the end of their authority, and look upon the people whose *servants* they are, as their *property*, which they may dispose of as they please'.[10] In words worthy of Lord Acton, Price asserts: 'All governments turn to despotism, and will end in it if no opposition checks them. Nothing corrupts more than power. Nothing is more encroaching, and therefore nothing requires more to be watched and restrained.' And, similarly pre-empting John Stuart Mill, Price declares: 'The safety of a free people depends entirely on their maintaining a constant and suspicious vigilance; and as soon as they cease to be quick at taking alarms they are undone.'[11]

Price admits that free governments 'are apt to degenerate into faction and licentiousness, and an impatience of all controul'; and he concedes that often 'exertions *apparently* the most ardent in favour of public liberty, have proved to be nothing but the turbulence of ambitious men, and a vile struggle for places and the emoluments of power'.[12] Price therefore insists: 'He that expects to be a citizen of the heavenly Jerusalem ought to be the best citizen of this world.' Meanwhile the state of Britain is sufficiently alarming:

> We see this nation (lately the first upon earth) reduced to a state of deep humiliation. Our glory departed – fallen from our high station among the powers of the world – devastation and bloodshed extending themselves round us – without colonies – without allies – some of the best branches of our trade lost – a monstrous burden weighing us down – and at war with *America*, with *France*, with *Spain*, with *Holland*, and in danger of being soon at war with all *Europe*.

Who was to blame? Do we blame the government? Do we blame Providence? Price provides the standard response: 'We are too corrupt to deserve the favour of Providence – Let us then accuse *ourselves*.'[13] What can the Christian citizen do in this crisis?

> If we see our country threatened with calamity, let us warn it. If we see our countrymen proud and insensible to the rights of mankind, let us admonish them. If the demon of corruption is poisoning the springs of legislation, and converting the securities of public liberty into instruments of slavery, let us point out to them the shocking mischief . . .[14]

As he wishes his hearers 'every comfort this world can give', and 'eternal happiness in that country beyond the grave', Price assures them: 'In that country alone I wish for honour; and *there* God of his infinite mercy grant that we may all at last meet!'[15]

It is often assumed that the political robustness of the Fast Sermons of Price and Priestley is not matched by other Unitarian preachers. Disney's Fast Sermon on 19 October 1803, as the fragile Peace of Amiens seemed about to fail, took as his text Revelation 19.6: 'Hallelujah for the Lord God Omnipotent reigneth', thus seeming to echo Price's theme of 22 years before. Yet Disney first told his Essex Street audience that he wished to avoid 'all political considerations not immediately involved in the issue of the present stupendously awful period...'[16] Unlike Priestley in 1793 and 1794, Disney is determined to eschew the application of scriptural prophecy to contemporary events. He fears that Christian apologists have 'not seldom injured the credibility of the Christian revelation in the opinion of some' by their 'bold, however ingenious conjectures, which they have derived partly from human learning, but chiefly from their own warm and fertile imagination'. Without impeaching their individual integrity, Disney prefers to ignore the speculation of such contemporary prophets, and stick to established proof:

> The mission of the Messiah, in the person of Jesus Christ, is an historical fact; and the destruction of Jerusalem, and the dispersion of the Jewish nation, are long and present existing facts, which jointly supply and confirm as much evidence for prophecy as is necessary.[17]

Disney regards Fast Days as well employed 'when they are devoted to the advancement of true and unfeigned piety towards almighty God, and of unaffected goodwill towards all mankind'.[18] But this has political as well as religious implications. Propaganda – what Disney calls 'partial representation' of the enemy – should be avoided. Demonizing our enemies was likely to have no other effect 'than to inflame the passions of the opponent'. Disney argues that preparations for national defence, and response to the prospect of defeat, 'must be built on a broader and more satisfactory foundation than that of merely gratifying our indignation at the avowed jealousies, asperities or resentments of an ambitious and sanguinary enemy'.[19] Public fortitude must be founded 'on the sober conviction of the justice and necessity of our engaging in our self-defence – on our high regard for our constitutional liberties – on a just sense of our own independent character' and on a determination 'not to survive the loss of all that renders our country dear and valuable to us'. The alternatives need to be starkly stated: 'the establishment of freedom protected by law, and untainted by licentiousness – or bondage, characterized by the most abject slavery, and accompanied with the most corroding and pestilential infamy'.[20]

There can be no doubt about the country's unanimity in patriotic resolve: 'If there is any subsisting contention among us, it is only who shall fill the front ranks of our armies, and who shall first advance to the post of danger in the defence of our country.'[21] In the autumn of 1803, the reality of the Napoleonic threat is clearly the overriding consideration. Yet even now Disney reminds his congregation that war has nothing to do with Christianity except 'in reprobating that wicked disposition and those malignant passions which produce alike private quarrels and public feuds'. And he quotes the words of the King of Israel, when sending a messenger to the King of Syria, as recorded in 1 Kings 20.11: 'Tell him, "Let not him that girdeth on his armour, boast himself as he that putteth it off".'[22]

The tone of Disney's 1803 Fast Sermon nevertheless contrasts strikingly with the sermon he preached at Essex Street ten years before, in commemoration of the 1688 Revolution. Congratulating his 1793 audience on the way in which England's example has 'been contemplated with horror by feudal despots, while it has been looked up to with reverence and envy by the friends of freedom through the world', he nevertneless urges the need 'to correct every defect in her political constitution, and every abuse which the hand of time hath engrafted on the labours of our forefathers'.[23] Europe was already at war: 'The invasion of the liberties of France by a beleagued conspiracy of foreign force' had faltered, 'happily for the liberties of mankind.' So the great principles that 'every nation is competent to settle its own government', and that 'it is sufficient reason for any form to be adopted that the people will it so to be', would now be universally received 'as axioms in the practice, as well as the theory of politics'. And he adds, in words that might be thought in tune with the Edict of Fraternity to be promulgated by the National Convention a fortnight later: 'Like the water that washes the coast and unites it with the most distant parts of the globe, the principles and blessings of a free government will travel to, and unite with every inhabited region of the earth.' America had 'already redeemed herself from colonial oppression, and erected herself into free and united states'.[24]

Poland's new constitution (1791) and newly acquired liberty had been short-lived, but Disney is persuaded that time 'will effect what unassisted internal resources have, for the present, been unable to accomplish'. He expresses the hope

> for the benefit of one part of mankind, and the admonition of the other, that the despotic conduct of the plunderers will, ere long, upon themselves recoil, and afford another example of the price that

> must finally be paid by one nation intermeddling in the internal government of another, with which it has no concern whatever.[25]

Citing the words from *Romans* 13.1 and 2 ('Let every soul be subject unto the higher powers...'), Disney dismisses the 'exploded doctrines of passive obedience and non-resistance, which have been proclaimed by tyrants and preached by priests', and suggests that such notions 'will be found to have no more agreement with the doctrine of the apostle, than Christ hath with Belial'.[26] He concludes:

> How elevated in the rank of nations would Britain be, if once her people were restored to their just and equal share in one branch of the legislature! We should soon observe the dogmatism of established theology and the chicanery of law to disappear; our code of criminal law to forward the reformation of morals, more than to thirst for the execution of its wretched subjects...

And his final sentence proclaims the promise: 'The reign of liberty would be the reign of happiness.'[27] Disney's anniversary sermon would not capture the headlines as Price's had done in 1789, but there is little to choose between the sentiments expressed by the two preachers.

Thomas Belsham, who succeeded Disney at Essex Street, was understandably at his least controversial when preaching a Jubilee sermon there in 1809 to mark the beginning of the fiftieth year of George III's reign. Belsham takes it for granted that there can be no individual in the country 'who does not venerate the personal character and virtues of the King'. The closing sentence of the sermon echoes the words of the prayer prescribed for national use: 'that peace and security may be restored to the people, and concord and independence to the contending and bleeding nations'.[28] But the address was not pure adulation. Belsham's text was from *Leviticus* 25.10: 'And ye shall honour the fiftieth year: and proclaim liberty throughout all the land, unto all the inhabitants thereof: it shall be a jubilee unto you.' The Christian jubilee proclaimed by Jesus, Belsham explains, 'may be regarded as the Jubilee of the world. It contains glad tidings of great joy to all nations. It proclaims the remission of debts...'[29] And although Belsham confidently announces that the 'Jubilee of the true church, the triumph over error and superstition, idolatry and persecution, is begun', he adds the reminder that when Edward III proclaimed a jubilee in 1362, in the fiftieth year of his *age*, it had been marked by the granting of 'many immunities'. Thus King Edward 'solemnly confirmed in parliament the great charter of English liberty. He issued an Act of Grace to forgive all offences, to release all prisoners, even those who were charged with high-treason, and to recall all exiles'.[30]

Whether or not, in 1809, Belsham was intentionally prompting George III on the need for further reform, the king's ministers had certainly been the preacher's target in the Thanksgiving Sermon preached in 1802, while he was still at Hackney. Rejoicing in the fact that 'amidst the violence of political ferment, the British constitution has retained so much of its purity and vigour', Belsham concedes that in the 1790s 'imprudent measures were adopted by some of the partisans of popular reform' which, if left unchecked, might have caused 'confusion and anarchy'. But there were also 'great stretches of power, and violent exertions of authority' on the part of the government:

> A spirit of alarm, and of violence bordering on persecution, was with great industry, and with too much success, propagated through the country; the Habeas Corpus Act, that palladium of personal liberty, was repeatedly and for a great length of time suspended; and many individuals were thrown into prison, and treated with unnecessary and unusual rigour, for charges which were never specified...

Among individuals suffering harsh sentences were 'men of unblemished character, and the highest literary reputation, whose principal offences were verbal indiscretions'. Severe restrictions, Belsham reminded his audience, 'were laid upon public discussion, upon liberty of speech, and liberty of the press', while government encouragement 'unknown to the best periods of the British constitution, was given to the odious and contemptible breed of spies and informers'.[31]

While recommending 'seasonable and temperate reformation, to cut off the pretence, and preclude the necessity of political revolution', and suggesting that the fate of the French royal family has 'proved an awful warning to other princes to avoid the follies and crimes of the Bourbons, if they would escape such a catastrophe',[32] Belsham emphasizes the need for loyalty, though of a qualified kind:

> Let us conduct ourselves as good christians and loyal subjects... cheerfully yielding that obedience to legal authority, which is enjoined by the law, provided it doth not interfere with the rights of conscience; for conscience is a power that is not amenable to a human tribunal, and her authority, when under proper direction, is paramount to every earthly jurisdiction.

Speaking for Dissenters in general, but for Unitarians in particular, Belsham adds: 'As professed Unitarians, we are exposed to the rigours of penal laws. In this instance, and this alone, let us disobey the laws of our country, and glory in our disobedience, for "it is right to obey God rather than man".'[33] It was a call to rebellion – though a passive rebellion for a strictly limited cause. The rhetoric of the Unitarian campaign was nothing if not consistent.

Part III

Undermining Establishments

7
Censuring Pitt

The Unitarians' disillusionment with Pitt began before the fall of the Bastille and the publication of Burke's *Reflections*. William Belsham, historian-brother of Thomas Belsham, pointed to the 1787 debate on the repeal of the Test and Corporation Acts as the defining moment:

> By arguing in defence of the equity and expediency of these justly obnoxious statutes, he deserted one of the clearest and most sacred principles of whiggism. Such a question might surely have been left to take its chance in the House of Commons, without having to encounter the eloquence of a minister who set out in life as an advocate of liberal reform.

Belsham considered that if Beaufoy's first motion for repeal had received 'the slightest countenance' from the Court, it would unquestionably have been passed: 'The Parliament and the Nation were ripe for this measure of policy and justice, but Mr Pitt employed his influence to counteract it.' By siding with the Tory and High-church party in the Cabinet, Belsham insists, Pitt had necessarily lost the confidence and esteem of the most intelligent and liberal persons in the community. Instead of encouraging his natural supporters, 'from step to step, Mr Pitt has completely abandoned his original principles of whiggism; and has at length become the greatest and most dangerous enemy of liberty that this Nation ever knew'.[1]

Pitt's desertion of the Dissenters in 1787 prompted Priestley's *Letter to Pitt*, published by Johnson in the same year. Priestley's long opening sentence was hardly likely to win over the Prime Minister:

> Sir,
> Having had the opportunity of hearing your speech against the repeal of the *Test and Corporation Acts*, and thinking I could perceive

> that you had not given sufficient attention to the subject, or seen it in a true point of light, I take the liberty which I conceive not to be unbecoming an Englishman, and which, being well intended, and respecting an object of great national importance, is not, I presume, without some title to gratitude, to suggest what appear to me to be clearer ideas than you seemed to be possessed of, and such as may be the foundation of a better policy than you have adopted.

Pitt's misapprehensions are blamed on his Cambridge tutors. Educated, as he had been, 'by clergymen, who are interested in the support of the present establishment', it was not surprising that Pitt 'should have adopted their ideas of its inseparable connexion with the political constitution of this country', or that he 'should have caught their fears on the subject'.[2]

Priestley responds to the Prime Minister's excuse, that innovations unwanted by the majority might be dangerous, by claiming there was little danger in innovations that ministers persuaded the public to think well of. On the contrary: 'The mischiefs which you now apprehend from a change, might arise from any attempt to prevent the change.'[3] Meanwhile the dangers were greatly exaggerated:

> If the safety of the state depended on their being no justices of the peace, among the more opulent of Dissenters, and no excisemen, &c. among those of the lower ranks, and on all members of corporations being true churchmen, I would agree that no such characters should be admitted to such stations. But, Sir, is not the apprehension of *danger to the state* from such a change as this perfectly chimerical and ridiculous?

There was no more danger of the constitution suffering from an influx of Dissenters into public office than of 'the river Thames rising so high as to overflow the whole city of London'. Pitt might as well propose 'the immediate raising of banks high enough to prevent so great a mischief'.[4] Repeal would not lead to Dissenters filling all the executive offices of government: 'If one in a hundred was so filled, it would be far less than the number of Scotchmen who have promotion in this country; and yet nobody apprehends that, in consequence of this, any thing will be done hostile to *England*, or more favourable to the interests of *Scotland*.'[5]

Pitt had been listening to too many bishops, who (says Priestley) are 'the most timorous, and of course the most vindictive of all men, apprehensive of danger from quarters which no eye but their own could have suspected any'. The Reformation had not been initiated by the bishops, 'and after it was made by the civil power, they voted against the repeal of the act which gave them the power of burning heretics'.[6] The Prime Minister ought to have imparted his own courage to the bench of bishops and 'to have persuaded them that the thing which to their distorted imaginations appeared to be a mountain, was, in reality, a molehill'. The Test Act had been recently repealed in Ireland (1782), without any damage to the Established Church 'and without any burning of the city of Dublin'. Even the despotic powers of Europe drew their troops from all religions: 'Must all other nations have the magnanimity to adopt liberal plans of policy; and is England alone to be kept back in the glorious contest, by a regard to the idle fears of bishops, and those of a prime minister governed by bishops?'[7]

In his speech (continues Priestley), Pitt had referred to some Dissenters being 'of a more dangerous complexion than others, in consequence of their being enemies to all ecclesiastical establishments'. Priestley was proud to reply: 'I avow myself to be of this class of Dissenters and I glory in it.' But Christianity would not be saddled with establishments for ever: 'Our posterity will even look back with astonishment at the infatuation of their ancestors, in imagining that things so wholly different from each other as *Christianity* and *civil power* had any natural connexion.' Priestley's uncorrupted Christianity disdained the support of the civil power: 'It wants no support that you, Sir, as a statesman can give it, and it will prevail in spite of any obstruction that you can throw in its way.'[8]

To allay the fears of those who were so apprehensive of 'the dangerous attempts of such furious sectaries as myself and my friends, and the terror which they have conceived from our gunpowder plots &c.', Priestley offers the assurance that the method they propose to employ is 'not *force*, but *persuasion*'. He continues: 'The *gunpowder* which we are so assiduously laying *grain by grain under the old building of error and superstition*, in the highest regions of which they inhabit, is not composed of saltpetre, charcoal and sulphur, but consists of arguments.' And since Priestley and his associates sought not demolition but debate, 'if we lay mines with such materials as these, let them countermine us in the same way'.[9] The aim was to enlighten the minds of the people, and to show them how much error and superstition there was in the church establishment, so that 'in proper time, they will take it down of themselves, and either erect something better in its place, or dispose of the materials (if they should think them of any value) for some other purpose'.[10] Pitt could hardly have found this reassuring.

Non-enforcement of the surviving penal laws was not enough: 'If you would make the toleration *complete*, you must give us a power of doing that by *law*, which we now do by *connivance*, that is the power of declaring and defending our religious principles.' And Priestley makes clear that he is thinking of Unitarian principles:

> You must, in the first place, repeal the act of King William, which makes it *blasphemy* to impugn the doctrine of the Trinity. I think it my duty to attempt the utter overthrow of this doctrine, which I conceive to be a fundamental corruption of the religion which I profess, the greatest of those that mark the Church of Rome, and which was left untouched at the Reformation.[11]

If there must be a state religion, Priestley suggests in the same provocative vein, let it be 'rational and intelligible'. Let it be 'something that mankind may see to afford a natural foundation of good conduct here, and of reasonable expectations hereafter; and such is the *Unitarian doctrine*, as opposed to your Trinitarian worship in the book of Common Prayer'. He warns Pitt that Unitarian doctrine has taken deep root in the church itself, and 'is a plant of strong constitution, and makes vigorous shoots'. And its growth was being quickened by controversy. Thus, if the Established Church insists on retaining its Trinitarian doctrines and keeping up the subscription to them, 'it must in time fall with them'.[12]

Targeting the subscription tests imposed at Oxford and Cambridge, Priestley cannot have pleased Pitt (Cambridge graduate and University MP), by contrasting the English universities so unfavourably with Dissenting Academies, which 'being formed in a more enlightened age', were better suited to providing 'a truly liberal education'. Thus 'while your Universities resemble pools of *stagnant water*, ours are like *rivers*, which, taking their natural course, fertilize a whole country'. The Dissenters' educational programmes 'embrace a much greater variety of objects; and the minds of our youth, being unfettered by subscription, are certainly more open to the impression of truth'.[13]

Despite such disobliging comparisons, Priestley's pamphlet seeks to underline the peaceful character of his campaign to overthrow the establishment. He would not be understood, he insists,

> to be an advocate for any *violent* change. Anything of this kind would counteract and defeat my purposes. Every desirable step in the whole progress will be effected by the operation of reason alone,

> aided by free enquiry; and on no consideration would I have anything done by the governing powers, but with the hearty concurrence and at the requisition of the people.

All he asks of Pitt's ministry in the meantime is 'to lay no undue bias on the minds of men'.[14]

While expressing the hope that the Prime Minister's mind might yet be 'open to conviction', Priestley cannot resist a Parthian shot on the subject of electoral reform:

> I cannot conclude this address without observing that from you, Sir, we were led to expect a reform in the state of representation in this country, and other measures of public utility; and sorry I am to say that it yet remains to be seen whether you are a real friend to such measures, and choose to have your name enrolled among the very few truly and honest and upright statesmen...

The alternative judgement was that Pitt belonged to that much larger group of politicians who consulted only 'their own interest or ambition' and practised 'all the arts of deceit', and who 'beginning with imposing upon their country, have at length never failed to involve themselves in that ignominy and disgrace which they have been the means of bringing upon others'.[15]

Priestley would later concede that his *Letter to Pitt* 'gave great offence'. But he excused its excesses on the grounds of Pitt's provocative refusal to repeal the Test Acts: 'I appeal to the impartial public, whether, though written with some degree of indignation at recent, and as we thought unjust treatment, there be anything in it unbecoming men and Englishmen, unjustly and ignominiously treated.'[16] The public proved anything but impartial. Priestley admitted that hostility to Dissenters now went beyond demanding continued exclusion from civil offices, and made them objects of 'general odium and punishment'. Sermons delivered against him in Birmingham were matched by 'hundreds, I may say thousands, that were echoed from other pulpits, charging the Dissenters, in opposition to all history, and even to recent and existing facts, with principles inimical to the government of the country and to the prince upon the throne'.[17]

Not surprisingly, the Commons debate on further motions for repeal of the Test and Corporation Acts in 1789 and 1790 showed that Pitt was not 'open to conviction', as Priestley had somewhat naively hoped.

By the time of the 1790 debate, Price had committed his own act of rhetorical incendiarism, and Burke was already at work on his *Reflections*. Meanwhile debates on the question of repeal, held at Guildhall in February 1790, were reported in the *Gentleman's Magazine*. It recorded of one speaker: 'The Doctors Price and Priestley, Mr Birch observed, had spoken out pretty plainly – that the Constitution was their object; nay Dr Priestley had given the bishops public warning, scorning to take them by surprise, that he meant to begin with them.'[18] Two months later the same journal devoted eight pages to reporting the Commons debate on the Test and Corporation Acts, including Burke's reference to a 'letter' of Priestley's, 'in which he talks of a train of gunpowder being laid to the Church Establishment'.[19]

This is not quite what Priestley said in his *Letter to Pitt*, where he was careful to explain that his explosive mixture was made up of arguments. Nor does the notorious 'train of gunpowder' occur in his earlier *Reflections on the Present State of Free Inquiry*, which was published with the printed version of a sermon delivered in Birmingham on 5 November 1785. What he then said was: 'We are, as it were, laying gunpowder, grain by grain, under the old building of error and superstition, which a single spark may inflame, so as to produce an instantaneous explosion . . .'.[20] The 'train of gunpowder', with its implication of more active and deliberate demolition, appears in the reported account of Sir William Dolben's speech in the Test Act Repeal debate of 1787, in which he quoted the offending passage from Priestley's 1785 pamphlet. The parliamentary report reads: '[The pamphlet] stated that their silent propagation of the truth would in the end prove efficacious; for they were wisely placing, as it were, grain by grain, a train of gunpowder, to which the match would, one day be laid, to blow up the fabric of error . . .'.[21] It looks as if Burke (who had not attended the 1787 or 1789 debate) was in 1790 quoting the report of Dolben's 1787 speech, rather than Priestley himself.

As a chemist, Priestley was an expert in combustion, but however apt the gunpowder metaphor may have seemed in a postscript to a Guy Fawkes Day sermon, Priestley was hoist with his own rhetorical petard, long before the storming and demolition of the Bastille. And he was unwise enough to return to the gunpowder image in his *Letter to the Rev. Edward Burn* (1790), and to link it with events in France. In those parts of the preface which he had separately printed and circulated to all bishops and MPs before the 1790 debate, Priestley suggests that the vehement defenders of the establishment

> are assisting me in the proper disposal of the grains of *gunpowder*, which have been some time accumulating, and at which they have taken so great an alarm, and *which will certainly blow it up at length*; and perhaps as unexpectedly, and as completely, as the overthrow of the late arbitrary government in France.

In resisting 'reasonable repairs' to the Established Church, the Anglican clergy were labouring for its destruction more effectively than Priestley himself: 'If I be laying *gunpowder*, they are providing the *match*, and *their* part of the business seems to be in greater forwardness than mine.'[22]

Writing after the destruction of his Birmingham laboratory and meetinghouse in the 1791 riots, Priestley complained that 'it was even asserted that I had conveyed gunpowder into one of the churches, and had contrived that it should explode during divine service, and some pious ladies, I am well informed, forbore going to church under the apprehension of it'. The report was strengthened, he adds, by another that 'two barrels of gunpowder were certainly found in my house.'[23] He himself quotes lines from a song entitled *Old Mother Church*, describing Dissenters:

> Sedition is their creed
> Feign'd sheep but wolves indeed
>   How can we trust?
> Gunpowder Priestley would
> Deluge the throne with blood
> And lay the great and good
>   Low in the dust.
>
> Hist'ry thy page unfold
> Did not their sires of old
>   Murder their king?
> And they would overthrow
> King, lords and bishops too,
> And while they gave the blow
>   Loyally sing
>
> O Lord our God arise
> Scatter our enemies
>   And make them fall.
>   &c &c &c [24]

The self-imposed mantle of 'Gunpowder Joe' proved impossible to discard. However unfairly, Priestley was now cast in the role of Guy Fawkes.

Priestley's opposition to the religious establishment took the form of a personal attack on Pitt. Other Unitarian polemicists concentrated their fire on the bishops. The alliance between Pitt and the bishops, complained of by Priestley, had been highlighted in 1787 by the reprinting of Bishop Sherlock's *Vindication of the Test Acts* (1732), with a dedication to Pitt. Indeed some of the arguments deployed by the Prime Minister in 1787 and 1789 seem to have come from Sherlock.[25] Disney, who published (also in 1787) the works of his former Cambridge tutor, John Jebb, wrote a direct attack on a bishop who had blatantly interfered in local politics. His *Address to the Bishops* (1790) reprinted a letter from an unidentified bishop to the clergy of his diocese, urging them not to re-elect the sitting member because of 'the part he took in the late attempt to overthrow our ecclesiastical constitution by the repeal of the Corporation and Test Acts'.[26]

Parliament itself was attacked, notably by George Walker FRS, minister of High Pavement Chapel, Nottingham, and former mathematics tutor at Warrington. In his *Dissenter's Plea* (1790), Walker reminded the government that Parliament represented not only members of the Church of England, but 'all the free sons of Britain'.[27] According to Gilbert Wakefield, Fox regarded the *Dissenter's Plea* as the best pamphlet in the campaign for repeal.[28] There was no lack of competition. The *Analytical Review* listed 74 such publications appearing during the first six months of 1790, while Disney's *Arranged Catalogue* lists 95 pamphlets published or republished in 1790.[29] Even the normally self-effacing Robert Garnham, who (while remaining in Anglican orders) had resigned his curacies in 1789, now publicly repudiated the Christian doctrine of the Incarnation and described the 1698 Blasphemy Act as 'an antichristian act of parliament, in which the legislature arrogated powers that belong solely and exclusively to Christ as delegated by the Most Highest'.[30]

The failure of the Unitarians in May 1792 to secure the suspension or repeal of the Blasphemy Act, had followed swiftly on the rejection (30 April) of Grey's motion for parliamentary reform. John Gifford, editor of the *Antijacobin Review* and Pitt's first major biographer, would later record Pitt's contribution to both these 1790 debates. Pitt opposed Fox's motion on behalf of the Unitarians

> as it seemed to be acknowledged, on all hands, no practical evils had resulted, or were likely to result, from the laws in question, and as

> danger might possibly accrue from the repeal of them. He thought it probable too that the public might imbibe false ideas of the motives which had influenced the repeal of them; concluding from appearances, that *the House of Commons had become indifferent to the established religion, and careless of what infringements were made upon it.*[31]

And in opposing Grey's motion:

> He had seen, with concern, that those gentlemen of whom he spoke, who were members of that House, were connected with others, who professed not reform only, but direct hostility to the very form of our government. This afforded grounds for suspicion that the motion for reform was nothing more than the preliminary to the overthrow of the whole system of our present government. If they succeeded, they would overthrow, what he thought, the best constitution that ever was found on the habitable globe.[32]

On the same day Dundas proposed discussion of a proposal to form county associations, and on 21 May the royal proclamation was issued 'for the preventing of Tumultuous Meetings and Seditious Writings', the text of which Gifford would print as an appendix.[33] Gifford would also print an account of the meeting chaired by Priestley, at the King's Head in February 1791, to establish the Unitarian Society for Promoting Christian Knowledge, or (as Gifford prefers) 'in order to prove their eagerness to intermeddle in politics'. Gifford gives a list of toasts proposed on that occasion, culminating in: 'May the example of one revolution make another unnecessary.'[34]

Gifford's *Life of Pitt* took a posthumous revenge on Priestley. Commenting on the riots in Birmingham, Pitt's biographer claims that Priestley was 'a most dangerous subject; all his writings, for years, had a tendency to create dissatisfaction, in the minds of the people, with the existing institutions of the country, and to render them at once infidels and rebels'. He suggests that 'the Doctor should have been the last man in the world to complain, and that the populace, *so* irritated, and *so* inflamed, were the objects more of pity than of indignation'.[35] Grey's later tribute in the Commons to Priestley, as 'a great man' and '*a respectable person, whose character does honour to human nature, and* WHOSE WORKS DO NOT CONTAIN A SINGLE *principle hostile to government*', is ridiculed. Gifford retorts that 'independently of his wish, constantly expressed, for the downfall of the Hierarchy, and the destruction of the Established Church, in his letters to Mr E. Burke, already quoted [Priestley] praised the American Revolution as having set a glorious example to the whole world, of course including England . . .'.[36]

Almost six years after Priestley had emigrated to America, Gifford's *Antijacobin Review* for January 1800 would give prominence to *Elements of Christian Theology* by George Pretyman, Bishop of Lincoln and Pitt's former Cambridge tutor. Noting approvingly that it 'will guard the young divine against the erroneous assertions of Dr Priestley', the *Antijacobin* quotes Pretyman's claim that 'those who acknowledge the divinity of Christ and the Holy Ghost are never called heretics by any writer of the three first centuries'.[37] In January 1792, before the vote on the Unitarians' petition for relief, the Archbishop of Canterbury had written to Pitt thanking him for 'the able and effectual support, which on all occasions you have given to our Church establishment'.[38] Politically, it was hardly realistic of Priestley to expect Pitt to go against the bishops, and the tone of the *Letter* was seen as counter-productive – even by Unitarians. William Enfield disliked the constant attacks on the Church of England, believing that a religious establishment was needed for practical reasons. Nor did he believe that polemics furthered the pursuit of truth: 'His attitude towards truth was both more sceptical and more ecumenical than that of Priestley.'[39]

Enfield, though praising Priestley's *Letter to Pitt*, expressed the hope that its publication would persuade 'the world that all polemical disputes are futile and unsatisfactory . . . and that it is high time for us all to meet on the broad ground of Common Sense'.[40] The outbreak of the French Revolution and Burke's polemical response to Price's London Revolution Society sermon, together with Unitarian reluctance to condemn the execution of Louis XVI, would soon show that Enfield's irenical approach could not be sustained.

8
Challenging Burke

Priestley's response to Burke's *Reflections on the Revolution in France* was instantaneous. *Reflections* appeared in November 1790. In January 1791, Priestley's *Letters to Burke* was already being reviewed in the *Analytical*. And by April the *Monthly Review* was noting facetiously: 'Dr Priestley condemns and analyzes several of the Right Hon. Gentleman's highly rarefied and attenuated vapours; and finds them to contain a greater quantity of noxious and impure gas than of wholesome respirable air'.[1] The *Monthly*'s bantering tone did not match the pained recriminations of Priestley's preface to the first of the *Letters*.

Regretting that he and Burke found themselves on opposite sides, Priestley sadly observed: 'I must now no longer class him among the friends of what I deem to be the *cause of liberty, civil* or *religious*.' Yet Burke had been 'greatly befriended by the *Dissenters*, many of whom were enthusiastically attached to him'. And the Dissenters 'always imagined that he was one on whom we could depend, especially as he spoke in our favour in the business of subscription, and he made a common cause with us in zealously patronizing the liberty of America'.[2] By invoking the American Revolution, Priestley immediately exposed the divide that had opened up between the former fellow-campaigners in the colonists' cause. For while Priestley expressed astonishment that 'an avowed friend of the *American* Revolution should be an enemy to that of the *French*, which arose from the same general principles, and in a great measure sprung from it', Burke saw the French Revolution as arising from dangerous principles, utterly different from the American Revolution or that of 1688.[3]

Priestley's preface charges Burke with having abandoned the principles of 1688 as well as those of 1776. If Burke's newly expounded constitutional principles were accepted, 'the *church* and the *state*, once established, must for ever remain the same'. This, claims Priestley, is the

> real scope of Mr Burke's pamphlet, the principles of it being, in fact, no other than those of *passive obedience and non-resistance*, peculiar to the *Tories* and the friends of arbitrary power, such as were echoed from the pulpits of all the high-church party, in the reigns of the *Stuarts*, and of Queen Anne.[4]

In the first of the *Letters* Priestley describes Burke as appearing 'not to be sufficiently cool to enter into this serious discussion'. His imagination is 'evidently heated' and his ideas 'confused'. Priestley continues:

> The objects before you do not appear in their proper shapes and colours; and, without denying them, you lose sight of the great and the leading principles on which all just governments are founded, principles which I imagined had long been settled, and universally assented to, at least by all who are denominated *Whigs*.[5]

As for the upheaval in the French government, 'for all the evils arising from the change, you should blame, not the framers of the new government, but the wretched state of the old one'. Priestley asks (naively as it now seems) why the French should not succeed in avoiding political confusion, just as the Americans have done, 'especially as they have no enemies to contend with, and interrupt their proceedings?' Meanwhile he expresses his 'wonder that the Revolution was brought about with so much ease and so little bloodshed'.[6]

In the second *Letter* Priestley castigates Burke's dismissive treatment of the National Assembly, noting that its members are undoubtedly 'a truer representation of the French nation than our *House of Commons* is of ours'. There might be a preponderance of lawyers in the French legislature, but 'if the lawyers of *France* do as well as the lawyers of *America*, they will soon wipe away the reproach they may now lie under, and become the object of respect, perhaps of dread, to those who at present despise them'.[7] Burke's chivalrous defence of Marie Antoinette is gently mocked: 'On this subject you give the most unbounded scope to your eloquence, as if you were her *knight*, pledged to defend her honour.' There is some difficulty, Priestley suggests, in accounting for 'the fall of this queen from the height of popularity, to the abhorrence and contempt into which, you tell us, she is sunk, without supposing something very material to her prejudice, though I do not pretend to say what that is'. And he adds more ominously that, if she was 'that intriguing woman, and that enemy to their liberties, that the French people in general imagine her to have been, she may think herself fortunate to have escaped with life'.[8]

Reverting to the 1688 Revolution, the centenary of which Dr Price and the London Revolution Society had been celebrating, Priestley challenges Burke's objection to 'the doctrine of *kings being the choice of the people*', a doctrine (says Priestley) 'advanced, but not first advanced by Dr Price in his Revolution sermon'. Burke also reprobates the notion of the king being the servant of the people rather than 'our sovereign lord'. But Priestley quotes Burke's own admission that 'kings in one sense, are undoubtedly the servants of the people, because their power has no other rational end than that of general advantage'. A stern footnote reminds Burke:

> This title of *sovereign lord*, derived from the *Feudal system*, given to a king of England, is by no means agreeable to the nature and spirit of our present constitution, which is a *limited* monarchy, and not *unlimited* as that title implies. Our only proper sovereign is the parliament.[9]

According to Priestley, it is only Price's *words* that Burke quarrels with: 'Your ideas are, in fact, the very same with his, though you call his "doctrine", not only "unconstitutional" but "seditious"; adding, that it "is now publicly taught, avowed and printed", whereas it was taught, avowed, and even printed before either you or Dr Price were born.'[10]

The 1688 Revolution recognized, says Priestley, 'the right of a subject to resist a tyrant, and dethrone him', and what is this except 'in other words, shocking as they may sound to your ears, dismissing or *cashiering a bad servant*, as a person who had abused his trust?'[11] Burke had commended, in a much admired passage, 'that generous loyalty to rank and sex, that proud submission, that dignified obedience, that subordination of the heart that kept alive, even in slavery itself, the spirit of an exalted freedom'. Priestley retorts: 'I think it much easier, at least, to be preserved *out* of a *state* of servitude than *in* it. You take much pains to gild your chains, but they are chains still.'[12] If Price was at fault in expressing from the pulpit his sympathy for the French Revolution, what should be said of Anglican clergy who preach 'in defence of *arbitrary power*' on the anniversary of Charles I's execution?[13]

Priestley would later complain that it had taken Burke and his fellow parliamentary critics two decades to decide that his published political ideas were subversive:

> My 'Essay on the First Principles of Government', which, of all my writings, may be thought the most offensive to the friends of arbitrary power, was published more than twenty years ago, and never proceeded farther than a second edition, which also has been on sale for almost twenty years; so that it could not have given any recent provocation.[14]

Who, Priestley asks, has been provoking whom? If Burke fears any mischief arising from political writing, 'it has been wholly occasioned by his own'. Priestley cannot believe that 'even in this most arbitrary government ... it would be deemed treasonable, or seditious, to maintain in argument that there might be, and that there actually were, better forms of government than theirs'.[15]

Priestley's *First Principles of Government* (1768) had been cast in Lockean natural-rights language, but drew a distinction between political and civil liberty: 'POLITICAL LIBERTY, I would say, consists in the power, which the members of the state reserve to themselves, of arriving at the public offices, or, at least, of having votes in the nomination of those who fill them.' Civil liberty, Priestley defines as 'that power over their own actions, which the members of the state reserve to themselves, and which their officers must not infringe'.[16] To all intents and purposes, rulers are 'the *servants of the public* and accountable to the people for the discharge of their respective offices'. If such rulers abuse their trust, then the people 'have the right of *disposing*, and consequently of punishing them' – though Priestley concedes that this will be easier in small states than in large ones.[17]

Applying these principles to the British Constitution in 1768, Priestley had written that 'it seems to be agreed that *septennial parliaments* have brought our liberties into very imminent hazard, and that *triennial*, if not *annual* parliaments would be better'.[18] He observes that, thanks to the failure of James II, and the providential arrival of William III:

> the government of this country is now fixed upon so good and firm a basis, and is so generally acquiesced in, that they are only the mere tools of a court party, or the narrow-minded bigots among the inferior clergy, who, to serve their own low purposes, do now and then promote the cry, that the church is in danger.[19]

Yet in the next breath, Priestley defends the execution of Charles I. Were Priestley's 'first principles' republican in an anti-monarchical sense? He asserts that 'every government, in its original principles, and antecedent to its present form, is an equal republic'.[20] Consequently every man 'when he comes to be sensible of his natural rights, and feel his own importance, will consider himself as fully equal to any other person whatever'. In this context, considerations of wealth and power are irrelevant: 'Whoever enjoys property or riches in the state, enjoys them for the good of the state, as well as for himself.' Magistrates who do not consult the public good and 'who employ their power to oppress the people, are a public nuisance, and their power is abrogated *ipso facto*'. Priestley admits that 'governors will never be awed by the voice of the people, so long as it is a mere voice, without overt acts', and that such maxims imply violent action. 'But,' he asks, 'is not even a mob a less evil than a rebellion, and ought the former to be so severely blamed by writers on this subject, when it may prevent the latter?' [21]

Opinions, Priestley insists, even potentially seditious opinions, should be no concern of government. Nor should actions that have no bearing on public order: 'The greater part of human actions are of such a nature that more inconvenience would follow from their being fixed by laws, than from their being left to every man's arbitrary will.'[22] Political and civil liberty are closely connected, since 'governors will not consult the interest of the people, except it be their own interest too, because governors are but men'. So the more political liberty people have, the safer is their civil liberty.[23] He lists the safeguards against arbitrariness, provided by the British constitution, before adding:

> Whenever the *House of Commons* shall be so abandonedly corrupt, as to join with the court in abolishing any of the *essential forms of the constitution*, or effectually defeating the great purposes of it, let every *Englishman*, before it be too late, re-peruse the history of his country, and do what *Englishmen* are renowned for having formerly done in the same circumastances.[24]

Despite such hints of revolutionary menace, Priestley's *Essay* is concerned predominantly with the religious aspect of civil liberty. Defining the object of government as 'the making provision for the secure and comfortable enjoyment of this life, by preventing one man from injuring another in his person or property', Priestley cannot think the office of magistrate to be in any great danger of being encroached upon 'by the methods that men might think proper to take to provide for their happiness after death'.[25] Even atheists should be tolerated, since they can wield no terrors for the security of the state 'but what the magistrate himself, by his ill-judged opposition, may give them'.[26] And if atheists are not to be tolerated, the definition of God would need to be carefully drawn 'or otherwise *Epicureans* and *Spinozists* might be no *Atheists*; or *Arians* or *Athanasians* might be obnoxious to the law'.[27]

The 1771 edition of Priestley's *First Principles of Government*, with its associated tracts (as reprinted by Rutt), devotes nearly two-thirds of its 144 pages to questioning the need for religious establishments. Precisely the same proportion appears in Rutt's reprinting of the *Letters to Burke*, where the percentage of pages challenging religious establishments is 64 per cent – compared with 62.5 per cent for the earlier tract. The preface to the *Letters* recognizes that, although most readers will be drawn to the author's defence of the new constitutional arrangements in France, his prime concern is to refute what Burke 'has advanced on *civil establishments of religion*, which makes no small figure in his performance, and which appears to be a subject not generally understood'.[28] The sixth of the fourteen *Letters* is entitled: 'Of the Interference of the State in Matters of Religion in general'. It contains an uncompromising rebuttal of Burke's defence of the Established Church. Priestley writes: 'Religion I consider as a thing that requires no civil establishment whatever, and that its beneficial operation is injured by such establishment, and the more in proportion to its riches.' Noting that Burke offers, as a foundation for an established church, 'that man is by his constitution a religious animal', Priestley retorts that man is constitutionally an eating and sleeping animal, but asks whether it follows that 'civil government has any thing to do with his eating or sleeping'.[29] Why, Priestley asks, 'must every thing once established, be, for that reason only, for ever maintained?' He presumes that, had Burke lived in Turkey, he would have been a Moslem, and in Tibet 'a devout worshipper of the Grand Lama'.[30]

Priestley chides Burke for considering the Christian religion 'as having no respectability, without being *established*', whereas on the contrary 'Our Saviour declared that *his kingdom was not of this world*, which must mean that it did not resemble other kingdoms, in being supported by public taxes, and having its laws guarded by civil penalties'.[31] Priestley gives short shrift to the claim that the repeal of the Test and Corporation Acts would endanger the church. He reminds Burke that 'the *church of Christ* is built upon a rock, and we are assured that *the gates of hell will not prevail against it*'; and he suggests that, if the Church of England had 'been made of proper materials, and constructed in a proper manner, had it been built on this rock of *truth*, it would never have had any thing to fear. Its own evidence and excellence would have supported it'.[32] Instead, 'thinking people' must judge what must befall a church

> whose fundamental doctrines are disbelieved by men of sense and inquiry, whose articles are well known not to be subscribed *bona fide* by those who officiate in it, while the truly enlightened either keep out of the church, or relinquish their preferment in it?[33]

Burke is censured for his unexpected opposition to the latest (1790) petition to repeal the Test and Corporation Acts. As he had not opposed the two earlier petitions for repeal, the Dissenters had supposed that 'having been in other respects a friend to *equal liberty*, especially in *America* and *Ireland*, where, as well as *Scotland*, no such tests are known, you would have been a friend to us'. He ought surely to recognize that 'as we derive no *advantage* from the Established Church, we ought not to suffer any unnecessary *disadvantage* from our nonconformity to it'.[34] Though Priestley claims to speak for all Dissenters, the Unitarians see themselves as particularly victimized: 'We boldly assert the *unity of God*, and the purity and simplicity of his worship. We exclaim against all usurpation of our only law-giver, Jesus Christ, by priests or kings, by councils or parliaments.' By attempting to outlaw such opinions, Priestley warns, 'you raise a storm, the force of which you and your church will not be able to stand'.[35]

Only in his final *Letter* does Priestley return to the French Revolution. Recent events in France, as in America, 'teach the doctrine of *liberty*, *civil* and *religious*, with infinitely greater force than a thousand treatises on the subject. They speak a language intelligible to all the world, and preach a doctrine congenial to every human heart'.[36] The tone of this last *Letter* is rhapsodic:

> How glorious, then, is the prospect, the reverse of all the past, which is now opening upon us, and upon the world! Government, we may now expect to see, not only in theory and in books, but in actual practice, calculated for the general good, and taking no more upon it than the general good requires; leaving all men the enjoyment of as many of their *natural rights* as possible, and no more interfering with matters of religion...[37]

In his *Letters to Burke*, as in his *First Principles of Government*, Priestley seeks a political system that will allow full scope to religion, while freeing it from the authority of the state. *First Principles* had appeared in both its editions before the American Revolution, but during the campaign against clerical subscription to the Thirty-nine Articles. The *Letters to Burke*, though prompted by *Reflections on the Revolution in France*, reflected Dissenters' dismay at the retention of the Test and Corporation Acts.

Apart from Priestley's riposte to Burke's *Reflections*, a further 14 hostile replies by British authors appeared before Paine's *Rights of Man*. One of the first was *Vindication of the Rights of Men* by Mary Wollstonecraft, friend and neighbour of Richard Price, protégé of the Unitarian Johnson and frequent contributor to the *Analytical Review*. The *Analytical's* founder-editor, Thomas Christie, had himself attended Essex Street during his days as a medical student.[38] His *Letters on the Revolution in France* did not appear until May 1791, but Capel Lofft, another member of Essex Street, and a former Cambridge pupil of Jebb, was so swift in his response that a notice of his reply to Burke appeared in the *Critical Review* for December 1790. At this early stage in the Revolution, the *Critical* strongly supported Burke, but it nevertheless called Lofft's 100-page pamphlet 'one of the most reasonable and judicious answers to Mr Burke that has yet occurred'.[39] Lofft himself admitted that his was a hasty production, penned 'at no easy hour'. The *Monthly Review* nevertheless reckoned that the author had proved 'to our satisfaction that the right to depose unjust kings for their misconduct, to chuse their own governors, and to frame a government for themselves, was included in principle and asserted in practice' by the 1688 Revolution.[40]

The *Monthly's* reviewer (in a long footnote extending over two pages) endorses Lofft's view that the Christian cause could not be 'injured by the errors of atheism or infidelity'. The *Monthly* also commends Lofft's pamphlet for 'that mild and gentle, that kind and courteous air, which runs through the whole of it'. The review continues: 'He writes with the politeness of a gentleman, and with the benevolence of a sincere Christian. He appears not to contend for victory, but to seek for truth; and seems as happy to find it in his opponent as in himself.'[41] Besides commenting that 'the reader will perceive how much better the true nature of the social compact is understood by Mr Lofft, than by Mr Burke', the *Monthly Review* quotes a long extract listing the benefits of the French Revolution, including:

> the abolition of LETTRES DE CACHET; the vindication of liberty of conscience; the introduction of liberty of the press; the trial by jury,

> where life, liberty or reputation are concerned; the substitution of the representative will of a great people in place of the arbitrary will of an individual or of secret favouritism; the extinction of seigneurial privileges, and particularly of the game laws.

If such achievements are not sufficient reason for joy, Lofft is at a loss to know what can occur 'till the final dissolution, at which a friend of liberty and mankind can have cause to rejoice'.[42]

Besides Priestley's *Letters*, and Price's reply to Burke in the preface to the fourth edition of his Old Jewry sermon, two of the early challenges to Burke came from antitrinitarian Dissenting ministers. David Williams, Dissenting minister successively at Frome, Exeter, Highgate and Margaret Street, would later attract censure for his friendship with Roland, the Girondin Minister of the Interior. In the 1770s, Williams had published a liturgy of his own devising, together with *Essays on Public Worship, Patriotism and Projects of Reformation* (1773) and *The Nature and Extent of Intellectual Liberty* (1779). Now, in mid-November 1790, he published *Lessons to a Young Prince*. Reviewing the sixth edition in March 1791, the *Monthly* noted that 'a *tenth* Lesson is added in which the ingenious author attacks Mr Burke's Revolution-pamphlet in a strain of irony, which may produce a greater effect in the minds of many readers, than the more serious and elaborate compositions of Mr Burke's most argumentative opponents'. But the *Monthly* also records that Williams charges Burke with 'bombast, scurrility, ill-humour, indelicate allusions, distorted imagery, &c. &c.', and that he characterizes Burke's angry tone as 'not the emotion of a great and good mind; it is that of Milton's *Fiend*, contemplating the innocence of our first parents and the possible happiness of their race'. The reviewer is compelled to exclaim, 'Surely this is too severe!'[43]

Joseph Towers, close associate of Price at Newington Green, and Williams's successor at Highgate, published his *Thoughts on the Commencement of a New Parliament* in December 1790. It carried an appendix, attacking Burke's *Reflections*, and defending both the Constitutional Society and the Revolution Society against Burke's misrepresentations. On the French Revolution itself, the *Analytical Review* notices that Towers 'considers what has been done with respect to the church lands, as not only dictated by the exigencies of the state, but by the abuses and corruptions also of the ecclesiastical establishment'.[44] Towers complains that Burke 'seems much delighted that, in this country, religion "exalts the mitred head in courts and parliaments"; and that the nation pays so much honour to the "high magistrates of its church".' But (says Towers) it may 'be remarked that these "high magistrates of its church", are a sort of people of whom we read nothing in the New Testament'. He adds that Burke 'is inclined to make the most liberal provision for the bishops; but in his theory of government, he does not make, at least in this world, a very comfortable provision for the poor'.[45] Towers follows Lofft in ridiculing the notion that Christianity itself faces extinction – an outcome 'of which no man who believes its divine origin can possibly entertain any serious apprehensions!'[46] Towers ends with an appeal to the people of England to cultivate French friendship. He has no doubt what the answer of the people of England would be, if they were consulted as to 'whether the people and parliament of England have not also a right to adopt that mode of government, which they conceive to be most conducive to their own advantage'.[47] But Towers, like Priestley, has the civil disabilities of Dissenters very much in mind when he contrasts Frenchmen's newly acquired equality before the law, and career open to talent, with the British Government's retention of the Test Acts.[48]

Seven of the first 15 British responses to Burke in late 1790 and early 1791 came from antitrinitarian Dissenters, or those like Mary Wollstonecraft and Catherine Macaulay who mixed in Arian or Socinian circles. And that leaves out of account Anna Laetitia Barbould's *Address to the Opposers of the Repeal of the Corporation and Test Acts*, also published by Johnson in 1790. Mrs Barbauld – 'the first Unitarian poet' – blamed Burke, and those who opposed the removal of the Dissenters' civil disabilities, for thus uniting a highly articulate Dissenting opposition, for which Unitarians provided much of the intellectual leadership: 'If we are a party, remember it is you who force us to be so.'[49]

9
Campaigning for Peace

The most notorious Unitarian pamphlet challenging the war policy of the Pitt ministry was written before hostilities between France and Britain began. William Frend's *Peace and Union* (1793) ended with the words:

> At this moment perhaps the decree is gone forth for war. Let others talk of glory, let others celebrate the heroes, who are to deluge the world with blood, the words of market women will still resound in my ears, we are sconced three-pence in the shilling, one fourth of our labour. For what![1]

Frend devoted the second of two appendices (written after the outbreak of war, and together amounting to barely five pages) to a brief account of the overheard complaint of a group of poor women going to market. Frend could not bring himself to explain why Britain was at war: 'What is the beheading of a monarch to them? What is the navigation of the Scheldt to them? What is the freedom of a great nation to them but reason for joy?'[2] He had no hesitation, however, in proposing a remedy to his readers:

> Let the first magistrate, the peers, the representatives of the people, the rich men of the nation, all who are for war, be sconced one-fourth of their annual income to defray the expence of it. Let them be the first sufferers, let the burden fall on them, not on the poor.[3]

The first of Frend's appendices focused on the execution of Louis XVI which had 'afforded an excellent topic for parliamentary rhetorick'. But if we 'strip the subject of figures of rhetorick', the execution need cause no alarm to Englishmen: '[Louis] was accused of enormous crimes, confined as a state prisoner, tried by the national convention, found guilty, condemned and executed. What is there wonderful in all this? Our revolution, the boast of the present days, pursued the same conduct as far as possible.'[4] James II had escaped trial by fleeing the country, but 'the laws against himself and his son', and the experience of the years 1715 and 1745, 'must convince the most superficial reasoner, that the maxims of the english and french nations with respect to the dethroning of kings, are exactly the same'. Louis XVI's trial and execution were no sufficient reason for Britain to go to war:

> If Louis Capet did, when king, encourage the invasion of his country, however we may be inclined to pity the unfortunate man for the errour of his conduct, we have no right to proclaim him innocent in point of law. It is in short no business of ours, and if all the crowned heads on the continent were taken off it is no concern of ours.[5]

The provocative tone of Frend's two postscripts to *Peace and Union* is not always matched by the pamphlet itself, which claims in its opening sentence to have been prompted by 'the royal proclamations and the number of associated bodies on various pretexts in different parts of the kingdom'. Frend recognizes on the first page that 'the assassinations, murders, massacres, burning of houses, plundering of property, open violations of justice, which have marked the progress of the French revolution, must stagger the boldest republican in his wishes to overthrow any constitution'. The response of Englishmen should be to learn from such excesses, and 'instead of exasperating each other by useless invectives, to unite cordially in their endeavours to promote the common good, and to remove those grievances, if any such there be, which occasion the present discontent'.[6] The 'peace and union' of the pamphlet's title are to be promoted within the conflicting factions at home.

Britain must not, says Frend, seek to imitate the new French constitution: 'It has not received the sanction of experience, and we must wait till the wretched despots, who with unparalleled insolence dared to interrupt its course, consent to leave a nation in possession of the undoubted right to form its own internal government.' The example of America was less relevant still, and even if we could be offered 'the most perfect system that ingenuity can devise', we should not necessarily be justified in 'forcing the acceptance of it on our fellow countrymen'. The present generation must not be sacrificed to posterity. It would be wiser to 'leave to future generations the care of bringing government to the utmost pitch of perfection'.[7]

Frend makes two proposals for modest constitutional reform. He recommends triennial parliaments as a compromise between the existing septennial act and the reformer's demands for annual parliaments; and he suggests the transformations of 'rotten boroughs' by forcing them gradually to enlarge their electorate to at least a thousand. The current methods of election would need to be reformed, in order to avoid 'the bribes, the quarrels, the riots, the drunkenness, the profaneness, the blasphemies, the perjuries' that customarily surround the hustings.[8] By adopting such moderate reforms, 'we should not confound republicans with levellers'. Meanwhile the disadvantages of Utopia should not be discounted: 'To hear some persons talk of perfect representation, one would imagine that it must be the precursor of a second golden age.' It was a mistake to focus solely on parliamentary reform. We should 'seriously recommend to the contending parties to employ their thoughts on other topicks', lest they are distracted from 'the abuses, which may gradually undermine the peace and happiness of society'.[9] Among such abuses Frend instances the game laws, the inadequacy of poor relief and the frustrating complexities of the judicial system. Both legislature and public need to be 'seriously persuaded that internal good government is more productive of general happiness, than interference in foreign politicks and the triumphs of a victorious navy'.[10]

Up to this halfway point in the pamphlet, Frend has been seemingly evenhanded and (to modern eyes at least) persuasive. But, like his fellow Unitarians, he now offers hostages to fortune by attacking the Anglican establishment. The church of England, he insists, 'can be considered as only a political institution', and, with the monarch as its titular head, may become a threat to the two houses of the legislature: 'For ten thousand men in black under the direction of an individual are a far more formidable body than ten thousand that number in arms, and more likely to produce the greatest injury to civil society.'[11] But it was the vituperative tone of his dismissive description of Anglican sacraments that gave colour to accusations of blasphemy. His reference to 'the priest in every age, whether he celebrates the orgies of Bacchus, or solemnizes the rites of the Eucharist', and his characterization of the sacraments of baptism, marriage and burial as 'superstitious prejudices'[12], explain the speed with which the Master and Fellows of Jesus College condemned Frend for 'prejudicing the clergy in the eyes of the laity, or degrading in the publick esteem the doctrines and rites of the established church, and of disturbing the harmony of society'.[13] Even the *Monthly Review*, sympathetic to Dissenters and already critical of the war with France, thought Frend's tone 'must serve rather to disgust than to convince'. And the reviewer considered that, if the author wished to promote peace and union, he should not have been so ready 'to insinuate that the great body of Christians are guilty of idolatry, and to accuse the laity of being like brute beasts because they allow the clergy to baptize, marry and bury them'.[14]

Frend, like Priestley, diverted attention from persuasive arguments for constitutional reform, and from justifiable criticism of Pitt's 'just and necessary war', by the seeming violence of his rhetorical imagery. But more moderate Unitarian voices could be heard. Barely two months after Britain declared war on France, Mrs Barbauld published her discourse for a Fast Day, *Sins of Government, Sins of the Nation*. Like the first part of *Peace and Union*, the pamphlet adopts a conciliatory tone. The author begins with an implied warning to Pitt: 'Public functionaries, being intrusted with large powers for managing the affairs of their fellow-citizens . . . are very apt to confound the executive power with the governing will.' They need therefore to be 'frequently reminded of the nature and limits of their office'. But campaigners for reform also need to be restrained:

> Reformers, conceiving of themselves as of a more enlightened class than the bulk of mankind, are likewise apt to forget the deference due to them. Stimulated by newly discovered truths, of which they feel the full force, they are not willing to wait for the gradual spread of knowledge, the subsiding of passion, and the undermining of prejudices.[15]

Barbauld nevertheless warns opponents of reform: 'If you oppose conciliatory measures, you are answerable if others shed blood . . .' But she concedes, conversely, that if 'we have lessened the reverence due to constituted authorities, or slackened the bonds which hold society together; ours is the blame when the hurricane is abroad in the world, and doing its work of mischief'.[16]

Mrs Barbauld contrasts the behaviour of the ministry and its supporters in their private and public capacities: 'They would not join with a gang of housebreakers to plunder a private dwelling, but they have no principle which prevents them from joining with a confederacy of princes to plunder a province.'[17] It is clear whom Barbauld is targeting. When it comes to war, 'as both parties may be to blame, and most commonly are, the chance is very great indeed against its being entered into from any adequate cause'. Britain has been insulated from the 'calamities of war', and has had direct experience only of the 'wasteful expense of it'.

So 'sitting *aloof* from these circumstances of personal provocation', Parliament has 'calmly voted slaughter and merchandized destruction – so much blood and tears for so many rupees, or dollars, or ingots. Our wars have been wars of cool calculating interest, as free from hatred as from love of mankind'.[18]

The word 'war' needs to be translated 'into language more intelligible to us,' Barbauld suggests. When approving the army and navy estimates, we should set down 'so much for maiming, so much for making widows and orphans, so much for bringing famine upon a district, so much for corrupting citizens and subjects into spies and traitors, so much for ruining industrious tradesmen and making bankrupts . . .' We must fix our eyes

> not on the hero returning with conquest, nor yet on the gallant officer dying in the bed of honour – the subject of picture and of song – but on the private soldier, forced into the service, exhausted by camp-sickness and fatigue; pale, emaciated, crawling to an hospital with the prospect of life, perhaps a long life, blasted, useless and suffering.[19]

Barbauld is opposed to that 'species of patriotism, which consists in inverting the natural course of our feelings, in being afraid of our neighbour's prosperity, and rejoicing in his misfortunes'. She deplores the fact that 'we are not ashamed to use that solecism in terms *natural enemies*; as if nature, and not our own bad passions, made us enemies'. We behave like 'animals of prey, solitarily ferocious, who look with a jealous eye on every rival that intrudes within their range of devastation'. This language, Barbauld complains, 'is heard in a christian country, and these detestable maxims veil themselves under a semblance of virtue and public spirit'.[20]

As if war is not bad enough, Barbauld's Christian feelings are outraged by 'the impiety of calling upon the Divine Being to assist us in it'. When nations 'send out their armies to desolate a country, and destroy the fair face of nature, they have the presumption to hope that the Sovereign of the Universe will condescend to be their auxiliary in it'. Their prayer, if put into plain language amounts to this: 'God of love, father of all the families of the earth, we are going to tear in pieces our brethren of mankind, but our strength is not equal to our fury, we beseech thee to assist us in the work of slaughter'. As the majority of wars are 'the offspring of mere worldly ambition and interest', we should carry them on as other secular enterprizes are carried on, and 'not think of making a prayer to be used before murder'. Bad actions are made worse by hypocrisy: 'An unjust war is in itself so bad a thing, that there is only one way of making it worse – and that is, by mixing religion with it'.[21]

Mrs Barbauld's father had taught at Warrington Academy for 17 years, and had been there in the early 1760s when Priestley (then still an Arian) was tutor there. One of Priestley's Warrington pupils was Benjamin Vaughan, future correspondent of Jefferson, and editor of the first edition of Franklin's works. In the summer of 1793, Vaughan published his *Letters on the Subject of the Concert of Princes*. It was an edited version of letters that had appeared in the *Morning Chronicle* between July 1792 and June 1793 over the pseudonym of 'A Calm Observer'. The preface to the published collection of letters denies the right of foreigners to interfere in the internal government of other countries. Although Vaughan focuses on Russia's occupation of Poland and her suppression of its 1791 constitution, his purpose is also to censure the coalition against France – as the full title of the pamphlet makes clear.[22] Indeed the preface encourages the British people to remonstrate against the war, and urges ministers to negotiate with France in order to end it. In a seven-page notice, the *Monthly Review* concedes that 'the postscript will by some be thought tinctured with party politics', but notes that 'when parties, fortunately for the people, have once separated on grounds purely of principle, the philosopher is necessarily a partizan'. The reviewer agrees that Prussia deserves censure for first encouraging the Poles to defend their new constitution, and then 'at the first breath of Russian displeasure', failing to support the rebels.[23] The coalition of princes , Vaughan argues, seeks to 'bring the military forces and the revenues of *all* nations, to act, when requisite, upon the *people* of any *single* nation'. As a counter-coalition of peoples is impossible, the despotic powers clearly intend that 'princes shall legislate at their own discretion; and that no nation shall ever be able to right its own wrongs'.[24] Vaughan insists that the real threat to the European balance of power comes from Austria, Prussia and Russia: 'Blinded then by the smoke and vapour of French politics, we forget the real fire from an opposite quarter that may soon devour Europe.'[25] James Currie, author of *Letter Addressed to Pitt* (1793) thought that Calm Observer's letters to the *Morning Chronicle* displayed 'a perspicuity and force of reasoning that nothing can surpass. The whole series of letters far exceeds any similar production of the English press'.[26]

Coleridge, journalist as well as poet, had himself written for the *Morning Chronicle*, and relied heavily on reports from the opposition dailies when compiling his own short-lived weekly, the *Watchman*. In the third issue he reprinted a two-column comparison from the *Morning Post*, which matched the changing objectives against the successive failures of Pitt's war policy. The objectives declared in December 1792 – to prevent the opening of the Scheldt, to save Holland, and to prevent the aggrandizement of France – are matched by the Scheldt 'being solemnly opened' and Holland being conquered, and 'by France conquering territories almost equal in extent to her own'. Similarly the restoration of the French monarchy is 'obtained' by 'establishing a Republic, and seeing those who voted the death of Louis the XVIth appointed to the supreme government of France'.[27] The first issue of the *Watchman* (1 March 1796) carries a 'Review of the Motions in the Legislature for a Peace with France', from Fox's motion of 14 December 1792 to Grey's motion of 15 February 1796. The reported parliamentary responses include Lord Sheffield, 'who averred *the impossibility of negociating with a gang of robbers and cut-throats, with a murderous and savage banditti*'; Lord Loughborough, 'who stated the *Atheism* and *Ambition* of the French, as motives for the War against them'; the Duke of Portland, 'who considered the War to be merely grounded on one principle – the preservation of the CHRISTIAN RELIGION'; Earl Spencer, who 'conceived the vigorous prosecution of the War with France the only means of *preserving the British Constitution*'; and Lord Grenville, who opposed Grey's motion on the grounds 'that it was impossible to treat with men who had changed the worship of God into Idolatry of Personified Abstraction'.[28]

Coleridge's *Watchman* was published after the passing of the 'Gagging Acts' (curtailing freedom of assembly and of the press) which he had so vehemently attacked in his Bristol lecture of November 1795. So the *Watchman's* political criticism prudently took the form of reprinting without comment the words of government ministers and their supporters – though with a liberal use of italicized passages and exclamation-marks. Ironically the greatest damage to the *Watchman* was self-inflicted, by the flippancy with which Coleridge treated Fast Days. His 'Essay on Fasts', with its tastelessly provocative text from Isaiah ('Wherefore my bowels shall sound like an Harp'), was later credited with losing Coleridge many of his subscribers, even among a largely Dissenting readership. In the second of his 1795 Bristol lectures, published as *Conciones ad Populum*, he condemned those who, in the face of military calamities, sought to appease 'the anger of Heaven'.[29] Now, in the *Watchman*, Coleridge complains that 'the devotional compositions appointed for all churches and chapels, contain each year an abridgement of the Minister's latest harangues against the French', while 'the good people of this country, "in the most devout and solemn manner", tell God Almighty all that the Minister has told *them*'. His irony is directed against Trinitarians:

> For, to be sure, we ought to acknowledge with penitent hearts that we (the church-people) have been blessed beyond other nations in the knowledge of the truth (i.e. the Athanasian Creed and the Thirty-nine Articles), and the undisturbed profession of it (no Test-acts and Birmingham mobs against *us*), and in the long possession of abundant temporal prosperity.[30]

There is, however, no mistaking the serious Christian message, taken from Isaiah, with which the essay ends:

> Wilt thou call this a fast and an acceptable day to the Lord? This the Fast that I have chosen, *to loose the bands of wickedness, to undo the heavy burthens, and to let the oppressed go free, and that ye break every yoke*: to deal thy bread to the hungry, to bring the unhoused poor to thy table, and when thou seest the naked that thou cover him.[31]

Much of Coleridge's poetry, too, may be considered as directed against the war – most obviously his *War Eclogue*, written in 1796–7 and published in the *Morning Post* (8 January 1798). But poems focusing on the plight of the poor, written by Coleridge and Wordsworth during their brief but productive period of co-operation that resulted in *Lyrical Ballads*, can fairly be regarded as anti-war poetry.[32] And it was the sufferings of the poor, exacerbated by the war, that prompted the poet, George Dyer (former Christ's Hospital pupil, Cambridge associate of Coleridge and late convert to Unitarianism), to write the prose work that would outlast his poetry.

Dyer's *Complaints of the Poor People of England* (1793) was written before Britain's declaration of war against France, but it was read against the background of war experiences. The topics painstakingly listed on the title-page include the ignorance of the poor, 'disproportion between crimes and punishments', workhouses and poor rates, 'price of provisions and labour', and rules for provident societies. Dyer explains in his preface that he has decided not to publish his *Complaints* 'at large', since to do so after the recent proclamation against seditious writings 'would have argued rashness, or a species of ambition that invites persecution'.[33] This did not prevent the *Monthly Review* from noticing the second edition. Remarking that 'to attend Mr Dyer through all his wide excursions, would be to give a summary of all the present political complaints', the reviewer focuses on Dyer's criticism of the system of poor relief in pre-Speenhamland England.[34] Dyer's 'insuperable objection' to the existing system is that 'people who themselves require support, are obliged to contribute to others'. He argues that 'in America, Scotland and Ireland there are no poor rates; but the poor are not therefore neglected', whereas in England he insists that 'the poor rates are highly oppressive, and that the laws professedly for the relief of the poor, are, in some instances, penal'.[35]

In his introductory chapter Dyer celebrates contributions made by the poor in other ways:

> The prosperity of nations depends on the poor. They dig the ore out of the mine, and the stone out of the quarry. They build our houses, work our vessels, and fight our battles: yet, while the rich enjoy almost all the benefit, the poor undergo all the labour. The rich have little to do but give orders, or to sign their names, and sometimes not even that. As to the poor, what they eat, and what they wear, their firing, their candles, window-light and small beer are taxed... What do they meet in return? They are oppressed and insulted by government.[36]

As for the poorhouses, Dyer confesses that in Cambridge castle, and in many London prisons, 'people may lodge with much greater safety to their health than in several workhouses in London'. He writes of narrow lanes, 'where no air can arrive', such as St Bride's workhouse in Shoe-lane. In order to provide healthier sites, Dyer does not hesitate to say that the 'the houses of fifty rich people ought to be levelled to the ground, sooner than three or four hundred of the poor, who have spent their best days in the service of the public, should be smothered'.[37] Dyer here emerges as a 'leveller' in a literal sense.

As a Unitarian, Dyer predictably attacks the Anglican establishment. The French (he notes with approval) have 'sold their church lands, shut up their monasteries, sent their silver chests and images to the mint, and can afford England shiploads of refractory priests, gratis'. If America and France 'have found out a truth, how idly are more than three millions [of pounds] employed in England!'[38] Making clear that he opposes impressment, and prefers a militia to a standing army, Dyer grudgingly concedes the need for a navy 'while the rage for shedding human blood, and the pride of conquest last'. But he adds emphatically: 'Wars for mere conquest, however, are the wars of governments and princes; they are never beneficial to the people.'[39] Similarly, Coleridge's *Religious*

Musings, written in 1794 and published two years later, addresses Dyer's suffering poor:

> ye who weekly catch
> The morsels tossed by law-forced charity,
> And die so slowly, that none call it murder!
> O loathly suppliants! ye that unreceived
> Totter heart-broken from the closing gates
> Of the full Lazar-house: or, gazing, stand
> Sick with despair! O ye to glory's field
> Forced or ensnared, who, as ye gasp in death
> Bleed with new wounds beneath the vulture's beak!

Coleridge points his accusing finger, not only at the despotic powers, 'Austria, and that foul Woman of the North/The lustful murderess of her wedded lord!', but also at the Fast-day prayers and sermons of the Church of England.[40]

Robert Garnham's *Outline of a Commentary on Revelations XI: 1–14* (1794) sought a narrower readership than Dyer and Coleridge – though his Cambridge sermons appear in the catalogue of books distributed by the Unitarian Society for Promoting Christian Knowledge.[41] Garnham's exposition equates the Apocalyptic beast ascending from the bottomless pit with the Declaration of Pillnitz: 'The Confederates of Pillnitz have combined "to put a stop to attacks made on the throne and the altar"; that is to restore despotism and superstition, and consequently extirpate every trace of liberty'. And in a footnote Garnham notices a report in the *Star* for 26 July 1794, commenting: 'The committee of the legislature of Massachusetts, one might almost imagine, were expounding this passage of St John, when they said, "We consider the present war of Europe as a war of principles; a combination of kings and nobles temporal and spiritual against the equal rights of men, civil and religious".'[42] Unitarians were not alone in thinking that Pitt's 'just and necessary war' was the wrong war fought with the wrong allies, but the accents of biblical prophecy were seldom absent from Unitarian political protest, whether in poetry or in prose.

Part IV
Sparks of Sedition

10
National Networks

In *Peace and Union* (1793) William Frend argued that the main Dissenting denominations posed no threat to the Church of England. They were (he said) distinct bodies, normally jealous of one another, which only Parliament's refusal to repeal the Test and Corporation Acts had compelled into joint action. Were that objective to be achieved, they would 'retire to their different camps, and be separated from each other by the usual marks of theological hatred'.[1] Two decades earlier, at the height of the campaign against subscription to the Thirty-nine Articles, Priestley had written to William Turner of Wakefield: 'The Dissenting Committee waver much about their application to Parliament. Some of them have been influenced by courtiers. What they will do, I cannot tell, nor do any of themselves know.'[2]

The old Dissenting denominations – Presbyterians, Baptists and Independents/Congregationalists – had co-operated as early as the 1730s. In 1732 Dissenters had set up a representative body of laymen, the Committee of Deputies of the Three Denominations, which worked in conjunction with the General Body of London Dissenting Ministers. And in 1735 the London Dissenting ministers organized a programme of weekly sermons against Roman Catholicism, which were delivered at Salters' Hall and ran for four months.[3] But effective co-operation begins in March 1772, when a committee of 15 members was set up by the London and Westminster representatives of the three denominations, under the chairmanship of Edward Pickard. Price and Kippis were both on the committee, as was Philip Furneaux, who had challenged Blackstone in arguing that the magistrate's penal powers 'should be directed against *overt acts* only which are detrimental to the peace and good order of society, let them spring from what principle they will . . .'[4] The purpose of the committee was to argue the case against the subscription requirement for Dissenting ministers, tutors and schoolmasters. Pickard hotly denied the Bishop of Bristol's claim that the campaign was designed to promote 'Arianism, Socinianism, any schism, any heresy that any fanatic or incendiary may advance'. Pickard explained to the General Body of London Dissenting Ministers:

> It is not for or against Athanasianism or Arianism, it is not as Calvinists or Arminians, or Baxterians that we have applied and prosecuted this great affair... Sir, the principles upon which we have acted are Liberty of Conscience, the Right of Private Judgment, the Sufficiency of Scripture, and the Authority of our Divine Master and Saviour.[5]

Not all Dissenters agreed. Indeed it was claimed that, if the laity were counted alongside ministers, the number of orthodox Dissenters who 'have cause to wish that matters remain as they are', would outweigh supporters of the subscription campaign.[6] The gulf between rational and many orthodox Dissenters on this issue is illustrated by Kippis's argument that the Test Acts excluded nonconformists only 'from the enjoyment of certain civil honours and preferments, whereas the penal statutes deprive us of the common rights of human nature and of Christianity'. Toleration, he thought, should not be confined to Christians: 'I am of the opinion that the magistrate hath no right to interfere in religious matters so as to lay any restraint upon or prescribe any test to those who behave as peaceful subjects.'[7] Kippis was chairman of the committee of Dissenting ministers that negotiated the abolition of subscription to the Articles in the 1779 Act, and, though he was not pleased with the declaration of Protestantism that replaced it, he and his committee secured the deletion of 'whole' from the assertion that the Scriptures 'do contain the whole revealed will of God'.[8] In 1785 Kippis presented to Pitt a resolution from the General Body in response to the Registration Act of 1783, which had excluded Dissenters from the requirement to pay the new Stamp Duty on the registration of births, marriages and burials. Asserting the willingness of Dissenters to pay the duty in order to secure the benefits of legal registration, the resolution spoke of their 'most affectionate disposition to share in this and every other tax'. The Act was swiftly amended to include all Protestant Dissenters.[9]

John Gifford's *Life of Pitt* (1809), reporting the Prime Minister's speech in the 1790 debate on the motion to repeal the Test and

Corporation Acts, ironically records Pitt's reference to these earlier concessions:

> Dr Kippis, a man of no inconsiderable rank and esteem among [the Dissenters], in his letter on the subject, declared that, after obtaining the toleration in question, they would ask no more of the legislature, but would retire, graceful and content, to their books and closets, impressed with a becoming sense of the great indulgence with which they had been favoured.[10]

Gifford, in a concluding comment on the debate, expresses his 'astonishment' that, 'after this clear and full development of the views and designs of the Dissenters, *one hundred and five members* of the House of Commons should have voted for supplying them with the power of carrying their plans into effect'.[11]

In the 1780s, Kippis and his fellow Unitarian minister, Joseph Towers, spent much time closeted with their books. The years 1780–93 saw their joint production of *Biographia Britannica* in five volumes. By 1780 Kippis already had several publications to his credit, and in 1781 he launched the *New Annual Register*. Towers, self-taught by being apprenticed (like Benjamin Franklin) to a printer, was already by 1766 'a reader at the British Museum, examining papers and acquiring that kind of knowledge, which enabled him afterwards ... to vindicate freedom and its friends'.[12] After writing pamphlets in the 1770s against John Wesley and Dr Johnson, Towers published in 1778 *Observations on Mr Hume's History of England*, which challenged Hume's version both of the Reformation and of the Stuart monarchy. Towers finds Hume 'no friend to Protestant principles, that all men have a right to examine for themselves the foundations of those religious opinions which are proposed to them'; and he contradicts Hume's contention that (as Towers puts it) 'the people of England did not know before the reign of James the First that they held any of their privileges by any other tenure than the pleasure of the prince'.[13] As for Hume's claim that Charles I's assent to the Petition of Right 'produced a change in the government, as was almost equivalent to a revolution', Towers retorts that 'the liberties and privileges claimed by this petition were unquestionably founded on the ancient laws of the kingdom'.[14] In 1782, Towers replied to Dean Tucker's pamphlet attacking John Locke's 'levelling principles'. In his summary of Locke's theses, Towers concludes with the assertion that 'kings and princes, magistrates and rulers of every class, have no just authority but what is delegated to them by the people; and which, when not employed for their benefit, the people have always a right to resume, in whatever hands it may be placed'.[15] It is no surprise to find Towers challenging Burke in 1790, and republishing his own defence of Locke in 1796.

In the mid-1780s, however, responsibility for lobbying Parliament on behalf of the Dissenters lay with the more moderate Edward Jeffries and his special committee of 21 lay deputies. After the failure of the second motion for repeal of the Test Acts in 1789, a request for a London meeting was signed by 44 Dissenting ministers and laymen, including, Kippis, Towers, Price and Lofft.[16] The Dissenting Deputies and the General Body of Dissenting Ministers decided against a meeting, but in January 1790 the Jeffries Committee drafted a circular to provincial committees suggesting 'the necessity of making application to every member of Parliament within your district to give his attendance and support when the motion [for repeal] shall be made in the House of Commons'. Attached to the circular letter were lists of those MPs who had supported the Dissenters in the votes of 1787 and 1789.[17] After the third defeat, in 1790, the Jeffries committee was superseded by the Standing Committee of Protestant Dissenters in England and Wales. Although there seems to be no documentary evidence that the proposed convention of 42 delegates from the counties, and 21 from the Deputies, was actually convened, it is clear that the committee met early in 1791 under the chairmanship of Michael Dodson, London barrister and member of the Essex Street congregation.[18]

Essex Street Chapel was important, not only because of its links with members of both Houses of Parliament, but because of its distribution network that linked London with Unitarian congregations in the provinces. The Society for Promoting Knowledge of the Scriptures was set up by Lindsey, Disney and Jebb in 1783. Among its 41 members at the end of the year were: Lee and Brand Hollis (MPs), Edmund Law (Bishop of Carlisle), Tyrwhitt and Lambert (Cambridge University), Priestley and William Russell (Birmingham), William Tayleur (Shrewsbury), William Christie (Montrose) and Major John Cartwright. The object of the Society, Lindsey told Tayleur, was 'to circulate rational sentiments of Christianity among the people'. A committee to select tracts for publication comprised Dodson, Kippis and Jebb.[19] Disney, as secretary, soon established links with Priestley's *Theological Repository*, and extended the Society's activities, from mere circulation of existing publications, to publishing tracts in its own right. Tayleur, writing to Lindsey early in 1784, reported that individuals he had consulted 'think your present plan by no means well adapted to render the gospel level to the capacities of the common people' – which in Tayleur's view had been the original objective.[20] More serious than Tayleur's misgivings was the unexpected death of Jebb in 1786. But already by the end of 1785, a lack of suitable tracts for publication led the Society to waive the membership subscription for the following year.[21]

An effective Unitarian network dates from 1790, when Disney, Dodson, and Belsham drew up a plan which (according to Lindsey) would involve correspondence being conducted 'with friends in every great town and district in the Kingdom'. Lindsey added that 'Ireland and Scotland also by and by may come in'.[22] The new Unitarian Society for Promoting Christian Knowledge and the Practice of Virtue held its first meeting in February 1791. It defined its Christian objectives as:

> To advance the interests of truth and virtue; to promote peace, liberty and good order in society; to accelerate the improvement of the species; and to exalt the character, and secure the greatest happiness of individuals, by disseminating the right principles of religion, and by exciting the attention of men to the genuine doctrines of revelation.

And its method was described as 'distributing such books as appear to members of the society to contain the most rational view of the gospel, and to be most free from the errors by which it has been long sullied and obscured'.[23]

The same statement of aims defined 'Unitarian' so as to exclude Arians:

> The fundamental principles of this society are, That there is but ONE God, the SOLE Former, Supporter, and Governor of the universe, the ONLY proper object of religious worship; and that there is one mediator between God and men, the MAN Christ Jesus, who was commissioned by God to instruct men in their duty, and to reveal the doctrine of a future life.

Some members of the earlier society – notably the Cambridge University contingent – withdrew their support in protest at so exclusive a definition. Lindsey and Belsham, surprised by the objections, had opposed concessions on Christology. Lindsey told Tayleur he suspected the objections 'originated in a secret apprehension, perhaps unknown to themselves, of appearing in print as Unitarians'.[24] The Arian Dr Price nevertheless subscribed ten guineas to the new society. The clearer sense of identity, imparted to the new society by its exclusive definition of membership, is seen in its campaign to free Unitarians from the stigma and continuing proscription of being 'Blasphemers of the Trinity'. The Society's increasing radicalism, after the failure of the Unitarian Relief Bill of 1792, is reflected in its choice of publications for circulation. These include: Samuel Heywood's *High Church Politics* (1791), Benjamin Flower's *French Constitution* (1792), Robert Jacomb's *Letter vindicating the Dissenters from the charge of Disloyalty* (1793), Jeremiah Joyce's *Account* of his arrest (1794), and the second edition of Priestley's *Observations on the Increase of Infidelity* which was published simultaneously in Pennsylvania and London in 1796.[25]

In his *Reflections*, Burke poured ridicule on networks for book distribution, and described the Society for Constitutional Information as

> intended for the circulation, at the expense of members, of many books, which few others would be at the expense of buying; and which might lie on the hands of booksellers to the great loss of a useful body of men. Whether books so charitably circulated were ever as charitably read, is more than I know.[26]

Joseph Towers responded angrily, claiming that the Constituional Society was 'wholly unconnected with booksellers', and that its publications consisted of 'political tracts, essays, &c from Sydney, Locke, Trenchard, Lord Somers, &c'.[27] Ditchfield has shown that the London bookseller, Longman – even before taking the Unitarian Owen Rees into partnership in 1797 – would notify Lindsey when he had a consignment to send to the provinces. A regular recipient was the Shrewsbury bookseller, Joshua Eddowes. In 1766 Eddowes had seceded from the mixed congregation of Presbyterians and Independents at High Street Chapel on the arrival of an Arian assistant minister, newly qualified from Warrington Academy. William Tayleur joined High Street Chapel in 1780, when it adopted the Essex Street liturgy, with service books supplied by Lindsey from London, in a choice of black or coloured bindings.[28]

Responding in 1792 to Burke's charge against the Unitarians, Priestley wrote: 'As some evidence that the *Unitarian* Dissenters are the enemies of the constitution, [Burke] alleged the toasts that were given at the first annual meeting of the Unitarian Society, none of which, however, were at all disloyal, or breathed a spirit unbecoming Englishmen.' Priestley continued:

> Mr Burke was ignorant that the *Unitarian Society* by no means represents the Unitarians of England, being nothing more than an association of a very few of them for the purpose of distributing

> books, and certainly are not one in a thousand of the Unitarians in England. That society has no political object whatever, and the toasts were quite an accidental thing, owing to the company of some strangers, who chiefly suggested them at the time, none of them being provided beforehand.

According to Priestley, 'Unitarianism bears no relation to any system of politics, and in fact there are Unitarians among the friends, as well the enemies, of what is called *government*...'.[29] Yet Priestley's protestations cannot conceal an underlying political motivation. As Lindsey wrote to Tayleur that summer: 'July reminds me of the 14th, when the anniversary of the French Revolution is proposed to be celebrated at the Crown and Anchor near us, where I was last year and intend this.'[30] The evidence of Godwin's list of Unitarians present at the London Revolution Society's celebratory dinner on 4 November 1789 (see preface) helps to explain Burke's suspicion that 'the Revolution Society, hitherto a non-political club of Dissenters, had been taken over by political extremists for use as a "front organization".'[31]

Jebb had died three years earlier, but his political radicalism is shown both in his involvement with Christopher Wyvill in establishing the Yorkshire Association in 1780, and in his persuading the Westminster Association to pursue its own more radical line of annual parliaments, universal manhood suffrage and equal electoral districts – demands that the Chartists would later take up.[32] Jebb had shared with Cartwright, Capel Lofft and Brand Hollis the early shaping of the Society for Constitutional Information. Among the Society's 136 members by 1783 were Kippis, Price, Samuel and Benjamin Vaughan, and Joseph Towers. Disney, who edited Jebb's works and also compiled a life of Brand Hollis, would describe the latter as 'an active promoter' of the Society for Constitutional Information, who continued to be a member of it till nearly its dissolution in 1794'.[33] It was in 1794 that Towers wrote to Wyvill that he saw 'no prospect of any Reform, till events shall have rendered it inevitable'.[34] And it was in 1794 that Jeremiah Joyce, tutor to Stanhope's sons, proposed the Constitutional Society's address to those sentenced to transportation: 'Our best wishes will ever attend you; and we do believe that the day is not very distant when we shall again receive you, on British Shores, the welcome children of a *free and Happy Country*'.[35] Joyce, who was himself arrested and imprisoned as a committee member of the Constitutional Society, was described by Horne Tooke as one of 'the most quiet and peaceable men in the world'. After Horne Tooke's acquittal in the 1794 treason trials, the charges against Joyce were dropped.[36]

Following the failure of the campaigns for parliamentary reform and repeal of the Test Acts, Unitarian political opposition continued in the form of criticism of the government's war policy. A recent historian of Dissent records: 'The anti-war movement of the 1790s was predominantly a Dissenting affair, and its provincial base often the local Unitarian chapel'.[37] By contrast, the main body of Dissenters went to ground. The Wesleyan Methodist ministers in conference in 1792, and already effectively separated from the established church, had resolved that 'none of us shall, either in writing or conversation, speak lightly or irreverently of the Government under which he lives'. Admittedly the Baptist, Robert Hall, while stoutly defending freedom of the press, also criticized the war, arguing that 'if the re-establishment of the ancient government of France be any part of the object; if it be a war with freedom, a confederacy of Kings against the rights of man; it will be the last humiliation and disgrace that can be inflicted on Great Britian'.[38] He also pledged his support for those who, like his Baptist colleague at Plymouth, were put on trial for alleged treasonous activities. Yet Hall dismissed the Unitarian Coleridge as 'a very ingenious young man, but intoxicated with a political and philosophical enthusiasm, a sophic, a republican and a leveller'; while the Unitarian bookseller, Benjamin Flower, a member of Hall's Particular Baptist congregation in Cambridge, came to regard Hall as a political apostate.[39]

Flower's own *French Constitution*, circulated by the Unitarian Society in 1792, marked an important departure, as Ditchfield makes clear: 'The real significance of this, Flower's first work for the Unitarian Society, was that it began that stream of pamphlets in favour of Revolutionary France, which, after 1792, began to emanate from Essex Street Chapel.'[40] Lindsey resigned the pulpit at Essex Street in 1793, and was in any case an unlikely leader. Augustus Toplady, after hearing Lindsey preach, recorded: 'He seems to be a man of much personal modesty and diffidence, and, I verily believe, acts upon principle, but he has no popular talents. He is no more qualified to figure as head of a party, than I am to command the navy.'[41] The network he had set up through the Unitarian Society for Promoting Christian Knowledge was nevertheless to prove more effective than some historians have thought. To publish Priestley's continuation of his *History of the Christian Church* (1802) and his *Notes on Scripture* (1803–4), the Society raised £800 'in the name of four Trustees', while the Duke of Grafton gave £50. And in 1807 the Society enrolled 1200 supporters for Belsham's translation of the New Testament. By 1803 the Society had adopted William Vidler's *Universal Theological Magazine*, with a view to using his subscription list as a means of extending the Society's network of book distribution. In 1806 the journal was renamed the *Monthly Repository*, and the same year saw the establishment of the Unitarian Fund, with Aspland as secretary, in an attempt to target a more socially diverse readership.[42]

How far did the aspirations and activities of the metropolitan Unitarians find echoes of applause or imitation in the provincial Unitarian societies? The next three chapters will attempt to answer that question.

11
Midlands and the North

The nature of the Unitarian provincial network in the 1790s is illustrated by Coleridge's contacts on his tour of Midland and Northern cities in search of subscribers for the *Watchman*. Leaving Bristol in January 1796, having enrolled an initial 400 names in the south west, Coleridge stopped first in the cathedral city of Worcester, where he was told that the Anglican clergy were too dominant and too hostile for him to have any hope of obtaining subscriptions. In Birmingham, where he was welcomed by the Lloyd family, Coleridge delivered two sermons 'preciously peppered with politics'. John Edwards, Priestley's successor as minister at the New Meeting, had defended pulpit-politics three years earlier when he argued that it was as logical to protest against politics being brought into the pulpit, as it was to 'exclaim against a volume of sermons being introduced into a manufactory'.[1] Midland Unitarians were prominent in manufacturing. From Birmingham, Coleridge went to Derby, where he met the cotton-spinner Jedediah Strutt, and Erasmus Darwin of the Birmingham Lunar Society. He missed meeting Peter Crompton, alumnus of Warrington Academy and founder-member of the Derby Constitutional Society. Crompton would stand in the 1796 Nottingham election, gaining 561 votes against his opponents' combined total of 2279. Crompton's departure from Nottingham, after the election, was marked by a pitched battle in the city's streets.[2]

Coleridge's introduction to Nottingham was supplied by Strutt, who put him in touch with John Fellows of High Pavement Chapel – a future member of the Unitarian Society for promoting Christian Knowledge. Arriving in Nottingham in time for a public dinner in honour of Fox's birthday, Coleridge was invited to preach the annual charity sermon for the benefit of High Pavement School. He wrote to Josiah Wade, describing the Nottingham congregation as '*all* sorts – Arians, Trinitarians, &c.'

and to Edwards explaining: 'I have got among the first families in Nottingham, and am marvellously caressed.'[3] After Nottingham, Coleridge was put in touch with a Unitarian businessman, Samuel Shore, in Sheffield. Here James Montgomery, editor of the Sheffield *Iris*, was in prison for libel. Possibly sobered by this evidence of the vulnerability of editors, Coleridge visited Manchester and Lichfield before returning to Bristol.

Of all the towns where Coleridge had political contacts, Nottingham was the most politically active – as it had been in the 1770s. George Walker, minister at High Pavement Chapel since 1774 and formerly mathematics tutor at Warrington, described his own theology as 'tempered Arianism'. He had drafted the 1775 Nottingham petition in favour of reconciliation with America, which Dissenting ministers in the provinces are reckoned to have supported 'in the ratio of thirty-two to one'.[4] Walker campaigned for parliamentary reform in 1782 and 1784, and for the repeal of the Test and Corporation Acts in the late 1780s, serving as Chairman of the Associated Dissenters of Nottingham, Derbyshire and parts of Yorkshire. In 1779 he had preached to the Nottingham militia, assuring them: 'You are the soldiers of the people more than of the crown.'[5] In 1790 he published the *Dissenters' Plea*, in which he followed Priestley in challenging religious establishments. Walker claimed as basic principles that 'political society is for the good of all' and that 'religion is not within the jurisdiction of the civil magistrate'. From these principles he deduced that 'a religious Test, which opens or shuts the door to civil advantages, is the usurpation of a power that is not committed to the magistrate, and a violation of the rights of a citizen'.[6] Emphasizing that 'we ask not for offices of trust, but for simple eligibility', Walker explains that it is not a question of power but of principle. And he adds revealingly that Dissenters already possess sufficient power:

> Wisdom, character, industry, mercantile connections, real and personal estate, a right to elect and be elected to the seat of legislation, the freedom of speech and debate, are the sources of power, in comparison with which, all the benefits that would result from the repeal of the Test laws are as nothing.[7]

Walker was certainly right about 'mercantile connections'. He himself was a partner in Major John Cartwright's cotton mill at Retford, and acted as Cartwright's agent in Nottingham. Other mill-owners worshipping at High Pavement Chapel were Robert Denison, who subscribed to the *Watchman* and whose factory was burned down in 1801, and Thomas Wakefield, who owned a cotton mill at Mansfield. During the last quarter of the eighteenth century, 12 of the 15 successive mayors of Nottingham came from the High Pavement congregation.[8] How far did Walker share Cartwright's political aims as well as his business interests? In 1793 Walker drew up a petition signed by 2500 citizens in favour of manhood suffrage.[9] That was after the failure both of the campaign against the Test Acts and of the Unitarian Relief Bill, when Dissenters could be forgiven for thinking that only a change in the electoral system could advance their cause. But Walker's support for parliamentary reform dated from the end of the American War of Independence, and continued throughout the 1790s. In 1794, under a Tory mayor who actively encouraged the rioters, a loyalist mob targeted supposed Jacobins and their property, ducking the 'democrats' in the Trent or forcibly holding them under water-pumps.

By contrast, in the 1802 election, it was opponents of the government's war policy who marshalled the mob so effectively as to cause one of the Tory candidates to withdraw, for fear of bodily injury. The jubilation that greeted the election of the Whig, Joseph Birch, led John Bowles, Treasury hack and frequent contributor to the *Antijacobin Review*, to write from London condemning a procession 'altogether in the French Revolutionary style' and Jacobinical dances around a 'Tree of Liberty'. Bowles relied on a Nottingham informant, but the select committee conducting an inquiry found too many contradictions in eye-witness accounts. The Tory *Nottingham Journal* reported that the greatest good order had prevailed in the victory procession. The following year Fox challenged the House of Commons to name a town of Nottingham's size where fewer crimes were committed annually.[10]

Nottingham occupied a strategic role in the Unitarian network. When, in December 1789, there was encouragement from London Dissenters to concert their campaign against the Test Acts, it was Walker who drafted, for Deputies in Leicester from eight Midland counties, a resolution in favour of setting up 'a permanent mode of collecting the sense and uniting the efforts of the whole body of Dissenters of every denomination'. And in words that were echoed in Walker's *Dissenters' Plea* later that year, the resolution declared that the meeting implied no hostility to the established church, 'holding it as a maxim that nothing of this nature is within the province of the civil magistrate'.[11] The Leicester meeting on 12 January 1790 was chaired by Samuel Shore, the Sheffield Unitarian and correspondent of Wyvill. Shore's moderation is shown by his proposal to produce an expurgated edition of *Rights of Man*, which would remove all commendation of republicanism. Unexpurgated Paine had been held to explain why the Sheffield Constitutional

Society had so many members from the artisan class.[12] The Unitarian editor of the *Sheffield Register*, Joseph Gales, printed extracts from the first part of *Rights of Man* in his paper, and was a founder-member of the Sheffield Constitutional Society, which in 1795 would publish an abridged edition of Locke on civil government. Gales had led by example in the sugar boycott of 1791–2, personally giving up sugar as a contribution to the campaign against the slave trade. And in December 1792 he announced that he would increase the size of the *Register* to give fuller coverage of the parliamentary session.[13]

It was from Sheffield in January 1793 that an attempt was made to concert action between the Friends of the People, the Society for Constitutional Information and the London Corresponding Society. The Sheffield society proposed sending a circular letter to every reform society in the kingdom, requiring their views to be 'explicitly known, and candidly declared' so that the parliamentary campaign could be based on common objectives, which (the Sheffield Society made clear) should include annual parliaments and universal manhood suffrage. But Unitarian voices in Sheffield were on the side of caution. Gales himself wrote: 'To the Proprietor of this paper, the middle path appears the wisest.'[14] And a week later the *Register* carried a letter from Samuel Shore urging the reformers to avoid 'public rejoicings and processions' and to 'do nothing which can be conceived by others, except from wilful perversion, to be inimical to that Constitution one branch of which you profess it to be your design to restore to its due purity'. He urged them to persuade by 'peaceable behaviour' and by 'obedience to legal authority'.[15] His advice did not deter Sheffield citizens from burning Burke in effigy later that month, and it was Sheffield citizens who successfully defended Gales's house from being attacked by a loyalist mob.[16]

The *Sheffield Register*, with its circulation of 2000 a week, was supplemented by another periodical published by Gales, *The Patriot*, whose intended readership was 'the middle and lower ranks of people'.[17] Gales was not intimidated by the government any more than by loyalist mobs. In the spring of 1794 he composed the Address sent by the Sheffield Society to Muir and Palmer, awaiting transportation to Botany Bay, and published the society's *Address to the Nation*. Disclaiming any intention of seeking 'that visionary equality of property', the Address nevertheless announced an egalitarian programme that would 'make the slave a man, the man a citizen, and the citizen an integral part of the state; to make him a joint sovereign, and not a subject'.[18] In May 1794 the government began arresting reformers, starting in Norwich. Gales decided it was time to leave Sheffield, forestalling his own attempted arrest by departing for Derby 24 hours earlier. As he made his way to America with his family, two farewell addresses appeared in the *Register*. Gales observed wryly: 'It is in these persecuting days sufficient cause to have printed a Newspaper which has boldly dared to doubt the infallibility of Ministers, and to investigate the justice and policy of their measures.'[19] And to give his protest wider currency, he arranged for the publication of a handbill, *Appeal to Britons*.

After Gales's sudden departure, Benjamin Naylor, assistant to the outspoken Unitarian minister of Upper Chapel, Joseph Evans, provided James Montgomery with financial and editorial assistance to launch the *Iris*, in place of the defunct *Register*. Although Naylor's initial editorial on 4 July 1794 was notably more cautious in tone than that of Gales, Montgomery soon found himself in custody for publishing a poem (written in 1792) celebrating the French revolutionary cause. On emerging from three months' imprisonment, Montgomery broke with Naylor, and adopted a more radical editorial line – which landed him in prison again by the time of Coleridge's 1796 visit. Naylor may have turned his back on radical politics, and in 1803 would, like other Unitarian ministers, maintain the justice of a defensive war against Napoleon.[20] But in the mid-1790s, Sheffield Unitarians saw a different enemy. As Samuel Kenrick complained to James Wodrow, the government's 'sending of such men as Muir and Fyshe Palmer amidst a crew of malefactors, lost to every sense of religion, virtue and honour, manifests a cooler turpitude of heart, than Robespierre etc. up to their eyes in torrents of blood'. And in October, he told the same correspondent: 'It still remains with me a question which is the more effectual manner of effecting reformation – whether by violent or gentle means.'[21]

Kenrick's views were admittedly expressed in a private letter, and evidently embarrassed the recipient. Derby radicals became alarmed at the strident tone of Unitarian polemicists, not least of Priestley himself – now removed from the Midlands to Hackney. Henry Redhead Yorke, soon to be sent to strengthen the Sheffield reformers, had founded the Derby Constitutional Society in 1791, along with William and Joseph Strutt (sons of Jedediah), William Ward (editor of the *Derby Mercury*), Erasmus Darwin (friend of the Unitarian Wedgwoods) and the Unitarian Peter Crompton, who persisted so unsuccessfully in his attempts to enter Parliament.[22] In November 1792 the Derby Society (under Crompton's chairmanship) approved an Address to the French Convention. Yorke and William Brooks Johnson were deputed to carry the address to Paris. But the Derby Society's petition of 16 July 1792, in favour of parliamentary reform, was more cautiously worded than Sheffield's version.

Addressed to 'the Friends of Free Enquiry, and the General Good', the Derby petitioners declared 'that all true Government is instituted for the general good; is legalized by the general will; and all its actions, are, or ought to be, directed for the general happiness and prosperity of all honest citizens'. They expressed the belief that 'deep and alarming abuses exist in the British Government', questioned 'the necessity of the payment of seventeen millions of annual taxes', and viewed 'with concern the frequency of Wars'. The remedy was self-evident: 'An equal and uncorrupt representation would, we are persuaded, save us from heavy expenses, and deliver us from many oppressions'. The petitioners concluded by inviting 'the friends of freedom throughout Great Britain to form similar Societies, and to act with unanimity and firmness, till the people be too wise to be imposed upon, and their influence in government be commensurate with their dignity and importance'.[23]

At the end of 1795 the Derby reformers allegedly collected, 'in the space of two days only', 2291 signatures for a petition protesting against the 'Gagging Bills'.[24] Early the following year, Coleridge was told by Jedediah Strutt that he could count on finding 40 or 50 subscribers for the *Watchman* 'in Derby and round about'.[25] Twelve months later, John Thelwall was invited to lecture in Derby and to take over the editorship of one of the local papers. His lecture attracted violent intruders, and the editorial project proved a non-starter – though Crompton would still be corresponding with Thelwall in 1800. Coleridge had warned Thelwall against Derby audiences: 'Derby is no common place; but where you will find *citizens* enough to fill your lecture room puzzles me. At Nottingham you will surely be more likely to obtain audiences.'[26]

Coleridge's instructive comparison between the two cities recalls the 'Address to Dr Priestley', drawn up by the Derby Philosophical Society and printed in the *Derby Mercury* for 29 September 1791. Offering their condolences for the destruction of his library, apparatus and manuscripts, the address recognizes that his enemies have tried to counter rational argument by violence: 'They have halloo'd upon you the dogs of unfeeling ignorance, and of frantic fanaticism; they have kindled fires like those of the inquisition, not to illuminate the truth, but, like the dark lantern of the assassin, to light the murderer to his prey.' But the address goes on to express the hope that Priestley 'will not again risk your person amongst a people, whose bigotry renders them incapable of instruction', and that 'you will leave the unfruitful fields of polemical theology, and cultivate that of [natural] philosophy, of which you may be called the father'.[27] The aims of the Derby Philosophical Society and of the Derby Constitutional Society were not identical, though their membership overlapped. Erasmus Darwin, founder of the Derby Philosophical Society, linked Derby with Birmingham through his contacts in the Lunar Society, of which Priestley was also a member. One can nevertheless detect a hint, that Unitarian political activity in Birmingham was regarded as unduly provocative.

Priestley, who had been in Birmingham since 1780 when he arrived as assistant minister of the New Meeting, evidently intended to be provocative. These were the years that saw his pamphlet warfare with Bishop Horsley, his *Letter to Pitt,* and his *Letters to Burke*. Writing to Lindsey after the failure of the 1790 motion for the repeal of the Test Acts, Priestley noted: 'The high-church party have behaved with unexpected moderation here'. But he added: 'The church people in general think that we shall now be quiet, and give them no trouble a long time. When they find the contrary, they will be much chagrined.'[28] And in a letter to Lindsey nearly a year later, he expressed much interest in seeing both 'Mr Paine's answer to Mr Burke' and also 'the new plan for the Unitarian Society'.[29] Politics continued to go hand in hand with theology. After the Bastille Day Dinner and attendant riots in the summer of 1791, Priestley commented to his Birmingham Unitarian friend, William Russell: 'Had Dr Price been living, it is taken for granted that Hackney would have suffered as much as Birmingham, and that the College would not have been spared.'[30] Russell wrote to London's *Morning Chronicle* protesting at the account of the Birmingham Constitutional Society's Bastille Day celebrations, as reported in *The Times*. Describing the account as 'the most atrocious calumny that was ever laid before the public', Russell insisted that the report was 'materially untrue', and that 'the account given of the *first toast* in *The Times,* was a most flagrant falsehood. The toast had in fact been "The King and Constitution"'. Russell went on to list another 17 toasts, including tributes to the French Revolution, to the United States of America and to 'the late revolution in Poland'. In addition to such unexceptionable toasts as 'The Prince of Wales', 'Peace and good-will to all mankind' and 'Prosperity to the Town of Birmingham' were 'The Majesty of the People', and 'The Rights of Man'.[31] No wonder Priestley heard word that his new Hackney congregation would give him a mixed welcome: 'I have many friends in Dr Price's late congregation, but many of the elderly people, and especially the women, who are numerous in it, are apprehensive that my coming may excite another tumult, and be the means of bringing them into trouble.'[32]

Among many messages of condolence Priestley received from sympathisers, Condorcet wrote on behalf of the French Academy of Sciences, while 'The Society of the Friends of the Constitution, sitting at the Jacobins' declared: 'You have interrupted the course of your labours and discoveries in physics, to justify the French nation against the absurd charges brought against them and multiplied by their oppressors, who are driven from a land of liberty.'[33] As he prepared to leave Birmingham, Priestley reported to Lindsey an interview that Russell had had with the Prime Minister: 'Mr Russell owns that he has never had less satisfaction in any interview with Mr Pitt than the last. He says he clearly saw he had received unfavourable impressions of us.' The same letter records that Dundas had expressed 'great dislike of the Dissenters in general, and myself in particular, saying they were a different set of persons from the old Dissenters and did not know what they wanted'.[34] Priestley's departure did not mean that Birmingham Unitarians would now lie low. His successor, John Edwards, had been one of the first members of the Society for Constitutional Information in the 1780s. In 1796 Edwards could be found raising funds for the London Corresponding Society, with the help of Edward Corn, his fellow-minister at the New Meeting.[35] Corn was a friend of John Binns, who came to Birmingham as one of two representatives from the London Corresponding Society, before facing trial in 1797.[36] But Russell, whom Priestley recognized as the chief architect of their earlier efforts in Birmingham, had sailed with his family for America in August 1794, hard on the heels of the Priestleys. Corn might well complain that 'present circumstances render it somewhat difficult and dangerous to instruct mankind in the great and important principles of Politics'.[37]

When, in the summer of 1792, the Constitutional Society decided to distribute copies of Paine's *Letter to Dundas* to seven Midland towns, 100 copies each were earmarked for Bromsgrove, Leicester and Shrewsbury, 150 for Birmingham, 200 for Derby, but 1200 each for Sheffield and Manchester.[38] The named recipient for Manchester was the manufacturer, Thomas Walker, close friend of the Unitarian industrial chemist Thomas Cooper. In 1783 Cooper had been elected a member of the Manchester Literary and Philosophical Society, after reading a paper on 'The History of Physiognomy'. He became one of four vice-presidents of the society, but resigned in 1791 when the society refused to express sympathy for Priestley. Cooper described Priestley's *Essay on the First Principles of Government* (1768) as 'the first plain, popular, brief and unanswerable book on the principles of civil government'.[39] Cooper's own *Propositions respecting the Foundation of Civil Government*, read to the Literary and Philosophical Society in 1787 and first published in the Transactions of the society in 1790, advocates universal suffrage, arguing that 'public transactions do not require more than ordinary talents'. Cooper's views on government were given wider currency when published as a supplement to his *Reply to Mr Burke*.[40] Cooper was a leading member of the Manchester Constitutional Society, founded in October 1790 and included leading commercial and professional men. The chairman was Thomas Walker, who was corresponding with Paine before the end of 1791 and was instrumental in founding the *Manchester Herald*.

In April 1792, the Manchester Constitutional Society sent Thomas Cooper and James Watt Jr to Paris to present a congratulatory address to the Jacobin Club. Famously, the Manchester delegates took part in a procession to the Champs de Mars, with Watts carrying the British flag and Cooper a bust of Algernon Sidney. For this they were censured in Parliament by Burke, who characterized the French Jacobins as traitors and regicides, at a time (as Cooper reminded him) when 'the King of France is alive, and chooses his ministers from among this very Society'. Cooper explained that the Jacobins 'do nothing but debate political subjects, and now and then direct the publication of a political discourse'. If it was not improper for the philosophical societies of London, Paris or Stockholm to correspond 'for the Improvement of Chemistry or experimental philosophy', why should it be improper to correspond on political subjects? England and France were not enemies at the time, 'as Great Britain and America were, when Mr Burke corresponded with Dr Franklin and Mr Laurens'.[41]

Cooper's connection with the Jacobin Club was at a time when the Brissotins were still in the ascendant. He shared a common cause with Brissot in campaigning against the slave trade.[42] It was Manchester's Society for the Purpose of Effecting the Abolition of the Slave Trade, which demonstrated the effectiveness of political organization in the city. Cooper served on the committee which, in 1788, forwarded a petition to Parliament with 10 000 signatures. Less unanimity was achieved in the campaign against the Test and Corporation Acts. When Cooper chaired a meeting of Dissenters at Warrington in February 1790, the Baptists and Independents withdrew their support because the wording of the resolution went beyond an appeal against the Test Laws. Cooper, supported by the largely Unitarian Presbyterians, refused to divulge further steps along the same road – thus allowing Burke to claim that the abolition of the Anglican liturgy, and exemption from paying tithes, were the undisclosed objectives.[43] Thomas Walker would later claim that 'timidity and want of union amongst the friends of freedom' was responsible for the reform movement running into the sand.[44]

The Unitarian reformers of Liverpool certainly seemed to have held back. James Currie, who would soon (under the pseudonym 'Jasper Wilson') attack Pitt's war policy, argued in 1790 that the repeal of the Test Acts was 'perfectly consistent with the safety of the present establishment', and regarded the Warrington meeting, chaired by Cooper, as 'premature'.[45] In late 1792 Roscoe and Rathbone, in their Liverpool handbill *Equality*, made clear that their aim was not equality of property but 'an EQUALITY OF RIGHTS, or in other words, that every person may be *equally* entitled to the protection and benefits of society; may *equally* have a voice in the election of those who make the laws by which he is affected in his life, liberty or his property; and may have a fair opportunity of exerting to advantage any talents he may possess.'[46] Rathbone, who had undertaken to print and distribute the handbill, admitted privately that there was no immediate prospect of such reform. Yet in the following decade, he and Roscoe would be active in Liverpool's opposition to the Orders in Council (see Chapter 15).

Meanwhile Manchester's pro-French sympathies were not apparently diminished by the September Massacres. On 12 September a meeting of 'the friends of human liberty' was advertised for the 18th, in order to start a subscription for the relief of their French 'brethren' suffering from 'the calamities of a war instigated by a cruel combination of despots'.[47] And when 186 Manchester publicans denied their premises to meetings of reformers, Walker made his home and warehouse available. In December 1792 Cooper was urging a meeting, two days before the state opening of Parliament, to request the King 'to remove from his Councils all ministers hostile to the PEACE of the country; and to pursue such measures as may be most effectual to prevent the dangers of impending War'. Among those dangers, Cooper listed increased taxes, a fall in property values, and the damage to small manufacturers and their workers, as trade was curtailed.[48] On 14 December the London Constitutional Society ordered Cooper's address to be published in the newspapers, and proposed that 100 000 copies be printed by the society for distribution throughout Britain. But the *Morning Chronicle* and the *Morning Post* both refused to print it. Cooper's Manchester meeting on the 11th had taken a loyalist line, and that evening a mob shouting 'Church and King – Damn Tom Paine' attacked the premises where the *Herald* was published. The next night, Walker's windows were smashed.[49]

In March 1793 the proprietors of the *Herald* closed it down and left for America. In the summer of 1793 accusations of treason began circulating against Walker. He was said to have damned the King, and to be training men in the use of arms to support a French invasion. Walker's trial began in April 1794, on a charge of seditious correspondence rather than treason. Defended by Thomas Erskine and Felix Vaughan, Walker was acquitted. Samuel Shore, Walker's brother-in-law, attended the trial, and Cooper helped to ensure that the government's chief witness was convicted of perjury. That August, remarking that Walker's staying behind was 'probably rendered less unpleasant from some distant view of being a very great man in case of a Revolution', Cooper followed Priestley to America.[50] Four years later, with Walker still playing a leading role in Manchester politics, the United Englishmen were said to have more than 60 divisions in the city. James O'Coigly had arrived, en route to France, bearing a letter from the 'National Committee of Ireland' soliciting subscriptions. In that spring of 1798, members of the Manchester Constitutional Society were alleged to be distributing cockades in expectation of a French invasion.[51]

It was barely two years since Coleridge had set out on his subscription tour of the Midlands. Now, in a much-quoted letter, the former editor of the *Watchman* wrote that he had snapped his 'squeaking baby-trumpet of sedition'. He continued:

> I wish to be a good man and a Christian, but I am no Whig, no Reformist, no Republican – and because of the multitude of these fiery and undisciplined spirits that lie in wait against the public Quiet under these titles ... I chiefly accuse the present ministers – to whose folly I attribute, in great measure, their increased and increasing numbers.[52]

Coleridge often wrote what he thought his brother wanted to hear, but by 1798 'fiery and undisciplined spirits' seemed for a time to be taking charge.

12
Norwich, Bristol and the South West

The Octagon Chapel at Norwich is one of the most famous Unitarian meetinghouses in England. Opened in 1756 to replace an earlier Presbyterian chapel built before the Toleration Act, the new chapel was reckoned by John Wesley to be 'perhaps the most elegant in Europe'.[1] Yet it was not until Thomas Madge arrived from Bury St Edmunds in 1811 that (according to his biographer) 'Unitarianism was first brought prominently into the pulpit at Norwich'. One Unitarian considered that Madge found in Norwich 'an audience perhaps the most intellectual in our denomination'.[2] But when the Octagon Chapel was built, Unitarianism could not yet be called a denomination. John Taylor, the moving force behind the new chapel, had come to Norwich in 1733 to assist the Presbyterian minister, Peter Finch, who would serve his Norwich congregation for 63 years. Finch continued to instruct children in the congregation from the Scottish Presbyterian Catechism. Taylor, however, was Arian in theology, and persuaded the congregation to study Clarke's *Scripture-Doctrine of the Trinity*, 'having previously engaged in two solemn meetings for prayer for the divine assistance in their work'.[3]

Taylor, like many other Dissenters, disliked denominational labels. His *Paraphrase on the Epistle to the Romans* (1745) had been dedicated to 'the Society of Christians in the city of Norwich, whom I serve in the Gospel of our Lord Jesus Christ'. Praising the members of the Society for being a 'peaceable people', he assured them that they were 'a true church, built upon the foundation of the Apostles and prophets, Christ himself being the chief corner-stone'. They had 'the best reason in the world for adhering steadily to the cause you have espoused, the cause of Christian liberty...'[4] Two of Taylor's grandsons, John Taylor (a deacon at the Octagon) and Edward Rigby (a Norwich physician) would prove enthusiastic admirers of French liberty. Rigby was in Paris in July 1789, and attended a session of the National Assembly at Versailles:

> I have been witness to the most extraordinary revolution that perhaps ever took place in human society. A great and wise people struggled for freedom and the rights of humanity; their courage, prudence and perseverance have been rewarded by success, and an event which will contribute to the happiness and prosperity of millions of their posterity has taken place with very little loss of blood and with but a few days interruption to the business of the place.[5]

And when in November 1789, a second celebration of the anniversary of the 1688 Revolution was held in Norwich, 'The Trumpet of Liberty', written by John Taylor junior, was sung.[6]

In his account of the 'Norwich Jacobins', published in 1796, Richard Dinmore denied that Norwich reformers imported their principles from France: 'They are principles of pure English growth; Locke, Sydney, Marvell, Milton &c were their authors; for them Hampden bled in the field; for them the Anglo-Americans shed their purest blood, and exposed their bravest sons.' Among those principles, says Dinmore, are: their concern in religious matters with what a man does rather than what he thinks, their belief that 'immense wealth in the few produces corresponding misery in the many', and their detestation of all acts of parliament that cramp industry.[7] John Taylor junior was himself a partner in Thomas Barnard's wool and yarn factory. The William Taylors, father and son, were Unitarian textile manufacturers. William Taylor junior had gone to France in May 1789, carrying letters of introduction from Richard Price to Rochefoucauld, with the aim (like his namesake) of listening to National Assembly debates. On landing at Calais, Taylor 'kissed the earth on the land of liberty'.[8] The young William Taylor was also a member of the Tusculan debating society. In January 1794 the members (foreshadowing a notorious Oxford Union vote), asked: 'Are there circumstances that would justify us refusing to defend our country?'[9] Taylor was also a member of the Norwich Revolution Society, founded in 1791, of which his father was secretary.[10] The elder William Taylor was among the Norwich delegates elected to the Society for Constitutional Information. The list describes him as 'one of the first manufacturers' with 'William Firth, a considerable manufacturer; Thomas Barnard, ditto'. The only Dissenting minister in the Constitutional Society delegation was the Baptist Mark Wilks, who preached two 'collection sermons' to defray defence costs in the 1794 treason trials.[11]

It was Wilks who proposed a petition to George III against the 'Gagging Bills'. The address attracted 5000 signatures, and in his speech in support of the resolution, Wilks paid tribute to 'the philanthropy of our gracious sovereign', before adding more menacingly: 'It would be no easy task to make him a tyrant but should the... legislature frame tyrannic laws and prevail upon him to give reluctantly his royal assent and signature, it is to be dreaded they would, by that act, sign and seal his death warrant, build his sepulchre and toll his passing bell.'[12] Wilks's outspokenness contrasts with that of his Unitarian colleague William Enfield, minister at the Octagon Chapel from 1784 until his death in 1797. Former tutor and rector at Warrington, Enfield was one of 15 identifiable Liverpool Dissenting ministers who did not adopt an anti-government stance during the American War.[13]

In 1779, preaching at Cross Street, Manchester, Enfield had declared that the business of Christian ministers was 'to stop the progress of ignorance and error; to discourage superstition; to promote useful knowledge; to reprove the vices of the age in which we live'.[14] The previous year, he had begun a sermon at Lewin's Mead, Bristol, with the discouraging observation:

> To apply the speculations of philosophy to the regulation of human life and manners is no easy task. The theories which are formed in the closets of the studious, are commonly of so refined and abstracted a nature, and so remote from the general feelings and experience of mankind, as to be above the comprehension of the multitude, and of little use in practice.[15]

Yet the same published sermon spoke of 'the natural right which every man possesses, of framing his system of religious faith, and choosing the form of religious worship for himself'.[16] And in a sermon preached in November 1788 to commemorate the centenary of the 1688 Revolution, Enfield cited, as one of its legacies, 'an express contract between the King and his subjects, in which their mutual duties are clearly settled, and in which the prerogatives of the crown are restricted within limits that cannot be transgressed without hazarding the existence of the State'.[17] In Norwich, Enfield founded the Speculative Society and contributed to the *Cabinet*, urging the need for moderate reform that would not endanger the peace of society. Although his private correspondence (notably with William Roscoe) shows Enfield's radical sympathies, he and Pendlebury Houghton, his fellow-minister at the Octagon, seem to have left political activity to lay members of their congregation.[18] And when the Peace of Amiens was signed, one of those laymen, William Taylor Jr, took the opportunity to visit Paris again.[19]

William Windham, friend of Burke and MP for Norwich since 1784, was suspicious of the peace; but it was popular with the electorate. In the general election of 1802, Windham and Frere were displaced by Robert Fellowes (who had opposed Frere in the by-election of 1799) and the Unitarian William Smith.[20] Smith had been present at the first Bastille Day Fete of Federation in Paris in 1790, was steward for the Crown and Anchor dinner in 1791, attended the Crown and Anchor meeting addressed by Horne Tooke in May 1797, and earlier the same month was interrogated by the Privy Council. He defeated those who attempted to remove him as chairman of the Anti-Slavery Society, on the grounds that God could not be expected to bless the work of the society while it was headed by a Unitarian. In 1803 the 'Jacobin city' would support the government in the war against Napoleon, yet Smith continued to represent Norwich until 1830, becoming Father of the House, and in 1813 successfully piloted the Unitarian Relief Bill through the House of Commons.

In pre-industrial England, Norwich and Bristol had both claimed second place to London among provincial cities. In the 1770s, Bristol's MPs, Edmund Burke and Henry Cruger, sat in opposition to North's ministry, but rarely acted together. Burke was energetic in organizing petitions against the American War, working through the not altogether supportive Society of Merchant Venturers. Cruger, preferring to proceed independently by public meeting, produced an address which read 'more as if they were petitioning an eastern Tyrant than a British house of commons'.[21] By the autumn of 1775, loyalist forces in Bristol had gained the upper hand, while at Westminster the government's majority seemed so unassailable that, for several months, Burke and the Rockingham Whigs absented themselves from Parliament, whenever American affairs were being debated. Burke's support for Dissenting ministers and schoolmasters in 1779 did him no harm in a city with many Dissenters in a 5000-strong electorate. But his championing of Catholic relief, both before and after the Gordon riots, ensured his defeat in the 1780 election.[22]

The 1780s in Bristol were dominated by agitation against the slave trade. In the summer and autumn of 1783, *Felix Farley's Bristol Journal* reprinted articles from the American press, describing the barbarities of the trade, and in July 1785 the Bristol Quakers decided to distribute copies of Antoine Benezet's *Caution against the Slave Trade to Great Britain* 'to every Person concerned in any respect in the Slave Trade'. This was two years before a somewhat pessimistic Clarkson himself visited the city. In January 1788 a public meeting at the Bristol Guildhall set up a committee to prepare a petition against the trade. Among the leading supporters were the Dean of Bristol and Gloucester, the Baptist minister Caleb Evans, and the Unitarian John Prior Estlin.[23] Estlin was a continuous Unitarian presence in Bristol for 46 years. Agreeing in 1770 to come as an assistant at Lewin's Mead, he was ordained minister by William Enfield in 1778, and remained there until failing eyesight in 1816 compelled his retirement. According to Mrs Barbauld, 'the goodness of God, and the great practical duties of Christianity were his favourite themes'.[24] Estlin's *Evidences of revealed religion* (1796) was a reply to Paine's *Age of Reason*, and in 1797 he published his Bristol sermon on the nature and causes of atheism (with an epigraph from Coleridge's *Destiny of Nations*). In 1801 Estlin's *Apology for the Sabbath* sought 'to make the Sabbath a day of cheerful piety, and to include among things sanctioned on this day, the gathering of the fruits of the earth, in this uncertain climate, before and after religious service'.[25] It does not sound a very radical agenda.

Estlin's lectures, delivered to pupils at the school which he and his wife ran in Bristol, were published posthumously. In the preface, he not only paid tribute to 'that best of tutors, the Rev. Dr Aikin', who had instructed him at Warrington, but explained that his own aim was 'to lay before my pupils the plainest principles of Moral Science and of Natural Theology, and whatever is of the greatest practical utility, without any regard to the source from which it was derived'. And the first lecture opens with the words: 'Knowledge, next to Goodness, is the most valuable of all acquisitions.'[26] In Lecture XXV entitled 'On Rights, Laws and Government', Estlin defines natural rights as 'such as belong to a man, although there existed in the world no civil government whatever; adventitious rights are such as a person possesses and holds by the institutions of society.' Unsurprisingly, Estlin concludes that 'of our unalienable rights, the most important is that of worshipping God agreeably to the dictates of our conscience'.[27] He wants the Bible to replace the Thirty-nine Articles as the test of orthodoxy, and the introduction of 'a short and unexceptionable form of Prayer' for those who cannot conscientiously use the Book of Common Prayer. He also expects 'a repeal of the act of uniformity, and the legal recognition of *perfect liberty* in matters of religion', though conceding that the abolition of tithes must be a more remote objective.[28]

Estlin's reform programme did not extend to disestablishment, as he makes clear by his use of italics in asserting that

> *in this country, and in the present state of society; with our laws, our institutions, our manners and our habits, the total abolition of the establishment*

> *would be attended with more inconveniences than advantages*; in a word, that it is *the reparation of the structure which is to be wished for, and not its demolition*; or to speak in the plainest terms possible, the *reformation* of the church, and not its *subversion*.[29]

By the time Estlin was preparing his lectures for the press, the 1813 Unitarian Relief Bill had been passed, which drew the sting from much of the criticism of the establishment. But in 1792, at the first attempt to remove the stigma of the 1698 Blasphemy Act, Priestley had sought Estlin's help in obtaining signatures for the parliamentary petition: 'I depend upon your activity to get it signed by as many as you can in Bristol, and its neighbourhood, so as to be returned in a fortnight.'[30]

Despite the political and anti-hierarchical invective of the published lectures of the 21-year-old Coleridge and his continuation of the campaign in the pages of the *Watchman*, it cannot be claimed that Unitarians provided the focus for antigovernment sentiment in Bristol. Of some 50 separate titles published by Joseph Cottle between 1790 and 1800, only two titles (apart from the works of Estlin and Coleridge) are by indentifiable Unitarians. One is by David Jardine of Bath, and the other is a discourse given by John Rowe at Warminster in July 1799 'before the Society of Unitarian Christians, established in the West of England, for promoting Christian knowledge and the practice of virtue'. The membership list of the Society in 1805 includes 43 Bristol names out of 223, compared with 28 for Plymouth, 23 for Exeter and 22 for Bridport.[31] Among the Bristol names is Dr J. E. Stock, biographer of Dr Beddoes of the Bristol Pneumatic Institution. Beddoes's belief, that inhaling mixtures of gases could cure or relieve illnesses, has relegated him to the more laughable margins of history. Yet no less than one-fifth of Cottle's published titles (1790–1800) are by Beddoes. We need not endorse a correspondent's claim in the *Gentleman's Magazine* that Beddoes's '*philosophical* speculations had a direct tendency to Atheism', but he was not a professed Unitarian. And Cottle (a member of Broadmead Particular Baptist chapel) was passionately committed to Atonement theology, and would later express his 'unspeakable pleasure' at Coleridge's return to Trinitarian orthodoxy.[32] Cottle's boasted galaxy of Bristol *literati* includes (apart from the future Lake poets) John Morgan from the Unitarian family of Bristol wineshippers, and Charles Danvers who appears in the 1813 membership list of the Society of Unitarian Christians in the West of England – alongside Estlin, Rowe and two members of the Morgan family.[33]

It was Beddoes rather than Estlin who led Bristol's opposition in the 1790s. Himself a contributor to the *Watchman*, he published a 200-page pamphlet attacking Pitt's policies at home and abroad, together with a defence of the Bill of Rights against the 'Gagging Bills'. He and William Long Fox chaired the protest meetings against the two Bills in November 1795, while Beddoes's vociferous concern for the impact of war and industrial processes on the suffering poor, finds echoes in *Lyrical Ballads*, printed by Cottle in 1798. But neither Beddoes's pamphlets nor *Lyrical Ballads* could loosen the grip of the Merchant Venturers. As Robert Lovell, one of Cottle's protégés wrote in 1794:

> Low in a drear and gloomy Vale immur'd,
> By mud cemented, and by smoke obscur'd,
> A City stands, and BRISTOL is its name,
> By trade and dullness consecrate to fame,
> *That* o'er her Sons in form of Philos reigns,
> And binds their groveling hearts in golden chains;
> *This* to their brain a leaden mask imparts,
> And makes their heads as callous as their hearts.[34]

An annuity from the Unitarian Wedgwoods enabled Coleridge to write poetry in Somerset rather than become (as Estlin had hoped) a Unitarian minister. But even after deciding to accept the annuity, in preference to going as minister to Shrewsbury, Coleridge told Estlin, 'I most assuredly shall preach often.' He added that he planned to assist alternately Toulmin at Taunton and Howell at Bridgwater 'on one part of every Sunday, while I stay at Stowey'.[35] Taunton was probably a more important Unitarian centre in the south west than Bristol. Bradley regards the 'charismatic leadership' of Joshua Toulmin as significant as that of George Walker in Nottingham.[36] A close friend of Priestley, Toulmin had laid stress in his own *History of Taunton* (1791) on the importance of impressing 'on the minds of the present, and future generations, a conviction of the great importance, in which their ancestors regarded the revolution [of 1688]'.[37] Toulmin had been minister of an Arian Presbyterian congregation at Colyton, Devon, in the early 1760s, but, developing scruples about administering infant baptism, he moved in 1765 to the General Baptist Chapel in Mary Street, Taunton. Here he remained until his move to Birmingham in 1804. His Socinian views date from about 1770: by 1771 he was already proposing to write a life of Socinus, which he eventually published in 1779.[38]

In 1788, preaching at Bridport, Toulmin reminded his hearers that Christ's kingdom was not established in the way that the Apostles had expected: 'They do, indeed, triumph in the name of their master. They do enlist subjects to his sceptre. They do see the kingdom of Christ opening, and thousands flocking into it. But no sword is unsheathed: no throne is erected: no banners are displayed.' And he adds: 'The weapons of their warfare are spiritual; the words of truth and grace, and the miraculous gifts of the Spirit.' The aim of Unitarians, among other Protestant Dissenters, he told his audience, besides that of 'preserving the spirit of piety in your own hearts, or the cause of religion in the world, is to stand fast in the liberty wherewith Christ hath made you free, and to recover Christianity from the gross corruptions, that have disguised and enervated it, to its original purity and simplicity.'[39]

Less than four years later, Paine would be burned in effigy outside Toulmin's front door. Their house was saved from attack on that occasion, but the Toulmins abandoned the school they had been running, and Mrs Toulmin gave up her bookselling business. In the winter of 1792–3, their house was attacked nightly, while their son, the Rev. Harry Toulmin, was confronted by a mob carrying 'Guns and Swords, and an effigy of Paine'. In May 1793, Harry left with his family for America, and (according to Brand Hollis) the elder Toulmins seriously considered following with their entire congregation.[40]

Joshua Toulmin had admittedly commended the Taunton Revolution Society (founded in 1789), and had written to its parent body in London that such societies were 'highly useful to awaken attention to the "RIGHTS OF MEN"'.[41] And in 1792 the London Constitutional Society had sent him 100 copies of Paine's *Letter to Dundas* for distribution.[42] Toulmin had taken a vocal part in the campaign against subscription in the 1770s, demanding in his *Two Letters* (1774): 'Give us back our full natural rights!' And in his *Present State of the Church of England* (1779), he had defended Dissenters' rights to state offices and emoluments: 'Can different ideas or speculative points, or different rituals in religion, be pleaded in bar against *political* merits?'[43] But his most powerful polemic was directed against the American War in a published sermon preached twice in Taunton within a week. He deplores the decision to fight against those 'who are your countrymen and your subjects, whose useful hands have been accustomed to pour in upon you the riches of commerce, and to reap for you the blessings of harvest'. While conjuring up a bloody scenario – 'What promiscuous carnage! What mangled limbs! What hideous cries! Fields covered with ghastly corpses! Green pastures crimsoned with human gore!' – Toulmin warns of the long-term consequences:

> Be not too warm in congratulating yourselves; the glory of your triumphs is tarnished with the sorrowful countenances and mourning garbs of orphans and widows – with the silence of your ports that used to hear the voice of merchandize – with the increased burdens which an exhausted treasury, multiplied taxes, and a diminished trade will entail on your posterity. The unborn may weep at the mention of victories in which their sires exulted.[44]

Taunton had its own Dissenting Academy, and two-thirds of the population of the town were Dissenters, though it was governed by an Anglican corporation. So it is scarcely surprising that the town was one of the most active centres of opposition to Lord North's government.

Yet Toulmin was one of only three Dissenting ministers to sign the 1775 Address pleading for conciliation with America. (North had just become Honorary Recorder of Taunton.)[45] In 1776 Toulmin urged his congregation to pray for peace, beseeching God 'to inspire all orders and ranks of men with a commanding sense of the excellency and value of our government.' But the force of his patriotic exhortation was somewhat blunted by his calling also for prayers 'that corruption may be destroyed; that the senate and council of the nation may be actuated by disinterested zeal for the public good'.[46] Aspland might not consider Toulmin 'eminent for originality or boldness of thought'.[47] But at Taunton, as elsewhere, Unitarian rhetoric of the 1790s was unchanged from that of the 1770s. By the time Toulmin reached Birmingham in 1804, however, Napoleon's advent had altered the parameters of debate.

13
Scottish Convict, Irish Exile

The two leading Unitarian radicals to figure respectively in Irish and Scottish politics were members of the same Cambridge college, and both were pupils of John Jebb. Both would be indicted for distributing a seditious address, but while Archibald Hamilton Rowan escaped to France, Thomas Fyshe Palmer was confined in a Thames prison-hulk, before being transported to Botany Bay. Palmer died of dysentery in a Spanish prison on Guam, as he attempted the return journey; Rowan eventually received a royal pardon, and lived to 83 – long enough to see the passing of the Unitarian Relief Bill, Catholic Emancipation and the 1832 Reform Act.

Rowan once recorded of Palmer: 'We were fellow-collegians at Queens' College, and never was there a more regular, studious, and every way good man.'[1] Palmer, an Old Etonian who accepted Anglican ordination and became a Fellow of Queens', was one of the petitioning clergy against subscription to the Articles of Religion. But he did not embrace Unitarian views until the 1780s, in response to reading Lindsey and Priestley. Writing from Cambridge in July 1783 to William Christie at Montrose, Palmer complained of the established church: 'I consider her liturgy corrupt and anti-christian, and her articles to be not only an injurious violation of the liberty wherewith God and Christ have made us free, but a jumble of absurdity.' He had declined preferment rather than again swear to articles 'which I believe to contain so many gross and shocking falsehoods'. Palmer considers that Christie's Unitarian congregation would offer temporary asylum, where 'I could worship the Father of mercies according to my conscience' – and also study the Bible. He concludes: 'May the Father of mercies smile upon your little society; may it be the nursing mother to the whole kingdom, to bring it back to the long-lost truth – the worship of *only Him*.'[2]

William Christie's own biblical studies (according to the younger William Turner) had led him 'in consequence to embrace Unitarian opinions; in the open and avowed profession of which he at that time probably stood alone in the land of his birth'. Christie's congregation at first worshipped privately, but, on opening their meetings to the public, 'constituted the first religious society collected in Scotland whose worship was founded on Unitarian principles'. Christie's sermons were published in 1784 as *Discourses on the Divine Unity*, and are described by Turner as 'a valuable and learned work, which shows the author to be well versed in theological studies, and a complete master of the Unitarian controversy'.[3] Christie would stay at Montrose until moving to Glasgow in 1794, but Palmer left for Dundee as early as 1785.

Writing from Dundee that September, Palmer reports the first flowering of Unitarianism in Scotland:

> Dr Dalrymple and Dr Macgill are decided Unitarians, and teach their congregations of the Church of Scotland in Ayr publicly on the Unity of God, and on the other momentous truths to which they think the Scottish profession of faith is decidedly opposite. Dr Macgill has erected a seat in his garden with this inscription, 'To the memory of Dr Lardner, an Israelite indeed'.[4]

Palmer himself preached elsewhere in Scotland, gathering together several other communities of Unitarian worshippers, notably at Glasgow, Edinburgh, Arbroath, Forfar and Newburgh.[5] The Dundee merchant, Robert Millar, described as being in the 1790s, 'the personification of Dundee Unitarianism',[6] would later wonder whether the movement would ever take root in Scotland: 'I fear it is a plant that is not likely to thrive in this *Northern* climate in *my day*, neither has its culture in this country ever been under the best management. The belief and prejudices of almost every description of people are in opposition to it.'[7] Millar was a friend and supporter of Palmer, but thought that his appeal was aimed too much at the lower classes. Yet Millar's correspondence with Lindsey suggests that he does not consider the middle classes particularly fruitful ground. They are (he thinks) 'much immersed in care, and eager in the pursuit of riches, they therefore have too little leisure to enquire, and altho' rational sentiments more prevailed, it's to be feared that but few would dare to be singular, or, on account of religion, incur the world's "dread laugh".'[8]

Lindsey nevertheless seems to have regarded Dundee, on the eve of expansion in its jute manufacture, as one of the most important points of contact with radical Dissent outside the metropolis. Indeed, so much published material was despatched by Lindsey in the 1790s and early 1800s that 'Dundee merits consideration as an appendage of the Unitarian Book Society in London'.[9] Dundee's importance in Lindsey's distribution network owes much to the notoriety of Thomas Fyshe Palmer's trial for sedition, and the dismay aroused by his sentence. Lindsey would follow the trials of Palmer, Muir, Skirving, Margarot and Gerrald, and would visit Palmer and Muir in the hulks, besides raising £600 in support of their cause. And in 1797 he circulated Palmer's *Narrative of the Sufferings of T. F. Palmer and W. Skirving*.[10] As early as the summer of 1791, however, Millar was writing to Lindsey:

> A great reformation has been brought about in the minds of people here of late on the subject of *liberty* – and it is astonishing the execution Mr Paine's Pam[phlet] has done on this head. To hear people who a few years ago revered Religious Establishments, now reason against them, nay reprobate them, is such an internal sort of revolution as must please every friend of truth & the human race.[11]

At the time the first part of *Rights of Man* was published, Palmer was seeking to prove, in the pages of the *Theological Repository*, that the 'fallen angels' (2 *Peter* 2.4 and *Jude* 6) were the sons of Seth, spoken of in *Genesis*. As Palmer explains:

> When the sons of Seth left the place where the divine glory manifested itself, and went after the fair daughters of men, they were taught by them to apostasize from the Great Being, and worship the elements and stars. Idolatry brought with it its constant concomitant, depravation of manners . . .[12]

And in 'An Attempt to show that the Cock-crowing which Peter heard was the Sound of a Trumpet', Palmer remarks tartly: 'Surely its wears more the appearance of a miracle of Mahomet (for every prophecy is a miracle) to rest his veracity on the caprice of a dunghill-cock.'[13] How did such preoccupations cause Palmer to be charged with sedition?

Like other Unitarians, he undoubtedly welcomed the French Revolution. He wrote of Carnot's defeat of the French royalists of Brittany: 'The patriots have defeated the rebels at Nantes.' And he added: '8000 killed, 700 taken prisoner.' The words would be cited at his trial.[14] But his biographer thinks that Palmer's part in the Unitarian campaign made him 'as much an object of jealousy to the ruling powers and prevailing parties, as if he had been most deeply engaged in political agitations'.[15] Palmer's indictment for 'seditious practices' would make a point of referring to him as: 'Clergyman, sometime residing in Dundee, and commonly designed Unitarian Minister'.[16] He had attended a meeting of 'Friends of the People' at Dundee, where he was shown an address, drafted by an uneducated weaver. Objecting to some of the more inflammatory passages, Palmer undertook to redraft the document and have it printed. The amended address focused on reform of Parliament:

> Is not every new day adding a new link to our chains? Is not the executive branch daily seizing new, unprecedented and unwarrantable powers? Has not the House of Commons (your own security from the evils of tyranny and aristocracy) joined the coalition against you? Is the election of its members either fair, free or frequent? Is not its independence gone, while it is made up of pensions and placemen?

After claiming a readiness 'to assert our just rights and privileges as men' – the chief of which was universal suffrage – the address continues:

> *Fellow citizens*
> The time is now come, when you must either gather round the fabric of Liberty to support it, or to your eternal infamy, let it fall to the ground, to rise no more, hurling along with it every thing that is valuable and dear to an enlightened people.

Objecting to having been plunged into war 'by a wicked Ministry and a compliant Parliament', and blaming the war for the loss of their 'invaluable rights and privileges', the address ends with a call to 'join us in our exertions for the preservation of our perishing liberty, and the recovery of our long lost rights'.[17]

Palmer was accused, not only of composing and printing the Address (which was undeniable), but also of distributing it. He certainly thought of doing so, writing to William Skirving: 'We want a copy to be sent to all the societies of the Friends of the People.' And writing to the Constitutional Society of London two weeks later, Palmer admitted: 'We do not know how to circulate it among the different societies in England but as some of your members are in parliament, you may be able to frank some to Leeds, Sheffield, Nottingham, Derby, Manchester etc.'[18] While his defence counsel went so far as to plead that Palmer's extravagant religious beliefs prevented him from being considered an altogether rational person in other respects, Palmer's own defence (which was never presented to the jury) drew a distinction between attacking the constitution itself and attacking merely the administration of it.[19] When the sentence of seven years transportation was announced, Palmer told the court that his life had 'for many years been employed in the dissemination of what I conceived to be religious and moral truths; truths which I supposed to be of the greatest importance to mankind'. But during 'the late great political discussions' it had been impossible for a man of his 'sanguine disposition' to remain an 'unconcerned bystander'. He considered politics 'a great branch of morals'. He hoped that all who knew him would agree 'that it has been the tenor of my life to endeavour to add if possible to the sum of human happiness'. He had suffered for his principles before, and if he was called on to suffer again, he hoped that 'my sufferings will not be wholly lost, but will, by the blessing of that great Being whom I serve, be rendered efficacious to the good of my fellow-creatures'.[20]

In January 1794 Lindsey, still hoping that the order for transportation would not be implemented, suggested to Millar that, should Palmer be sent to Botany Bay, 'we may not doubt God's sending him, and that he will be an instance of much good to that country, both he and Mr Muir'. Lindsey had admired reports of Muir's speech to the jury, in which he had displayed 'his virtue and integrity, as actuated by true principles and regards to a future immortal life, brought to light by Jesus Christ'.[21] And while he languished on board the *Stanislas* hulk at Woolwich, Palmer received a consoling address from his Dundee congregation:

> We mourn your absence; but while we have no doubt of being remembered by you in your prayers, you shall not be forgotten in ours. In the mean time we most fervently pray that the God and Father of all, whose mercies are not confined to prosperous situations, may impart to you divine consolations, that if your heart and flesh should at any time be apt to fail, He may be your never-failing support...[22]

To his Unitarian flock, Palmer remained the Christian pastor, not the subverter of the state.

Maurice Margarot was the only one of the four to return to England. Skirving died in Australia, and Palmer during his attempted voyage home. Muir escaped from Sydney on an American ship, and spent his last days in France. A letter from Sydney Cove, dated 9 November 1794 and signed by Palmer, Skirving and Muir, was addressed to Jeremiah Joyce, Unitarian minister and editor of Palmer's *Narrative*. The letter referred to an accusation 'as unexpected as it was horrible in its nature' that the trio had led a conspiracy to 'murder the master and crew, in order that they might carry the ship into some foreign harbour'. Because of this allegation they were confined in a manner 'to justify in their minds the continual alarm of assassination'. Having nevertheless survived the voyage, honour compelled them to declare that 'Mr Margarot was an accessory to the wrongs they have suffered, was even an instigator of their accusation in collusion with master of the Transport'.[23] Joyce printed the letter (which had already appeared in the press) in his introduction to the *Narrative*. It is uncannily apt that the false accusation of an intended mutiny should reproduce in microcosm the accusations levelled by Burke, Pitt and the antijacobins against Unitarian reformers as a whole.

Robert Millar would later remark to Lindsey of Palmer's time in Scotland: 'It was deeply to be lamented that he ever troubled himself about Politics – and certainly contrary to my earnest entreaties.'[24] Turner has no doubt about the impact of Palmer's transportation on Unitarianism in Scotland: 'Of the small Unitarian societies in Scotland which owed their temporary existence to Mr Palmer's exertions, scarcely any survived the shock arising from his removal.'[25] The Montrose society did not outlast the departure of Christie; the congregations at Edinburgh and Glasgow soon temporarily died out; only at Dundee did Millar succeed in holding things together, though 'every letter he received was previously opened by the agents of government'.[26] Yet in 1811 Richard Wright of the Unitarian Fund preached four times at Dundee to 'full, and most of them crowded congregations, who were very attentive'.[27]

Archibald Hamilton Rowan's Unitarianism is less well documented than Thomas Fyshe Palmer's. We know that his maternal grandfather, William Rowan, was Unitarian in his beliefs. His will began with the words: 'In the name of the ONE only self-existing Being.' Besides requiring Archibald Hamilton to take his benefactor's name, the will decreed that he should attend a British university – and not return to Ireland until he was 25. It also expressed the hope that he would become 'a learned, sober and honest man', who would live 'unbribed and unpensioned, zealous for the rights of his country, loyal to his King and a true Protestant, without bigotry to any sect'.[28] We also know that, in his latter years, Archibald Hamilton Rowan himself worshipped at Strand Street Chapel, Dublin – a Unitarian congregation. When his wife died shortly before him in 1834, the *Bible Christian* recorded that her commitment to study of the scriptures had 'enabled her to overcome the prejudices of early education, and to adopt the principles of Unitarian Christianity as the true religion of the Bible'.[29] When the same journal reported Rowan's own death later that year, it only hinted at Unitarian beliefs, but noted that 'he claimed the right of serving God according to the dictates of his own conscience, and held that all men are justly entitled to the full enjoyment of the same right'. The report adds: 'His religion taught him to "do justly, love mercy, and to walk humbly with his God" – that God whom he honoured and adored as the Universal Father, Friend and Benefactor'.[30] And it was William Drummond, joint Unitarian minister of Strand Street Chapel, who followed Rowan's funeral cortege and edited his autobiography.

At some stage during his student years, Rowan had connections with William Enfield and the Aikins at Warrington, where Anna Laetitia Aikin (the future Mrs Barbauld) is said to have been Rowan's first love. He may have gone there when Jebb took his leave of Cambridge.[31] Rowan married in Paris in 1781, and remained there for two years before returning to Ireland. But he continued to correspond with his old tutor until Jebb's death in 1786. The year before (in response to a letter from Rowan) Jebb wrote: 'I fear neither your heart or your head; and trust now you are settled in your own country you will be eminently useful to your generation – the highest praise of man.' He offered his former pupil some wholly characteristic advice: 'Explore with the utmost exertion of your faculties political truth, and having found it, avow it with firmness and perseverance. In the end it must succeed, and your character be stamped with honour. Temporizing expedients are always injurious, when contrary to natural right and natural feelings.' Jebb was convinced that Christianity would flourish 'without the aid of the bishops in the House of Lords'. He is sure that a reformed parliament would recognize this, 'while the clergy see it already, and therefore are your enemies'. He insists that 'a reformed parliament is therefore the first point to be aimed at', and, failing the adoption of 'Major Cartwright's plan', suggests a householder franchise to 'check the power of the great landowners'.[32]

This particular correspondence with Jebb grew out of Rowan's involvement in the Irish Volunteers. Originating in the American War, when Belfast's request for troops to defend them against possible French attack, elicited an offer of 'only half a troop of horse and half a company of invalids', the Volunteers would soon give self-defence a new meaning.[33] In July 1784, at a review of Volunteers in Belfast (attended by Rowan, as a private in his father's regiment), an address was presented to 'General Earl of Charlemont' expressing collective satisfaction at

> the decay of those prejudices which have so long involved us in feud and disunion – a disunion which, by limiting the rights of suffrage, and circumscribing the number of Irish citizens, has in a high degree, tended to create and foster that aristocratic tyranny which is the foundation of Irish grievance, and against which the public unanimously complain.[34]

When, two years later, Rowan commanded his own regiment of Volunteers, he explained that, when he first enlisted, 'it was not for the parade of a red coat, nor the merriment of a review day: it was to assist in defeating the insidious policy of corrupt courtiers, who decried the institution because they dreaded its virtue'.[35] And in a letter to the Volunteers themselves, written on the same day, he urged them to persist not only in the privilege of bearing arms but in training to use them. 'Ministers (he assured them) may be insolent, the great and wealthy may be corrupt; but a free and intrepid yeomanry, with the arms of peace and of defence in their hands, will, I trust, preserve this once famous, but now tottering constitution.'[36]

The French Revolution gave a new impetus to such ambitions. In Dublin a 'National Guard' was formed with Rowan's active encouragement, the title 'citizen soldier' was adopted, and the harp surmounted by a cap of liberty, instead of a crown, became the preferred device.[37] It was too much for Lord Charlemont, who admitted that, though he was nominally their general, the Dublin Volunteers had 'in no instance' followed his advice. He complained:

> Their follies have brought shame on the institution: upon a late occasion their conduct has been absolutely indefensible. No Egyptian hierophant could have invented a hieroglyphic more aptly significant of a republic, than the taking the crown from the harp, and replacing it by the cap of liberty.[38]

It was against this background that the Society of United Irishmen was formed in the autumn of 1791, on the initiative of Theobald Wolfe Tone and Thomas Russell, and with James Napper Tandy as secretary. The members of the Society pledged themselves

> to forward a brotherhood of affection, and identity of interests, a communion of rights, and an union of power among Irishmen of all religious persuasions; without which every reform in parliament must be partial, not national, inadequate to the wants, delusive to the wishes, and insufficient for the freedom and happiness of the country.[39]

Rowan joined the United Irishmen without hesitation, and would soon serve as President. Thus (he records) 'circumstances led to an acquaintance with the popular leaders in Ireland, and transmitted the name of an insignificant individual to posterity'.[40] The popular leaders had already moved beyond campaigning for parliamentary reform, and (according to the admittedly biased Richard Musgrave) were already in touch with the Girondins in 1792.[41] By now Rowan was a major of the Dublin Volunteers, and it was among these 'citizen soldiers' that he was accused of 'wickedly, maliciously and seditiously' distributing 'a certain false, wicked, malicious, scandalous and seditious libel, of and concerning the government, state and constitution of this Kingdom'. Although Rowan had not written the Address, the indictment describes him as 'a person of wicked and turbulent disposition', and accuses him of 'maliciously designing and intending to excite and diffuse amongst the subjects of this realm of Ireland, discontents, jealousies and suspicions of our sovereign lord the king and his government', in order to 'over awe and intimidate the legislature of this kingdom by armed force'. To support this last charge, the indictment quotes from the words of the Address, including:

> *Citizen soldiers*, you first took up arms to protect your country from foreign enemies and domestic disturbance, for the same purpose it now becomes necessary that you should *resume* them.... CITIZEN SOLDIERS TO ARMS, take up the shield of freedom and pledge of peace; the motive and end of your virtuous institution...

Catholic emancipation was now considered as 'merely the portal to the temple of national freedom'.[42]

Rowan would later welcome the Act of Union, writing to his wife in 1799: 'It takes a feather out of the great man's cap; but it will, I think, put many a guinea in the the poor man's pocket.' And he wrote to his father that the Union would bring about 'the downfall of one of the most corrupt assemblies, I believe, ever existed'.[43] But in 1794 Rowan was sentenced to a fine of £500 and two years imprisonment, despite (as his defence counsel claimed) being well known in Ireland 'not only by the part he has taken in public concerns ... but still more so by that extraordinary sympathy for human affliction which, I am sorry to think, he shares with so small a number'. In declaring sentence, Mr Justice Boyd told the defendant: 'It is happy for you that this insidious summons to arms was not observed; if it had, and the people with force of arms had attempted to make alterations in the constitution of this country, every man concerned would have been guilty of high treason.'[44] Historians argue as to whether the United Irishmen of the early 1790s were as violent in their intentions as their counterparts in 1798, after Lord Camden's ruthless repression of Ulster had raised the stakes.[45] The address Rowan received in Newgate, from the United Irishmen, noted that 'corruption has been leagued with falsehood to misrepresent and vilify this Society', and reasserted their 'inflexible determination to pursue the great object of our association – *an equal and impartial representation of the people in parliament* – an object from which no chance or change, no slander, no persecution, no oppression shall deter us'.[46]

Thanks to his resourceful wife, Rowan escaped from custody and made his way to France, where he was temporarily jailed as a suspected spy. While in Paris, he became friendly with Mary Wollstonecraft, who continued to write to him after she left for Le Havre. But his reference to 'an American family, of the name of Christie', suggests that Rowan was not tied into the London Unitarian network.[47] Sailing for America on the *Columbus*, Rowan settled at Wilmington, near Philadelphia. It would be five years before he returned to Europe, and another three years before an official pardon allowed him to return to Ireland. He had disowned an attempt by his friends to obtain a pardon in 1796, as he was unwilling to 'sign any petition or declaration in favour of the British constitution in Ireland which embraces such flagrant abuses as I have witnessed, and of which I have been in some measure the victim'.[48] He had written to his wife from Wilmington: 'The fact is, that from education and principle, I was led to assert and attempt to support a reform of parliament, and equal liberty to all religious sects.'[49] And in a journal he kept for his wife during his American exile, he recorded, soon after arriving at Philadelphia: 'I am confounded by the various accounts I hear of Irish affairs. How often have I said, and to Wolfe [Tone] particularly, if they have a mind to destroy the United Irishmen, Volunteers, &c, they had only to do justice to the Irish Catholics!'[50]

It is difficult to believe that Rowan ever intended to overthrow the constitution by armed force – though in the early 1790s he printed United Irishmen handbills on his home printing press. One recent historian has concluded: 'Citizenship, with all its rights and all its responsibilities, was what the United Irishmen were after in political terms. In social and religious terms they sought the rights of individuals.'[51] The recall of Fitzwilliam, and the decision to impose a military solution – what Camden called 'a salutary system of security' – led to the Catholic violence of 1798.[52] By then, the United Irishmen were divided not only by religion, but by conflicting economic agendas. Yet Rowan's priorities remained clear. In 1814, back on his Irish estates, he reduced the rents of his tenants, who presented him with a testimonial of thanks for thus sharing 'the distress of the day with his tenantry'.[53]

Part V

Explosive Echoes

14
'Jacobin' Journalism

In the summer of 1798, the prospectus advertising the first issue of the *Antijacobin Review* announced that the new journal would confront those monthly reviews which 'have insidiously favoured the designs of those writers who labour to undermine our civil and religious establishments'. To this end, the *Antijacobin Review* would 'frequently *review* the *Monthly, criticise* the *Critical*, and *analyse* the *Analytical*, on the principle already adopted by the WEEKLY EXAMINER in its comments on the daily prints'.[1]

Of the *Antijacobin Review*'s three initial targets, the *Analytical* had been founded in 1788 by the nephew of William Christie, Unitarian minister at Montrose. Thomas Christie had been a member of Essex Street Chapel during his days as a medical student. He wrote the preface to the first bound volume of the *Analytical*, and in 1789 he published *Miscellanies*, which includes 'Observations on the Literature of the Primitive Christian Writers; being an attempt to vindicate them from the imputations of Rousseau and Gibbon that they were enemies to philosophy and human learning'.[2] In that year, Christie left for Paris with a letter of introduction from Richard Price. During a six-month stay, Christie made the acquaintance of Mirabeau, Siéyès and Necker. On the strength of his stay in France, Christie came to the defence of Price in his *Letters on the Revolution in France*, one of many Unitarian ripostes to Burke's *Reflections*.[3]

Joseph Johnson, who published the *Analytical*, had closer connections with Essex Street. Between 1766 and 1772, before Lindsey resigned his Anglican livings, Johnson published 12 books or pamphlets in support of the campaign against subscription to the Thirty-nine Articles. This was almost one-third of all the antitrinitarian publications of those six years. It was Johnson who gave Lindsey financial support by publishing his *Apology*, described by the *Critical Review* as a lasting monument to Lindsey's 'learning, modesty, zeal and integrity'.[4] And it was Johnson who published Lindsey's first Essex Street sermon, delivered in the temporary meetinghouse at Paterson's auction room. The sermon sold 500 copies in four days, and Johnson would go on to publish all Lindsey's further works. But his support of Lindsey went beyond this. He was responsible for acquiring the house in Essex Street and fitting it up as a permanent chapel, and he applied for the necessary magistrate's licence. When this seemed likely to be refused, Johnson went with Attorney-General John Lee (himself a member of the Essex Street congregation) to insist on the magistrates' compliance with the Toleration Act.[5]

Disney's *Arranged Catalogue* of publications relating to subscription and the Test and Corporation Acts, published by Johnson in 1790, gives a clear indication of his importance as publisher/bookseller. Of 122 publications and republications listed by Disney as arising from the attempted Test Act repeal of 1787, 1789 and 1790, no fewer than 38 were published by Johnson – again almost one-third of the total. And of the *Analytical Review*'s list of 86 titles published or republished on the topic, during the first six months of 1790, as many as 29 carry the Johnson imprint.[6] The first works published from St Paul's Churchyard, where Johnson established himself in 1770, had been works by Priestley– including his *Familiar Introduction to the Theory and Practice of Perspective*. In the early 1770s, Johnson published the sermons of William Enfield (head of Warrington Academy from 1770) and the works of Warrington's very first student, Thomas Percival, MD, FRS.[7] Besides publishing works by Priestley, Lindsey and Disney, Johnson was publisher to Capel Lofft, Garnham, Frend and Coleridge (all of whom had adopted Unitarian theology as Anglicans), and to those from Dissenting backgrounds – Thomas Belsham, George Walker (former mathematics tutor at Warrington), John Aikin of Warrington and his daughter Anna Laetitia Barbauld.

But the most notorious of Johnson's Warrington circle was Gilbert Wakefield, who had been ordained deacon in the Anglican Church, and was briefly Fellow of Jesus College, Cambridge (1776–78). In 1778, he withdrew from the mastership of Brewood School, Staffordshire, on finding he was required to subscribe to the Articles. After three brief curacies – two of them in Liverpool, where he denounced the slave trade from the pulpit – he married and moved to Warrington as classical tutor. When John Aikin senior died in 1781, Wakefield took over his course on the New Testament, publishing his own translation of St Matthew's Gospel, and revealing his Unitarian theology by denying the distinct personality of the Holy Spirit.[8] He soon extended his translation to the whole New Testament, and in 1792 published his memoirs, containing strictures on Hackney College where he had briefly been classical tutor.[9]

In 1794 Wakefield's *Spirit of Christianity* challenged the government's war policy. He professes himself '*a son of peace*; a lowly and insignificant, but conscientious follower of that *Saviour*, at whose coming *peace* was *sung* (Luke ii: 14), and at whose departure *peace* was bequeathed (John xiv: 27)'.[10] Wakefield reckoned that 'since this country engaged in a war with *France* only *twelve months* ago, *two hundred and fifty-thousand* lives have been lost in the field and on the scaffold; not to mention the numberless afflictions of the living connected with this horrible devastation'. He doubts whether the despotic powers would have moved against France without British support, and concludes that 'the shocking murders, which have taken place among the *French* themselves, from that of the King on the throne to the meanest peasant, are truly assignable to that fermentation, which the interference of the same combination has excited'.[11] The French crimes, 'so exaggerated and sounded forth', are described by Wakefield as '*occasional* and *incidental*; stricken out by the violent collisions of such an unprecedented conflict; which has given full scope to all the prejudices and passions of outraged humanity'.[12] By contrast, British wickedness is 'of a *deliberate* and *systematic* kind; abundantly transcending all the enormities of the *French*'. And yet the British 'dwell with the complacency of innocence on our *own happy government* and *reformed church*, in contrast with the *Atheism* and murders of the *French*'.[13]

As for the church, Wakefield asks: 'Do not *all* our *bishops*, without an individual exception, by their silence at least, and unresisting acquiescence, countenance these horrid scenes of ferocity and carnage, and thereby injure every pretence to the name and character of Christian?'[14] Wakefield had prudently declared in a footnote that 'nothing can be more remote from my intention than disrespect for the *person* of the sovereign; and that the errors of government, as I deem them, excite in my mind a most unfeigned sorrow'. The scholarly temperament, he explains, 'can have but little to hope from *violent revolutions*; where the *still small voice* of letters and philosophy is drowned in the din of arms and the clamours of enthusiasm...[15] And in his preface to the third edition, Wakefield explains that only two copies of the original print-run were sold before the publisher took fright.[16]

Kearsley rather than Johnson had published Wakefield's *Spirit of Christianity*, but Johnson did publish Richard Watson's *Address to the People of Great Britain* (1798), to which Wakefield wrote a famous reply. He did not expect the Bishop of Llandaff and his fellow bishops to 'view, with a suitable discrimination and a clear disinterestedness, the imperfections of our establishment, or profess themselves friendly to measures, which may remove the foundation on which they stand'. The existing system 'with all its corruptions must necessarily appear more eligible to men so situated, than the dangerous alternative of reformation'.[17] For Unitarians like Wakefield, the continuance in its present form 'of our most *happy* constitution in Church and State', would bring them

> the sure abhorrence of all good churchmen . . . persecution, and probably imprisonment, or even military execution in no long time hence, if we presume to assert the unalienable privilege of independent man in an open declaration of our sentiments; or, at best, an absolute isolation, through legal tyranny or popular opprobrium, from the reasonable benefits of society: in short, letters and philosophy, with neglect and poverty must be our lot.[18]

Responding to the Bishop's insistence on the 'necessity and justice' of continuing the war, Wakefield argues that the peace terms offered to France had invited rejection. Claiming that 'the interest of our corrupt and guilty ministers is *prolonged war*', he points to recent ministerial speeches, which continue to denounce France as 'the same *regicides* and *atheists* as before'. Meanwhile ministers have 'engendered sham plots, false alarms and visionary assassinations, for the purposes of deceiving the unwary, and to establish their own power by a military despotism in due time, over England, like that which now tramples bleeding Ireland to the earth'.[19]

What sounded like sedition, however, was Wakefield's prediction that the French would be welcomed if they landed in England with 60 000 or 70 000 men – though he added, 'which, nevertheless, appears to me utterly impracticable, with our present naval superiority'.[20] This was considered excessive by the *Monthly Review*, which thought the author 'too much animated by passion, and by his aversion to certain ministerial men and measures'.[21] It was also too much for the government, who first arrested Wakefield's publisher, Cuthell. Wakefield's own trial followed 'before the same jury'. He defended himself, unrepentantly saying of Pitt's ministers: 'Of men like these, let me never deserve the friendship, not regret the enmity. Their approbation is indelible reproach, their persecution the truest panegyric.'[22] He was sent to Dorchester jail, emerging in June 1801 – only to die of typhus three months later. Dr Samuel Parr would later characterize Wakefield 'as a very profound scholar, as a most honest man, and as a Christian, who united knowledge with zeal, piety with benevolence, and the sympathy of a child with the fortitude of a martyr'.[23]

Johnson's offence was merely to *sell* Wakefield's *Reply*, a book he had not published – though it was a response to a book he had both published and sold. Yet his indictment described him as 'a malicious seditious and ill-disposed person and being greatly disaffected to our sovereign Lord the King', and alleged that he 'wickedly and seditiously did publish and cause to be published a certain scandalous and seditious libel'. He was convicted on 17 July 1798, but not imprisoned until mid-November, and not finally sentenced until the following February. Between conviction and sentence he sought to convince the authorities that he had 'uniformly recommended the circulation of such publications as had a tendency to promote good morals instead of such as were calculated to mislead and inflame the Common people'.[24] Even the *Gentleman's Magazine* would later write of Johnson's prosecution and imprisonment: 'It was by many considered as the ungenerous indulgence of a long-hoarded spleen against him on account of publications not liable to legal censure, though displeasing to Authority.'[25]

Johnson was not the only Unitarian bookseller/publisher or editor to suffer imprisonment. In Birmingham, John Belcher was imprisoned in 1793 for selling the works of Paine, as was Priestley's printer/bookseller, John Thompson – though briefly, as the jury acquitted him. According to the *Sheffield Register*, Thompson, after being charged, 'was not allowed to return to his own house, even under guard, but was sent to Warwick gaol the same afternoon'. And when Gales and some friends tried to visit him in prison, they were denied access because it was the Sabbath.[26] Gales himself escaped prison by evading arrest, but his editorial assistant, James Montgomery (who started the *Iris* with Unitarian funding when the *Register* folded) had two spells in prison during 1795–6 for publishing what were judged seditious libels. Richard Phillips, editor of the *Leicester Herald* and founder of the *Monthly Magazine*, was jailed for two years – as the *Antijacobin Review* enjoyed reminding its readers. It was left to a Baptist, Robert Hall of Cambridge, to challenge the government in his *Apology for the Freedom of the Press* (1793).[27]

It was a Unitarian member of Hall's Baptist congregation who was probably the most influential provincial editor. Benjamin Flower, founder-editor of the *Cambridge Intelligencer*, was imprisoned in 1799 for libelling Richard Watson, Wakefield's antagonist. The first issue of the *Intelligencer* in 1793 had professed the paper's loyalty to the British constitution 'as settled at the GLORIOUS REVOLUTION'. But the editor makes clear that he could not 'rest contented with declaring himself a friend merely to the theory of our constitution', since 'the excellence of a theory consists in its being reducible to practice'. Although he wants a reformed House of Commons worthy to be called 'the REPRESENTATIVE OF AN EMPIRE OF FREEMEN', he insists that 'the only means he trusts his countrymen will ever adopt for this important object are *peaceable* and *constitutional*'.[28] The paper that Priestley referred to, early in his American exile, as 'all the English newspaper that I see', consistently maintained its opposition to the war against France.[29] In the summer of 1796, the *Intelligencer* regretted that 'Buonaparte has stained his laurels by threats and cruelties, as wanton as they were unnecessary. His Letters and Proclamations one would have supposed had been written by a Russian General, in the habit of burning towns, and massacring his fellow-creatures in cold blood.' But the *Intelligencer* equally execrated 'that abandoned administration, that plague of Britain and Europe, without whose machinations and pecuniary assistance, the horrid Tragedy, with all its dreadful scenes of fire, blood and devastation must have long since ceased'.[30]

Coleridge commended the *Cambridge Intelligencer* for 'fighting fearlessly the good fight against Tyranny, yet never unfaithful to the Religion, "whose service is perfect Freedom" ',[31] while the weekly *Antijacobin* (forerunner of the *Antijacobin Review*) called the *Intelligencer* 'a mass of loathsome ingredients, a sort of "hell-broth", made up of the worst parts of the worst public Papers that ever disgraced the Metropolis of any country, with added filth and venom of its own'.[32] Johnson was convicted two weeks before the first publication of the *Antijacobin Review*, which claimed credit for the collapse of the *Analytical*. In July 1799, after one year of publication, the *Antijacobin* denounced the *Critical*'s reviewers as '*semi-Christians*, when compared with the Analytical conductors of irreligious trash'.[33] The *Analytical* had unwisely welcomed publication of the *Manual of the Theophilanthropes*. This Parisian sect, though taken seriously in France, had been mercilessly ridiculed in cartoon and verse in the *Antijacobin Review*'s very first number. The *Analytical* reported that Theophilanthropists admitted 'no other dogma than the existence of God, and the immortality of the soul', and worshipped the 'Father of the Universe' in the open air.[34] It was indeed successor to Robespierre's Cult of the Supreme Being, but in June 1792 the *Analytical* had dismissed a defence of Natural Religion as 'pantheism, which confounds the ideas of God and the universe'. The reviewer insisted: 'Its moral system admits no distinction between the mechanical laws of nature, and the moral laws of God, and precludes all ideas of reward and punishment, except what arises from the necessary consequences of men's actions.'[35] The 'irreligious trash' of Johnson's *Analytical Review* was neither atheistic nor even deistic, but Unitarian. That admittedly meant hostility to the established church as well as to the Pitt ministry. Thomas Atkinson's shilling pamphlet in 1798 regretted that 'all these Reviews are in one interest; and *artfully arranged* to further one and the same cause'. But he reserved special condemnation for the 'abominable' *Analytical* which existed to propagate 'a destructive set of principles by which the venerable constitution of our ancestors, was intended to be gradually subverted'.[36]

The *Monthly Review*, founded by the bookseller Ralph Griffiths and still edited by him 50 years later, enrolled several contributors with Warrington connections. John Aikin senior and William Enfield both wrote for the *Monthly* in the 1770s. John Aikin junior (Anna Laetitia's brother) reviewed medical books for the *Monthly* from 1776 to 1784, and wrote over another hundred reviews for the journal between 1793 and 1799. Aikin was also active in setting up the *Monthly Magazine*, published by Richard Phillips, who continued to edit it from its launch in 1796 until 1806. Enfield, who moved to Norwich in 1784, reviewed for both the *Monthly Magazine* and the *Analytical*. William Taylor junior (also of Norwich) not only contributed 764 articles to the *Monthly Magazine* between 1796 and 1824, but is credited with a further 60 articles in the *Critical Review*. Taylor was introduced to the *Monthly Review* by Enfield, and from late 1795 took responsibility for the appendices dealing with foreign literature. He also contributed to Arthur Aikin's *Annual Review* and Flower's *Cambridge Intelligencer*.[37] Writing for the *Monthly Review* in 1797–98, Taylor reviewed both Barruel's alarmist *Memoir of Jacobinism* and Robison's *Proofs of Conspiracy*. His Unitarian biographer wrote that Taylor's reviews of these two authors had 'endeavoured by argument and by ridicule to dissipate the panic with which they were re-infecting the public mind'.[38] Barruel sent a letter of protest to the editor of the *Monthly Review*. Griffiths passed it to Taylor with the comment: 'What you will judge proper to do with it, I long to know. If you choose that we should descend with him into the arena, I hope the contest will not prove a very long one.' And he added revealingly: 'As to the concluding part of the article on Barruel, which I dared not print, you will find it in the parcel. I was indeed sorry to decline it, the phrases being so well turned.'[39]

In the preface to the third volume of the *Antijacobin Review*, the editor, besides claiming credit for 'the dissolution of one of our political and religious opponents, the *Analytical Review*', argues that both the *Monthly* and the *Critical* have been tamed. The editors of 'the two reviews which have most effectually contributed to give currency to principles of disaffection and hostility to the established order of things in this country', had been persuaded by the *Antijacobin*'s exposure of their 'profligacy' to change their tone. They had adopted 'a degree of wily prudence, and wary circumspection, which serve as a temporary mask to their designs'. This 'affected moderation' had led the *Antijacobin* to scrutinize back-numbers of the offending periodicals. This would have 'the two-fold advantage of shewing by what means the public mind was first poisoned, and of supplying an incontrovertible proof of the difference between the past *practice*, and the present *professions* of the literary despots'.[40] Yet the *Antijacobin* could still find present cause for complaint. In January 1800, it took the *Monthly Review* to task for its 'panegyric' on a poem by a Unitarian, Samuel Rogers. The *Antijacobin* sees Rogers as one of those overrated poets who 'have so far insinuated themselves into the public esteem, as to be applauded in terms which posterity can never sanction'.[41] And a year later, 'Academicus' challenges the *Monthly*'s favourable notice of a sermon by Joshua Toulmin, denouncing him as a representative of 'that abominable heresy, of which the Christian world was guiltless almost *sixteen hundred years*; which was generated by the hot brain of the turbulent schismatic *Faustus Socinus*'.[42]

Earlier the *Antijacobin* had bracketed the *Critical* and the *Analytical* together as propagators of Socinianism – and therefore of Jacobinism. Commenting on the *Critical Review*'s notice of James Stillingfleet's *National Gratitude*, the *Antijacobin* challenges the *Critical*'s reference to the preacher's 'narrow unchristian spirit' and its reviewer's complaint that 'we cannot perceive what concern the doctrines of The Trinity, original sin, imputed righteousness, &c., and harsh censures thrown out upon all who do not hold such sentiments, have to do with a day of national thanksgiving'. The *Antijacobin* concludes that, according to such critics, 'every clergyman who discharges his duty by supporting the true principles of the established church' must possess 'a narrow and unchristian spirit'.[43] The same issue of the *Critical* contained a hostile review of Samuel Horsley's *Critical Disquisitions on the Eighteenth Chapter of Isaiah*. The reviewer's regret, that 'the Critical Disquisitions on an ancient prophet should be embittered by the politics of modern times', draws a dismissive retort from the *Antijacobin*: 'Such Jacobinical insolence requires no comment. Simply to lay it before our readers is to expose it to contempt and detestation.' For its part, the *Antijacobin* had no hesitation in identifying the British as the Bishop's 'messenger people'.[44] Four months later the same journal's 'Reviewers Reviewed' section, not only describes the *Monthly Review* as 'the established vehicle of Arianism and Presbyterianism to the public', but exhibits the *Critical* as 'still breathing out the old *virus* of Presbyterianism, inflamed with the worser *virus* of new Arianism, or Socinianism, or new Deism'. These strictures are followed by a reminder of Kippis's connection with the *Monthly Review*, and of his 'open hostility to the church from the commencement to the close of the Doctor's life'.[45]

Kippis had died in 1795, having founded the *New Annual Register* in opposition to Burke's *Annual Register*, and from 1781 contributed a regular feature prefixed to the bound volumes. At the end of its historical narrative for 1792 (published in 1793), Kippis's *Register* was already pleading for peace with France: 'We cannot more religiously fulfil our duty towards [our country] than in wishing most fervently for the return of peace...'[46] In its notice of the *New Annual Register* for the following year, the *Antijacobin* deplored the advantage enjoyed by Kippis's editorial team: 'This work is constantly edited in less than *ten months* from the period of which the history is detailed; while the friends of our Church and King must wait *five years* before they can obtain any fair, honest or candid account of general occurrences, politics or literature.' The same critique notes that the *New Annual Register*'s publishers are the Robinsons, '*wholesale* booksellers, in London, who were convicted, 10 August 1793, at Bridgwater Assizes, for selling the second Part of "Paine's Rights of Man" '.[47] A month later, a continuation of the same critique, referring disparagingly to 'the author of the Register, and his accomplice, the Critical Review', observes:

> As the New Annual Register has contributed materially (aided by the Jacobinical Reviews) to propagate the most false notions respecting the French revolution, and the origin of the war... it becomes essential to render its errors so manifest, that its dangerous tendency may be clear to the plainest understanding.[48]

The new century opened with an attack, by a correspondent to the *Antijacobin*, on Priestley, Belsham, Kentish and Toulmin:

> My reason, Sir, for treating the New Annual Register, in this instance, with contempt, is because the celebrity of the Socinian school, founded upon infidelity, sophistry, and the little artifices of men who cannot reason, is so nearly extinct that I should deem it writing a libel on the common sense of Englishmen to enter, after what is past, into a laboured confrontation of such feeble attempts to give momentary vigour to the expiring flame.[49]

It would prove a premature epitaph.

15
Confronting Napoleon

Earlier chapters have cited published sermons as evidence of the continuities in Unitarian rhetoric. But was anyone still listening after 1800? The Bishop of Rochester thought not. A correspondent to the *Antijacobin Review*, at the beginning of 1802, objecting to the *Monthly Review*'s uncomplimentary notice of Horsley's diocesan charge to his clergy, remarked: 'Bishop Horsley having occasion to notice the baffled squadrons of Socinianism, says, "The Patriarch of that sect is *fled*, and the orators and oracles of Birmingham and Essex Street are dumb; or if they speak, speak only to be disregarded" '.[1]

Until his death in America in 1804, Priestley remained a target of antijacobin invective. In September 1800 a review, in the *British Critic*, of the second edition of the *Life of Bishop Horne*, prompts the *Antijacobin* to compare Priestley with the founder of Islam: '*Mahomet's* view was to raise a party against the Christian World; and the Doctor makes no secret of it, that he is actuated by a like spirit of proselyt[iz]ing.'[2] When Priestley died, the same journal devoted nine pages to attacking the Rev. John Edwards's memorial sermon. The review would have been briefer 'if Dr Priestley's ashes had been suffered, by his friends, to lie undisturbed ... if they had not most officiously, impertinently and injudiciously, placed him again on the public stage, as the best of men, as a martyr, and, indeed, as little less than a pattern of perfection ...' The reviewer challenges Edwards's account of the Birmingham riots, observing: 'But for the licentious proceedings of Dr Priestley and his friends, there had been no mob and no riot.'[3] And as late as 1807, a correspondent to the *Antijacobin* would call Priestley 'the arch-fiend of heresy'.[4]

Priestley was not the only figure from the 1790s to attract attention a decade later. Reviewing, in late 1802, the *Guilt of Democratic*

Scheming fully proved against the dissenters, the *Antijacobin* informs its readers:

> After alluding to Dr Priestley's 'train to overturn the present system of things', to the 'Evangelical Magazine', to the 'London Corresponding Society', and to its members Hardy, Gerrald and Skirving, all Dissenters, he makes a long extract from the inflammatory lectures of Robinson for the instruction of catechumens.

The author (who styles himself 'Inquirer') considers that Robinson's *Political Catechism* 'alone contains full proofs of a system of sedition against the laws of the land, that is against the constitution itself'. This echoes Burke's strictures in the 1790 debate on the Test and Corporation Acts. More topically, 'Inquirer', notices what the *Antijacobin* calls 'the factious conduct of the dissenters in 1801', which 'Inquirer' regards as being 'under pretence of petitioning for peace'.[5]

We know from Thanksgiving sermons that the peace of 1802 supplied Unitarians with a pretext for re-fighting the rhetorical battles of the 1790s. Benjamin Flower went so far as to quote from parliamentary speeches of the period, in a note appended to the preface of his *Reflections on the Preliminaries of Peace*. He cited Lord Loughborough's speech in the House of Lords on 29 March 1791, when the noble lord deplored 'the horrid spirit of insolence and ambition' that had afflicted His Majesty's ministers: 'Like a beast of prey, we roamed every quarter of the globe for victims. With astonishment and horror, we saw the system of the King's ministers taking a general sweep of all nations and kingdoms in one place, and insulting, meddling, irritating in another...'[6] Flower's 29-page pamphlet was reprinted from the *Cambridge Intelligencer* for 10 October 1801. Reminding his readers of Pitt's declared war aims – 'INDEMNITY FOR THE PAST, AND SECURITY FOR THE FUTURE' – Flower commented that most of those objectives had been relinquished, while 'the rest are left without any other security than we possessed at the commencement...' Calculating that 'HUNDREDS OF THOUSANDS OF BRITONS, MILLIONS OF EUROPEANS have fallen a sacrifice',[7] Flower asks whether, 'after his recent and violent philippic against the Chief Consul, characterizing him as "a man utterly destitute of good faith, the *Child and Champion of Jacobinism*" ', Pitt can sincerely applaud the peace terms.[8] Flower concludes:

> As MEN WE REJOICE that Europe is no longer a field of blood, and that the long and swelling catalogue of human woes, the consequence

> of the war, is about to close. As BRITONS WE REJOICE, in the hope that the restoration of PEACE will be followed by the restoration of those invaluable rights, of which our statesmen, during a period of war, have plundered us. As CHRISTIANS WE REJOICE that our established churches will no longer be profaned by insults offered to heaven, under the name of prayers, for success in a war of injustice, wickedness and folly . . .[9]

The *Monthly Magazine* (condemned by the *Antijacobin* in 1802 as 'a vehicle for the sentiments of all who are disaffected to our establishments, both in church and state') was slow to abandon hopes of a constructive peace with Bonaparte. Recalling the principle on which the war had been fought – 'that a people (the French nation) have not a right to choose a government for themselves' – the magazine went on to lament Bonaparte's misuse of his opportunities. Perhaps, the editors added optimistically, it was not too late: 'It is from the publications of this country alone that the great man can be acquainted with the voice of truth, and, unless we are greatly misinformed, he is not inattentive to them.'[10] By the following April, the same periodical had decided that, despite Napoleon's genius in the field, 'in his internal government he is more a man of promises than of performance'. His schemes are 'great, and even extravagant; but his means are totally inadequate to their execution'.[11] And after Britain had declared war on France, in May 1803, the same editors hailed Britain's united sense of purpose:

> The nation never was, at any period of its history, except perhaps in the latter years of the seven years war, under Lord Chatham's administration, so united as at this crisis. The friends of liberty, those who were stigmatized as Jacobins, are now the most forward to resent and to resist the odious tyranny of Bonaparte.[12]

The *New Annual Register* was no longer sympathetic to Unitarian friends of liberty. It noticed *Socrates and Jesus compared,* 'from the pen of Dr Priestley – a pen alas! That never shall move more', but added dismissively: 'We do not, however, admire such comparisons, or see any reason for them in the present day.' And the same volume for 1803 (published in 1804), commenting on the resumption of hostilities, concluded that, if peace with France could not be sustained, 'we must believe that a more favourable time could not have been chosen for the renewal of the war. In England the vigour of the government was nobly seconded by the heroism of the people'.[13] Unitarian publicists were not all so sanguine, or so unanimous in their patriotism. The *Monthly Review*'s 1804 notice of a publication by 'an ingenious and liberal writer' quoted the author's objection to the prevalence of press smears on Napoleon: 'There is neither *sense* nor good manners in the personal abuse with which the British newspapers are filled against him, and I really think *it unworthy of the nation.*' This produced a furious reaction from the *Antijacobin*'s 'Observator', who asked: 'How is it unworthy of the nation to shew in every respect how they detest and abominate a monster replete with everything that is horrible and accursed, and make manifest in what light they contemplate a murderer, who has sacrificed to his ambition . . . thousands of miserable wretches?'[14] The following month, while insisting that they radically disagreed with the Unitarian author 'on many points of religion and politics', the editors could not withold their 'tribute of applause from one of the most animated and eloquent discourses which has been published during the present contest' – Benjamin Naylor's *Right and Duty of defensive War.*[15] Yet as late as 1807, the Unitarian William Roscoe, Whig MP for Liverpool 1806–7, attracted vehement denunciation for his criticism of the conduct of the war.

Reviewing the second edition of Roscoe's *Considerations on the Present War* (1808), the *Antijacobin* cites, as evidence of the author's Jacobinism, Roscoe's poem written in the 1790s, and beginning:

> O'er the vine-cover'd hills and gay vallies of France
> See the day-star of liberty rise.

The reviewer mocks Roscoe's lack of consistency 'in praising the first efforts of the French to establish what *he* thought *liberty*, and is now forbearing to censure, or, in other words tacitly to commend, the present horrible system of despotism, which leaves to the subject not a shadow of freedom . . .' This 'weak and impudent calumniator', having made some mark as poet and historian, 'seems to think himself qualified to become the political dictator of the realm'. The *Antijacobin* concludes: 'We doubt not, however, that this apology for France and attack on England will prove as impotent and as contemptible as his insidious apology for Popish pollutions and attacks on Christianity in the soporific Memoirs of Leo X.'[16] The *Critical Review* treated the erstwhile historian of Leo X more respectfully. Noting that Roscoe showed 'that all the motives which were assigned for the stubborn prosecution of the late war, have no reference to the present', the reviewer bluntly expresses his own view of the war: 'We know and lament that in this *Christian country*, there has lately sprung up from the polluted seeds of loans, contracts, jobs and all the different species of political corruption, a host of men who are advocates for PERPETUAL WAR!!!'[17]

By 1808 the Unitarians' own periodical, the *Monthly Repository*, was in its third year. Founded in 1806 by Robert Aspland, who that year preached at Hackney an obituary sermon on Fox, the new journal attracted some well-known Unitarian contributors. Among those who wrote for it in its first year were: Rochemont Barbauld (Anna Laetitia's husband), Thomas Belsham, Benjamin Flower, Jeremiah Joyce, John Kentish, Henry Crabb Robinson, John Towill Rutt, Joshua Toulmin and William Hamilton Reid – the first editor of the *Orthodox Churchman*, who had turned Unitarian.[18] Among the aims of the *Monthly Repository*, as stated in its prospectus, were 'to blend literature with theology, and to make theology rational and literature popular; to be the advocate of Scriptural Christianity; to guard the Protestant privilege of liberty of conscience'.[19] The preface to the first bound volume expressed the hope that 'like the *Theological Repository*, edited by the venerable Dr PRIESTLEY', it would be accounted 'a valuable part of a theological library, and will be consulted in time to come as a collection of sound argument and rational criticism, as well as of authentic biography and interesting intelligence'.[20]

From the first, the *Monthly Repository* opposed the war with France. Among the selection of Thanksgiving sermons, briefly noticed after the victory of Trafalgar, was Jay's *Reflections on Victory*, preached on the text from 2 Samuel 19. 2: 'And the victory that day was turned into mourning.' Observing, rather unnecessarily, that national victories are different from 'the moral and spiritual victory of the Christian', the reviewer remarked of Trafalgar: 'The joy excited by this victory should be tempered with seriousness, prayer, praise, beneficence.' Hugh Worthington, in a sermon at Salters' Hall, warned his hearers that 'there must be no pride or self-conceit; no malignity against enemies; no inhuman delight in war; and no presumptuous confidence in futurity'. He also noted the ambiguous significance of Nelson's death 'in the very moment of victory'.[21] In March 1806 the *Monthly Repository*'s regular columnist, 'Gogmagog', launched an attack on Thanksgiving sermons:

1 They all agree in overrating the victory of Trafalgar. Judging from them, you would suppose that France, like Britain, was a maritime power solely...
2 They unite in extolling the spirit of war...

3 They conspire most indecently in praising the virtue and piety of Nelson...
4 They all, as if by mutual consent, pass over most courteously our national crimes...[22]

Two years later, the *Repository*'s 'Monthly Retrospect of Public Affairs or the Christian's Survey of the Political World' recorded of a recent Fast Day: 'As it is a day for the confession of national sins, care should be particularly taken, that we do not wilfully continue in one of a very atrocious nature, that of war, without an absolute necessity.'[23]

It is rather more surprising to find – almost a year after Trafalgar – the *Monthly Repository* commending Napoleon as a model of religious toleration. A correspondent informs readers that 'a late decree of the Emperor Napoleon orders every officiating Protestant Minister in the French empire to be accommodated with a house and garden; and the Government have engaged to keep the Protestant churches in repair at its own expense'.[24] In September 1806, the same correspondent asks: 'If, in the overthrow of the Germanic empire, the Emperor of the French has succeeded beyond any of his predecessors, may it not be owing as much to his tolerating principles of religion, as to the success of his arms?'[25] And a year later the *Monthly Repository* devotes four double columns to 'Religious Liberty in France'. Napoleon's reply to the Address of French Protestants, welcoming his victorious return to Paris, is quoted: 'You owe me no obligation; I wish not men to think themselves indebted to me, because I have merely been just. CONSCIENCE IS NOT WITHIN THE JURISDICTION OF HUMAN LAWS.' Disclaiming any attempt 'to find the hero in ancient prophecies' or to identify Napoleon with 'the man on the white clouds in the Revelations, with a golden crown on his head, and a sharp sickle in his hand to reap the harvest of the earth', the *Monthly Repository* boldly proclaims: 'WHEREVER BONAPARTE HAS GONE, RELIGIOUS INTOLERANCE HAS FLED BEFORE HIM.'[26]

The year 1807 closes with the hope that 'the measures now pursuing in France with regard to the Jews will lead to their restoration', though it is recognized that Napoleon's motives are 'no doubt political'.[27] Even his intervention in Spain is at first welcomed as a blow for freedom of conscience:

> Whatever may be the fate of the contending kings or the fallen minister, we look forward to objects of much greater importance: the restoration of religious liberty to the Spaniards; the downfall of the

> Inquisition; the abolition of monastic vows, and the weakening of the Spanish church to such a degree that Rome shall feel the shock to its very foundation.[28]

As in the 1770s and 1790s, Unitarians' sympathy for Britain's enemies was prompted by their admiration for the guaranteeing of religious freedom. Thus the 'Monthly Retrospect' notes the strangeness of Britain allying with the Spanish Bourbons, and asks: 'Is it for love of freedom, virtue and independence, or merely through hate and fear of a common enemy?' The writer concedes, however, that Napoleon is destroying the independence of a sovereign state, and warns that a conqueror's success is no proof of his own excellence: 'Nebuchadnezzar was raised to execute the just judgements of God, but was at last levelled with the beasts of the field.'[29]

The *Critical Review* recognized that the 'perfidy' of Bonaparte's conduct in Spain must alter attitudes to Napoleon, and, reviewing Whitbread's *Letter to Lord Holland,* decides: 'We hardly, therefore, agree with Mr Whitbread in thinking that this is a favourable moment for commencing a negotiation with France.'[30] Yet only two months before, the *Critical*'s notice of *Causes and Consequences of Continental Alienation* had applauded the late, shortlived Grenville ministry for refusing to subsidize Prussia, make a loan to Russia or send British troops to the Elbe and the Vistula. The *Critical* fears that 'there is too much truth' in the author's assertion

> that we are considered by the nations of the continent, as the most selfish people on the face of the globe; and that there is not one of them, either amongst neutrals, allies or enemies, but holds us in an aversion bordering on contempt. Everything that has happened of late years, the total failure of the war, and the long continuance of it to the total ruin of the continent has been imputed to us.

The reviewer adds his own endorsement: 'We subsidized the powerful, we menaced the weak; and we cemented one coalition after another, considering only our own interest, and regardless of the destruction which awaited our allies.'[31]

Similarly the *Critical*'s review of Roscoe's pamphlet, urging a negotiated peace, heaped equal censure on Bonaparte and the Portland ministry:

> The ministers of this country have informed us that they are determined to fight Bonaparte *with his own weapons*. We hardly need say

> that those weapons are fabricated on the anvil of Treachery, of Cruelty and Injustice. But are these the weapons with which our *Christian* ministers can ever promote the interest of Britain or diminish the power of France? Was the seizure of the Danish marine and the conflagration of the capital of Denmark designed as a specimen of the new mode of warfare which they are henceforth to prosecute?[32]

The *Critical* had already attacked the Orders in Council. Reviewing Alexander Baring's critique of their implication for the trade of neutral America, the journal complains that, on coming to power the present ministers 'seem to have resolved to make themselves *talked of*; and to impress the country with an opinion of their energy'. The reviewer quotes Baring's claim that the Orders in Council 'were of a description to produce a revolution in the whole commerce of the world, and a total derangement of those mutual rights and relations, by which civilized nations have hitherto been connected'.[33]

The Orders in Council of January 1807 – prompted by Napoleon's Berlin Decrees of 1806 – had been extended in November 1807, by the Portland ministry, to exclude neutrals not only from European ports, but 'from all ports or places in the colonies belonging to his majesty's enemies'. This prompted Liverpool merchants engaged in the American trade to draw up a parliamentary petition, and send it to London with three delegates. William Rathbone, expelled from the Quakers for Unitarian sympathies, was prominent in the agitation. He was supported by Roscoe and Whitbread, already influential in Liverpool politics through their opposition to the war. When the American merchants of Manchester and London followed the Liverpool lead, Rathbone was confident of success, writing to Roscoe: 'Be assured that these Orders in Council must be rescinded or the Ministry will fall. I do indeed fully expect both.'[34] The government agreed to an enquiry into the effects of the Orders in Council, but Rathbone was to be disappointed. Leeds and Birmingham did not press their case, while in Manchester pro-ministry petitions outweighed those of the opposition. And early in 1809, Rathbone died, described in tributes reprinted from the *Athenaeum* as 'this champion of peace and goodwill on earth'.[35]

The summer of 1811 saw Dissenters as a whole combine to defeat Lord Sidmouth's Bill, designed to amend the Toleration Act so as to curtail itinerant preaching. Thomas Belsham supported it as a means of excluding the uneducated from pulpits, but Dissenters in general saw it as a retreat from toleration. A correspondent to the *Monthly Repository* applauded the effectiveness of the opposition, 'for the *Toleration* was really *in danger*, and was rescued from its perils by the petitioners'.[36] Methodists joined the old Dissenting denominations in raising nearly 700 petitions, and, deprived of cabinet support, the Bill was defeated without a division.[37] The Dissenters' success encouraged a renewal of collective action against the Orders in Council. In December 1811, the *Liverpool Mercury* published resolutions from the city's American Chamber, blaming the Orders in Council for the dislocation of trade, and calling on the mayor to convene a public meeting in order to organize a petition. When he refused, the American merchants raised a petition nonetheless. The new Liverpool protest was supported by the Unitarian Wedgwoods in the Potteries. In Leeds and Sheffield, where Dissenters led the protests, a specifically Unitarian presence is harder to trace, though the *Leeds Mercury* had been bought in 1801 by Edward Baines, who divided his Sunday worship between Salem Congregational chapel and the Mill Hill Unitarian meeting.[38] The protests of the Midland and Northern towns were more effective than they had been in 1808, and on 3 March 1812 Brougham moved for a select committee on the effects of the Orders in Council. He conjured up the spectre of war with America, which would soon become a reality.[39]

As in the 1770s, the American trade and the East India Company had become linked. There was provincial anger at the proposed renewal of the East India Company's monopoly, which had been under negotiation since November 1811. At a Liverpool meeting on the East India Company in March 1812, Roscoe, who prepared the resolutions for approval, 'supported them in an address of considerable length'. The resolutions asserted a citizen's 'right to a free trade', and condemned the damage done by an 'exclusive traffic'.[40] And it was a Liverpool Unitarian minister who declared, at a public dinner for Roscoe's supporters in May 1812, that 'the spirit of reform is certainly rising'.[41] The government agreed to throw open the East India trade, and in June 1812 modified the Orders in Council so as to relieve American commerce. But before the news had crossed the Atlantic, the United States declared war on Britain. It is no surprise to find the *Antijacobin Review* supporting the Orders in Council, and taking a robust anti-American line. In May 1811 the *Antijacobin*'s lead review provides an excuse for supporting claims that the Madison administration exhibits Jeffersonian pro-French principles, and for describing a bill then before Congress as 'a full, unequivocal avowed adoption by the United States, of Bonaparte's continental system'.[42] By February 1812 the editors are urging war on the grounds that the American republic resembles 'in many respects, revolutionary France, particularly in her spirit of aggression and aggrandizement, at the expense of neighbouring powers'.[43]

Throughout the Napoleonic Wars, the *Antijacobin Review* remains a useful barometer of perceived Unitarian pressure on the establishment. The Belsham brothers had been targets since the first years of the new century. In 1802 Thomas Belsham's *Elements of the Philosophy of the Mind* and William Belsham's first volume of *Memoirs of the Reign of George III* were attacked in the same issue.[44] *Memoirs of George III* was reviewed over three issues and a total of 45 pages. And as late as December 1809, the editors could amuse their readers by wondering whether the Belsham, who is one of Dr Parr's 'excellent friends', is 'Mr Belsham the perverter of British history, or his brother the perverter of Holy Writ? The Jacobin historian , or the Unitarian preacher.'[45]

In 1809 the *Critical*'s reviewers were still under attack as 'zealous promoters of *heresy* and *schism*', and were accused of stripping Christianity of 'its most distinguishing and valuable peculiarities', and reducing it to 'little more than an improved system of heathenism; this they denominate *unitarianism*.'[46] Six months earlier 'Detector' had complained: 'Besides the *Critical* and *Monthly*, there are now the *Edinburgh* and *Annual* Reviews, which systematically and incessantly impugn the doctrines of our church and the measures of our government'.[47] Nor had accusations of Jacobinism disappeared. In March 1810 a correspondent refers to 'the Critical and Edinburgh Reviewers, and the whole body of *Deistical, Unitarian and Jacobin Reformers*', while the lead article for February 1812 quotes the author of the *Dangers of the Edinburgh Review*: 'I accuse it of *infidelity* in religion; *licentiousness* in morals; and *seditious and revolutionary principles* in politics.'[48] Unitarians were slower to recognize the *Edinburgh* as an ally. The *Monthly Repository* for January 1812 noted: 'The Edinburgh Review, the most powerful of our periodical publications, has at length taken up the cause of the Protestant Dissenters.' But the *Edinburgh* had reservations about Unitarians:

> The government has a right to do any thing that is for the good of the governed, and it is possible that a particular religious sect may be so notorious for dangerous political opinions, that their faith may be taken as a test, or mark, of their doctrines upon government. In the changes and chances of the world, Socinian doctrine may be firmly united to republican habits.

The *Monthly Repository* retorted: 'If, in spite of past history and present appearances, Socinians should become traitors, let them be punished, as the law has provided, though not for their Socinianism, but for their treason.'[49]

The *Edinburgh*'s print-run by 1805 was already 4000, compared with the *Monthly Repository*'s 1000 copies (including backnumbers) in 1809.[50] But the *Edinburgh*'s doubts did not dissuade Lord Liverpool's government from repealing (1812) the Five Mile Act and Conventicle Act of Charles II. The *Monthly Repository* gave credit to Sidmouth who had

> first united the Dissenters and next alarmed the magistrates, and hurried them into construction of the Acts of Toleration that could not be maintained consistently with the Dissenters' security, and thus again led them to unite their efforts which have been crowned by a most wise and beneficent law'.[51]

Nor was the government deterred from passing William Smith's Unitarian Relief Bill in 1813. The *Repository* itself records that the Bill passed the Commons 'without any debate', remarking, somewhat surprisingly: 'The new act indeed is not of much consequence in itself. The term Unitarian has lost the discredit some time ago attached to it; and for a long time no one has been debarred from professing this faith, from the fear of civil disabilities.'[52] The *Antijacobin* seems not to have thought the Act worthy of notice, preoccupied as its editors now were in defending the established church against the campaign for Catholic emancipation. In April 1812, before the amending of the Toleration Act later that year, the *Antijacobin* had asked:

> Do not petitions pour in upon us from the Papists of England and Ireland, modestly calling for the abolition of *all* tests and distinctions in matters of religion? Have not some degenerate Protestants been mad or foolish enough to make a similar call upon the legislature? Has not a member of the Lower House announced his intention of introducing a motion for carrying these notable propositions into effect? – Spirits of our forefathers arise and dispel the fatal delusion which envelopes your wretched posterity!'[53]

Catholic Emancipation was a campaign that Unitarians supported. Among five reasons for doing so, listed by a correspondent to the *Monthly Repository* that same month, the first was: 'Justice demands it'.[54] And a 'No Popery' meeting in Bristol, on 23 December 1812, was told by the Unitarian minister, John Rowe, that he regarded the protest as 'in the highest degree injurious in its tendency, to the cause of liberty, civil and religious, to the interests and even the safety of our country, and to the general welfare of mankind'.[55] In its upbeat 'Summary of Politics' at the end of 1813, the *Antijacobin* recorded, as the only troubling and unresolved question, 'the *emancipation of the Papists*, which the natives of Ireland seem determined to reserve as a constant bone of contention, to disturb the domestic peace and tranquillity of the country'. Elsewhere, it proclaimed, antijacobinism had triumphed: 'This is the triumph of reason over sophistry; – of law over anarchy; – of fidelity over treason; – of loyalty over usurpation.' The *Antijacobin* concluded that Britain owed her 'pre-eminence' to

> a wise and steady adherence, by her cabinet, to those grand, energetic and conservative principles of policy, which were infused into her councils and into the minds of her statesmen, by the great political saviour of Europe, Mr PITT. He incessantly laboured to promote that general co-operation against France which has at length been achieved, under more propitious circumstances, by statesmen trained in his school and wedded to his principles.[56]

The imminent collapse of the Napoleonic Empire robbed the anti-war protesters of their *raison d'être*. In January 1813 the *Monthly Repository* featured a new 'Peace Section' designed to report regularly on the campaign 'to put a stop to the crimes, miseries and horrors of War'. But its request for readers' 'communications on this subject' evidently elicited little response, as the feature was quickly discontinued.[57] Pitt's war policy appeared to have been vindicated after all. Yet the pressure put on the government over the Orders in Council, the East India Company's monopoly, and the eventual amendment of the Toleration and Blasphemy Acts was real enough. And the country would soon have to come to terms with the predictable consequences of so long a war.

Epilogue: Transatlantic Perspectives

In July 1793 Dr James Currie, close supporter of William Roscoe among Liverpool Unitarian radicals, wrote to his cousin and namesake in Virginia, predicting that America would become

> the refuge and asylum of those active and enterprising minds who cannot find, in Europe, scope for their exertions. Already large bodies of our manufacturers are preparing to emigrate; and those also, who, with a competence for their subsistence, pant after peace and quiet, and look for it in vain through Europe, are casting eyes on your peaceful shores. Of this number I confess I am one.

Currie never did return to America, where he had been employed in Virginia as a merchant's clerk in the 1770s. After attacking Pitt's policy in the early 1790s, he ended the decade helping to organize the defence of Liverpool: 'Pitt is, indeed, a great evil; but a French invasion is still greater.' Currie died two months before Trafalgar.[1]

In the 1770s, Price and Priestley had both been enthusiastic propagandists for the American cause, while other Unitarians preached support from their pulpits.[2] And as late as 1810, the *Monthly Repository* (which regularly carried correspondence from those who had sought asylum in America, and quoted from American newspapers and Unitarian magazines) reprinted George Dyer's poem on American Independence. The ninth and last stanza reads:

> Whilst we view yon lamp of fire;
> While we feel its genial ray;
> May Freedom British hearts inspire,
> May Honour rule with sovereign sway!

Hail Independence, reign supreme;
Ours be thy more than chartered plan;
And never will we Briton deem,
Who spurns the noblest rights of man.[3]

Priestley was only the most famous Unitarian to find self-imposed exile in what a correspondent in the *Gentleman's Magazine* unkindly called 'the Botany Bay of the whole world'.[4] Apart from Thomas Cooper, who took Priestley's sons across the Atlantic in 1793 to reconnoitre a possible site for settlement, the list includes: William Christie of Glasgow, Ralph Eddowes (Priestley's pupil at Warrington, and friend of Roscoe and Rathbone), Joseph Gales of Sheffield, Archibald Hamilton Rowan, William Russell of Birmingham, various members of the Vaughan family, and Joshua Toulmin's son, Harry. Toulmin senior, author of *The American War Lamented* (1776), seriously considered emigrating with his wife and entire Taunton congregation.[5] Even Coleridge's much ridiculed scheme for establishing a 'pantisocratic' community on the banks of the Susquehannah, belongs to his days as a young Unitarian in Bristol.[6] And writing to Thomas Belsham from Pennsylvania, two months after landing in America, Priestley shared the poet's optimism: 'I do not think there can be, in any part of the world, a more delightful situation than this and the neighbourhood, and the conveniences of the place are improving daily. The climate I like very much.'[7] He had yet to experience the Pennsylvania winter, and by December was explaining why he had decided not to accept the chair of chemistry at Pennsylvania University. He would have liked the employment and 'still more the opportunity it would have given me of opening an Unitarian meeting; but I must have spent four months in every year, and that in winter, at Philadelphia'.[8] Belsham commented: 'The offer was declined, much to the regret of many of Dr Priestley's friends at the time; but, as there is now reason to believe, not with any eventual detriment to the cause of Christian truth.'[9]

It was Belsham who had written the valedictory address that marked Priestley's departure from London:

> So little have you at any time interfered in national politics, it is but too obvious that the outrageous violence which you have experienced, and the atrocious calumnies which have been circulated with such unexampled industry... are entirely owing to that manly spirit with which you have avowed and defended what you firmly believed to be the pure and rational doctrines of the gospel, and to that truly Christian

> zeal with which you have entered your protest against the prevailing errors by which the religion of Jesus has been corrupted and debased.

Perhaps wisely, the society deleted a further sentence referring to 'anti-Christian hierarchies and establishments of religion', by which 'the meek and benevolent religion of the gospel' had been converted into 'an engine of sacerdotal tyranny and political oppression'.[10] Ten days later the Society of United Irishmen declared that 'the emigration of Dr Priestley will form a striking historical fact, by which alone future ages will learn to estimate truly the temper of the present times'. Recognizing that, despite his natural wish to be buried in England, Priestley was 'going to a happier world, the world of Washington and Franklin', the Irish address expressed the hope that 'the pure principles and genuine lustre of the British constitution, reflected from *their coasts* may penetrate into *our cells* and our *dungeons*'. The address concluded by beseeching 'a portion of your parting prayer to the author of Good for Archibald Hamilton Rowan, the pupil of Jebb', and for Muir, Palmer, Skirving, Margarot and Gerrald, who will be 'crossing, like you, the bleak ocean, but to a barbarous land'.[11]

Priestley's emigration was a well publicized event, not least in the pages of the *Gentleman's Magazine,* which noted that 'the peace and happiness of America depend so entirely on the life of Washington, that, in the uncertain state of sublunary things, it is staking a great deal when a man quits the old world for the new'. And it added the reminder that yellow fever had been raging at Philadelphia.[12] It was the profusion of congratulatory addresses, which greeted the Priestleys on their landing at New York, that provoked Cobbett into writing his bad-tempered pamphlet, *Observations on the emigration of Dr Priestley,* published in London as well as in Philadelphia. Cobbett claimed that Priestley had sought to impose himself on Americans as 'a sufferer in the cause of liberty', and accused him of being one of those 'system-mongers' for whom 'time, place, climate, nature itself must give way' and who wanted 'the same government [as the French model] in every quarter of the globe'.[13] Priestley would later complain that Cobbett constantly lampooned him in *Porcupine's Gazette* as 'the Firebrand Philosopher'.[14]

Priestley had hardly landed in America before he wrote to Lindsey: 'Here is a great field for rational Christianity, and many labourers will soon be wanted.'[15] And he wrote to Belsham of his hopes of establishing a college 'on the most liberal principles', with Belsham at its head: 'We could take our walks along the banks of the Susquehannah and ramble as I often do, in the woods, as we used to do about Hackney. Here we should have no apprehension of powder sugar being mistaken for gunpowder, or metaphorical gunpowder for real.'[16] A year later, Priestley is still lamenting his lack of opportunity 'to appear as a public preacher of Unitarian Christianity'. (The first sermon he had preached at the Presbyterian church in Philadelphia ensured that he was not asked again.) He confided to Belsham that 'if I have done any good, it has not been so much by preaching as by *writing*, and that my capacity for public speaking must necessarily decline'. And he added: 'I have no expectation of a chapel here till we build for the college, and then I shall make use of the common hall.'[17] In September 1795 he could report the arrival of the Russells at Philadelphia, where they took a house in which Priestley could stay on his visits to the city. In February 1796 he wrote to Lindsey: 'I am a guest with Mr Russell, where I am very agreeably accommodated, We found him engaged to drink tea with the President [Washington], where we accompanied him, and spent two hours as in any private family.'[18]

By 1796 Priestley was delivering addresses in the Universalist Church at Philadelphia. Published in both Philadelphia and London as *Discourses relating to the Evidences of Revealed Religion* (with a dedication to John Adams), Priestley did not pull his punches:

> It will at this stage be readily admitted that there are no peculiar powers conferred by *ordination*, or any peculiar sanctity in the character of *ministers*. Christian ministers become so by the choice of the *people*, to whom they officiate, and, like other *servants*, they cease to be ministers when they think proper to dismiss them.

He went on to explain that to worship both Jesus and the Holy Spirit, as if they possessed all the attributes of divinity, was in Unitarian eyes '*idolatry*, as much as worship of the *Virgin Mary*, or any other saints in the *Popish* calendar'.[19] Yet Henry Wansey reported that 'Dr Priestley preached a sermon, on the opening of the Universalist Church, at which almost every member of Congress attended'.[20]

The Russells chose to settle, not at Northumberland, but in Middletown, Connecticut. They hoped that Priestley might be persuaded to join them there. But he wrote to them from Northumberland, pointing out that, under Connecticut law, 'Unitarianism is a crime punishable, in the first instance, with incapacity for office, and, in the next, with exclusion from the courts of law; so that a Unitarian cannot recover a debt or have redress from any injury'. Priestley observed that there was no such law in Pennsylvania, 'or in France', adding that 'if ever we live together, it must be in a country of religious liberty at least'.[21] The Russells' son, Thomas, had commented on the isolation of Northumberland:

'The post only comes in once a week, and the intercourse by water is so uncertain that anything more bulky than a letter is sometimes longer coming from Philadelphia to Northumberland than it would have been coming from England to Philadelphia.'[22] That summer of 1796, Priestley would complain to Lindsey: 'I am very seriously concerned that I have had no letter from you or Mr Belsham these *three months*. The free communication of our sentiments, to persons who think or feel as we do, is the greatest charm of life.'[23]

Though studiously avoiding any involvement in American politics, Priestley still needed news from home. He followed the fortunes of Palmer and Muir, and told Lindsey he hoped that their Australian exile 'will serve for a furtherance of the gospel and the cause of liberty'. In a later letter to Lindsey, he protested: 'I feel as an Englishman and shall sincerely lament any evil that may befall my native country, though I condemn as much as ever the conduct of its rulers.' And writing to Lindsey again in March 1798, he begins:

> After many delays, I have, at length, received all the Morning Chronicles and Cambridge Intelligencers that you have sent me; I find I have them complete from the time of my arrival in this country, and I value them much, *especially the Cambridge paper*, and as it contains almost every thing that is of value in the other, I shall be very content to have that only.[24]

In the autumn of 1796 Priestley had written to Dyer: 'Here we have no poor; we never see a beggar, nor is there any family in want. We have no church establishment, and hardly any taxes ...'[25] And when, that same year, the second edition of his *Observations on the Increase of Infidelity* was published in Philadelphia, the preface proclaimed:

> Happily in this country, the *church* has no alliance with the *state*, every person being allowed to worship God in whatever manner he pleases, or not to worship him at all, if he be not so disposed, without being liable to any civil disobedience. In these circumstances, truth has the best chance of being heard ...[26]

The year 1796 had also seen Ralph Eddowes and William Christie establish a regular Unitarian meeting in Philadelphia, in a room at the University of Pennsylvania.[27] When in Boston, the Russells had visited the chapel where James Freeman presided over what Martha Russell called 'a very genteel congregation'.[28] Freeman's nominally Episcopal congregation had agreed to dissolve its connection with the diocese, and 'formally to engraft Unitarian views upon Episcopal usages.' Belsham would later describe the Boston liturgy as 'reformed nearly upon the plan of that which had been adopted in Essex Street, and perfectly Unitarian'.[29] Freeman did not, however, publish his views, or, it seems, even express Unitarian sentiments in the pulpit, whereas William Christie would later publish *Dissertations on the Unity of God*, as recorded in the *Monthly Repository* for 1811.[30] By then the Unitarian Society in Philadelphia was firmly established under Christie, with a programme of Winter Evening Lectures, and had started to build its own church. The new building was dedicated in 1813. But there had been a break in continuity: in 1800 Christie's original Unitarian meeting in Philadelphia had closed because of persistent outbreaks of yellow fever in the city.

Yellow fever was not the only hazard facing the immigrant Unitarians of Philadelphia in 1800. Thomas Russell, who had thought Priestley's congregation at the Universalist church there 'too wordly-minded to receive any lasting benefit from his teaching', was amused by the republican enthusiasm of a tutor, newly arrived from England. Meeting him at the home of Benjamin Vaughan, Russell decided that the new arrival 'had not yet stayed long enough in America to have his ardour cooled'.[31] Benjamin Vaughan, Samuel's eldest son and briefly MP for Calne, was a friend of Franklin and the 'Calm Observer' of *Letters on the Subject of the Concert of Princes* (1793). Arriving in America, by way of France and Switzerland, in 1796, he retired from active politics, and busied himself with editing the complete works of Franklin. He also corresponded with the first six American presidents.[32] While the eldest Vaughan settled down in America, becoming increasingly conservative in his political views, the Russells were getting restive. William Russell had left England with the firm intention of becoming an American citizen, and had so described himself during his enforced stay in France following capture en route to America. But in 1796–7 the unpopularity of the Jay Treaty made life in Connecticut uncomfortable for pro-French immigrants – as Martha Russell's journal makes clear.[33] So in 1800, Russell suggested that Priestley should accompany him to France (where the Russells owned property), and establish a Unitarian society in Normandy. Priestley preferred to wait until the coming of peace, while in 1801 Russell followed his family back to Europe and settled at Caen. He wrote to Martha that he was 'intending to turn a wilderness of a court into a *French* garden', and on 11 May 1807, he became a French citizen. Thomas followed his example in 1809, becoming a major in the *Garde Nationale*.[34]

Archibald Hamilton Rowan, whom the Russells had met in Paris in the 1790s, also decided against staying on in America. As early as 1796,

Rowan admitted to his wife: 'It is true I have not been, or ever can be, happy in America.'[35] And in November 1797, he comments on the anti-jacobin mood of Congress: 'Alien bills, naturalization bills and sedition bills are originating in each house of the senate [meaning Congress]; and the representatives seem to vie with each other who shall enact the most rigorous clauses.'[36] Like Priestley, who was initially threatened with deportation under the Alien Act, Rowan crossed swords with Cobbett.[37] Yet Rowan, the former United Irishman, still hoped that the United States would evolve a system of government 'better than any now known', and was 'fortified in this opinion from the great probability of a convulsion in this country, which has certainly theoretically the most free government existing'.[38] On 7 July 1800, Rowan embarked for Europe 'with a bag of bird-seed and a red bird, a dozen potatoes and a young opossum'.[39] After being intercepted and detained by a British cruiser, the ship eventually landed Rowan at Hamburg. After various false starts, he settled with his family at Altona, where there were 'many English, and some Irish residents, and a number of French emigrants of rank.'[40]

Priestley's continued residence in America had been made less irksome by Jefferson's election as President in 1801. In January 1803 Priestley wrote to Lindsey that he thought as well of this country 'as of any in the world; especially since the election of Mr Jefferson'. And a fortnight before his death, he wrote to another correspondent: 'Tell Mr Jefferson that I think myself happy to have lived under his excellent administration; and that I have a prospect of dying in it. It is, I am confident, the best on the face of the earth, and yet I hope to rise to something more excellent still.'[41] Priestley never lost his faith in the resurrection.

In 1804, the year of Priestley's death, the Unitarian Dr Henry Ware was elected Hollis Professor of Theology at Harvard; and in 1822 Jefferson would write:

> The pure and simple unity of the Creator of the universe, is now all but ascendant in the Eastern States; it is dawning in the West, and advancing towards the South; and I confidently expect that the present generation will see Unitarianism become the general religion of the United States.[42]

Thomas Cooper could be forgiven for thinking this over-optimistic. The Presbyterian establishment frustrated Jefferson's attempt to appoint Cooper to a professorial chair at the projected University of Virginia, and the same hostility dogged Cooper's 12 years as President of South Carolina College from 1821. Cooper accused the Presbyterians (who would later refuse to allow him to be buried in any of their churchyards) of wanting to revive religious persecution: 'I foresee another night of superstition, not far behind the Inquisition.'[43]

Although imprisoned under the 1798 Sedition Act for disparaging President Adams and the Senate, Cooper had become a judge of the Supreme Court of Pennsylvania during Jefferson's presidency. Harry Toulmin rose to be a judge of the Federal Court of Mississippi, and not only assisted in drafting the constitution of Alabama, but was commissioned to draft a legal code for the new state. It contained the provision:

> No person within this State shall upon any pretence be deprived of the inestimable privilege of worshipping God in the manner most agreeable to his own conscience; nor be compelled to pay taxes for any religious purposes. The civil rights and privileges of no citizen shall in any way be diminished or enlarged on account of his religious principles.[44]

Toulmin died in 1823. It was only five years earlier that homegrown American Unitarianism first found public expression. In 1818 William Ellery Channing, minister of the Federal Church, Boston, preached an ordination sermon – described as 'an outspoken and able defence of Unitarianism' – which provoked a pamphlet war. But in 1812 he had preached an even more outspoken sermon opposing war, and soon became a leading figure in the American peace movement. What is ironic is that the London *Antijacobin Review* used Channing to buttress its accusations against French sympathizers on both sides of the Atlantic. Noticing an earlier sermon Channing had preached in Boston, the *Antijacobin* observed approvingly: 'The main subject of this sermon, and an equally pious and patriotic object, is to rouse the people of America to a just sense of the danger to which they are exposed from the views and designs of the government of France.' The review goes on to quote Channing's words:

> As Christians, we ought to have a *strong and lively sensibility* to the miseries of the world in which we live, and especially to the miseries which threaten ourselves and those we love. As christians we have the deepest concern in the present state of the world; for *the interests of religion and morality*, as well as national independence and prosperity, are threatened by the great enemy of mankind.[45]

From the 1770s, through the 1780s and 1790s, and throughout the Napoleonic Wars, Unitarian political radicalism on both sides of the Atlantic was firmly rooted in Christian principles.

Notes

List of abbreviations used in the Notes

Sources are listed in the chapter notes that follow. Unless otherwise indicated, full bibliographical details are given at the first mention of the title. The place of publication is London, if not otherwise stated. References in subsequent chapters are abbreviated, but with a pointer to the initial reference *viz.* [Intro. 5] or [1.4]. J. T. Rutt, *Theological and Miscellaneous Writings of Joseph Priestley, LLD, FRS, etc.*, 25 vols (Sterling, Virginia, and Bristol, 1999: reprinted from London edition 1817–31) appears throughout as 'Rutt'. Other major sources are indicated by the following abbreviations:

AR	*Analytical Review*
ANReg	*Annual Register*
ANRev	*Annual Review*
AJR	*Anti-Jacobin Review and Magazine* [from 1808 *Antijacobin Review and Magazine*]. For convenience the latter form is used throughout the text
AJW	*Anti-Jacobin, or Weekly Examiner*
BC	*British Critic*
CR	*Critical Review*
DWL	Dr Williams's Library
ER	*Edinburgh Review*
EM	*European Magazine*
GM	*Gentleman's Magazine*
MMG	*Monthly Magazine*
MR	*Monthly Review*
MRep	*Monthly Repository*
MC	*Morning Chronicle*
MP	*Morning Post*
NANR	*New Annual Register*
PH	*Parliamentary Hiastory*
ST	*Star*
TRep	*Theological Repository*
W	*Watchman* in *Collected Works of Samuel Taylor Coleridge*, ed. Kathleen Coburn and others, 16 vols (Princeton University Press, 1969–2002)

Introduction: Unequal Toleration

1. *The Law and Working of the Constitution*, ed. W. C. Costin and J. S. Watson, 2 vols (Black, 1952) I. pp. 63–7. For Chandler and Herring *see* F. C. Mather, *High Church Prophet: Bishop Samuel Horsley (1738–1806) and the Caroline Tradition in the Later Georgian Church* (Oxford: Clarendon Press, 1992) pp. 8–9.

2. N. Sykes, *From Sheldon to Secker: Aspects of English Church History 1660–1768* (Cambridge: Cambridge University Press, 1959) pp. 166, 89.
3. *See* R. Thomas, 'The Salters' Hall Watershed' in C. G. Bolam and others, *English Presbyterians: from Elizabethan Puritanism to Modern Unitarianism* (Allen & Unwin, 1968).
4. Costin and Watson, I p. 67.
5. W. Blackstone, *A Reply to Dr Priestley's Remarks on the Fourth Volume of the Commentaries on the Laws of England* (Bathurst, 1769) pp. 11–12.
6. For a summary of the disabilities remaining after the 1689 Toleration Act *see* U. Henriques, *Religious Toleration in England 1787–1833* (Routledge, 1961) pp. 1–17.
7. *See* R. B. Barlow, *Citizenship and Conscience: A Study in the Theory and Practice of Religious Toleration in England during the Eighteenth Century* (Philadelphia: University of Pennsylvania Press, 1962) p. 208. The Test and Corporation Acts did not exclude Unitarians from Parliament, provided they took the appropriate oaths and subscribed to a declaration against transubstantiation.
8. *Act for the more effectual Suppression of Blasphemy and Profaneness* (1698). *See* Rutt, XV p. 391n.
9. *See* Chapter 10. For the shifting fortunes of eighteenth-century Arianism in the context of changing assumptions about the physical world *see* M. Wiles, *Archetypal Heresy: Arianism through the Centuries* (Oxford: Oxford University Press, 1996) pp. 93–164.
10. *The Substance of the Speech delivered by Henry Beaufoy, Esq., in the House of Commons upon the 28th of March 1787* (Cadell, 1787) pp. 46–7.
11. *Appeal to the Candour, Magnanimity and Justice of those in power to relieve from severe . . . Penalties a great Number of their Fellow Subjects* ([Johnson], 1787) p. 8.
12. For the Jeffries Committee *see* Chapter 10 and Barlow, pp. 224–31.
13. GM 57 (May 1787) p. 423. *See* J. Priestley, *History of the Corruptions of Christianity* (Birmingham, 1782). For Priestley's *Letter to Pitt* see Chapter 7.
14. *Debate on the Repeal of the Test and Corporation Act in the House of Commons, 28 March 1787* (Stockdale, 1787) p. 54.
15. W. Enfield, *Sermon on the Centennial Commemoration of the Revolution* (Johnson, 1788) pp. 16–18. For Enfield in Norwich *see* Chapter 12.
16. *Debate in the House of Commons . . . on the Eighth of May, 1789* (Johnson, 1789) p. 70.
17. *Debate of 8th May* pp. 90–4. Burke would echo Pitt's arguments, though in more dramatic language, when speaking on Unitarian relief. *See* Chapter 2.
18. *Two Speeches delivered in the house of Commons on Tuesday, the 2nd March 1790 by the Right Honourable Charles James Fox* (Debrett, 1790) pp. 34–5, 18–19.
19. *Speech of the Right Honourable William Pitt in the Commons on Tuesday, the Second March, 1790* (Stuart, 1790) pp. 12, 50.
20. *Debate in the House of Commons on Tuesday 2nd March, 1790, on the Motion of Mr Fox for a Repeal of the Corporation and Test Acts* (Stockdale, 1790) p. 45.
21. *Debate on Fox's Motion* 48–9. On Robinson *see* Chapter 2.
22. *Debate on Fox's Motion* pp. 54–5.
23. GM 60 (May 1790) pp. 423–6. But *see* Chapter 7 for Priestley's actual words.
24. Lindsey to Tayleur, 1 March 1791 in H. McLachlan, *Letters of Theophilus Lindsey* (Manchester University Press and Longman, both 1920) p. 67.

25. Lindsey to Tayleur, 7 April 1791 in McLachlan, *Letters*, p. 67.
26. J. Priestley, *Appeal to the Public, on the Subject of the Riots in Birmingham* (Johnson, 1792) in Rutt, XIX p. 390.
27. George III to H. Dundas, 16 July 1791 in J. Waddington, *Congregational History, 1700–1800* (1876) p. 654.
28. Lindsey to Tayleur, 15 February 1792 in McLachlan, *Letters*, p. 70.
29. PH XXIV 1393–5.
30. *Works of the Right Honourable Edmund Burke*, 12 vols (Rivington, 1803–13) X pp. 41, 48, 54–5.
31. *See Correspondence of Edmund Burke between the year 1744 and the period of his decease in 1797* ed. Charles, Earl Fitzwilliam and Gen. Sir Richard Bourke, 4 vols (1844) II pp. 255–61, 268–74. For the debate on the declaration, *see* Chapter 2.
32. For example, Henriques, p. 105
33. For a fuller extract *see* Henriques, p. 109.
34. Cited in Henriques, p. 111.
35. Henriques, pp. 113–14.
36. *See* Chapter 7 for Priestley's first use of the gunpowder image in his *Importance and Extent of Free Inquiry in Matters of Religion; a Sermon preached before the Congregations of the Old and New meetings of the Protestant Dissenters of Birmingham, 5 November 1785 to which are added Reflections on the Present State of Free Inquiry in this Country*... (London, Johnson; Birmingham, Swinney; both 1785). Rutt XV prints the sermon, but not the additional *Reflections* – which contains the gunpowder image.
37. *Debate of 28th March* [See note 9] pp. 54–5. For Priestley's clash with Burke over the French Revolution *see* Chapter 8.
38. *See* Barlow, p. 297.
39. *See* especially Chapters 14, 15 and epilogue.
40. J. Boucher, *A View of the causes and consequences of the American Revolution preached in North America between the years 1763 and 1775*... (Robinsons, 1797) in AJR II (Jan. 1799) pp. 86–7.
41. *See* Chapter 5 and Epilogue. *See also* E. Burke, *Reflections on the Revolution in France. A Critical Edition*, ed. J. C. D. Clark (Stanford, California: Stanford University Press, 2001) p. 74: 'The strangest omission in the *Reflections* was any comparison of the French Revolution with the American.'

1 Denying the Trinity

1. J. Priestley, *Prefatory Discourse relating to the present state of those who are called Rational Dissenters* (1782). He writes: 'I use the term *rational* and *Unitarian* Dissenter as synonymous.' (Rutt, XV p. 46.)
2. J. Priestley, *History and Present State of Electricity, with original experiments* (1767) and *History and Present state of discoveries relating to Vision, Light and Colour*, 2 vols (1782). For Priestley's millennialist theories *see* Chapter 3.
3. J. Priestley, *An Appeal to the Serious and Candid Professors of Christianity* (1770); 1791 edn in Rutt, II p. 384.
4. Priestley to John Whitehead, June 1778 in Rutt, IV pp. 144–50.
5. W. Chillingworth, *The Religion of Protestants a safe Way of Salvation* (1638).

6. *Autobiography of Joseph Priestley* ed. with an introduction by Jack Lindsay (Bath: Adams and Dart, 1970) p. 19.
7. *Memoirs of Dr Joseph Priestley, to the year 1795, written by himself, with a continuation by his son, J. Priestley; and observations on his writings by T. Cooper*... (Johnson, 1806) in Rutt, I. 1. p. 68.
8. Rutt, I.1. p. 69. *See* also Priestley's letter to Rev. C. Rotheram in Rutt, I.1. p. 315. Priestley expounded his materialistic theology in *Disquisitions relating to Matter and Spirit*... (Johnson, 1777).
9. *Corruptions* [Intro. 13] in Rutt, III p. 53.
10. *See* Wiles [Intro. 9] pp. 144–57.
11. Rutt, III pp. 81–5. *See* N. Lardner, *Letter writ in the year 1730 ... concerning the Question whether the Logos supplied a human Soul in the Person of Jesus Christ* (1759).
12. Rutt, III p. 90.
13. J. Priestley, *History of the early opinions concerning Jesus Christ compiled from original writers; proving that the Church was at first Unitarian* (Birmingham, 1786) in Rutt, VI p. 7. *See also* p. 45 where Priestley claims that Arians are no more entitled to be called Unitarians than Trinitarians are. In his revived TRep for 1788, he brackets Arians with Athanasians, calling them 'as revolting to common sense, as they are to Scripture, and being without a shadow of support from the history of the primitive times'. *See* Rutt, VII p. 485.
14. Rutt, VI pp. 15–17.
15. Rutt, VI pp. 20–4.
16. Rutt, II pp. 394, 397.
17. Rutt, II p. 402.
18. Rutt, VII pp. 241–2.
19. J. Priestley, *General History of the Christian Church to the Fall of the Western Empire*, 2 vols (Birmingham, 1790; 2nd edn Northumberland, 1803) in Rutt, VIII pp. 22–4.
20. J. Priestley, *Letters to the Author of the letters on Materialism to Dr Kendrick, Mr John Whitehead and Dr Horsley* (1777) in Rutt, IV p. 131.
21. J. Priestley, *Letters to a Philosophical Unbeliever. Part I containing an examination of the principal objections to the doctrines of natural religion and especially those contained in the writings of Mr Hume* (Bath, 1780; 2nd edn Birmingham, 1787) in Rutt, IV p. 366.
22. J. Priestley, *Institutes of Natural and Revealed Religion*... (Birmingham, 1782) in Rutt, II pp. 343, 319.
23. For D. Hartley, *Observations on Man, his Frame, his Duty and his Expectations*, 2 vols [1749] *see* R. E. Schofield, *The Enlightenment of Joseph Priestley. A Study of His Life from 1733 to 1773* (Pennsylvania State University Press, 1997) pp. 58–60.
24. *Corruptions* in Rutt, III p. 25.
25. Rutt, III p. 29.
26. Rutt, III pp. 59–61.
27. Rutt, III p. 69.
28. J. Priestley, *Letters to Dr Horsley in answer to his animadversions on the History of the Corruptions of Christianity*... (Birmingham, 1783).
29. *Letters from the Archdeacon of St Alban's in Reply to Dr Priestley* (1784) pp. 1–2.
30. S. Horsley, *Tracts in Controversy with Dr Priestley* (Gloucester, 1789).

31. *See* Mather [Intro. 1] pp. 55–61; *also* T. Belsham, *Claims of Dr Priestley in the controversy with Bishop Horsley re-stated and vindicated, in reply to the Animadversions of the Reverend Heneage Horsley* (Johnson, 1814).
32. *Institutes* in Rutt, II pp. xxii, 66.
33. *Letters to Philosophical Unbeliever* in Rutt, IV p. 369.
34. *Institutes* in Rutt, II p. 87.
35. Rutt, II pp. 70–1.
36. Rutt, II pp. 209–10.
37. Rutt, II p. 336.
38. J. Priestley, *Notes on the Old Testament* and *Notes on the New Testament* (Northumberland, 1804) in Rutt, XII, XIII and XIV.
39. Rutt, XIII p. 379.
40. *Corruptions* [Intro. 13] in Rutt, III p. 4.
41. T. Belsham, *Memoirs of Theophilus Lindsey* (Johnson, 1812) in Rutt, III p. 3n. For centenary edition of *Memoirs see* [3.17].
42. *Corruptions* in Rutt, III p. 495.

2 Opposing Subscription

1. Costin and Watson [Intro.1] I pp. 9–10.
2. Costin and Watson, I p. 69.
3. *See* P. Fraser, 'Public Petitioning and Parliament before 1832', *History* 46 (October 1961) p. 201, and E. S. Morgan, *Inventing the People: The Rise of Popular Sovereignty in England and America* (London and New York: Norton, 1988) pp. 225–9.
4. J. E. Bradley, *Religion, Revolution and English Radicalism* (Cambridge: Cambridge University Press, 1990) p. 416.
5. For the 1775 petitions *see* Bradley, especially pp. 315–409. Pitt, defending the 'Gagging Bills' in 1795, would explicitly deny the distinction between private and public petitioning.
6. F. Blackburne, *The Confessional* (London: Bladon, 1766; 3rd edn 1770), p. 50. He was probably the editor of *Collection of Letters and Essays in favour of Public Liberty*, 3 vols (Wilkins, 1774). *See* Barlow [Intro. 7] pp. 137–8.
7. *See* Mather [Intro. 1] pp. 9–10; *also* M. Fitzpatrick, 'Latitudinarianism at the Parting of the Ways: a Suggestion' in J. Walsh, C. Haydon and S. Taylor (eds), *The Church of England c. 1689–c. 1833: From Toleration to Tractarianism* (Cambridge: Cambridge University Press, 1993) pp. 209–27.
8. T. Edwards, *The Indispensable Duty of Contending for the Faith which was once delivered unto the Saints* (Cambridge, 1766) p. 10.
9. Subscription at Cambridge was required before proceeding to MA, though before taking the BA degree a declaration was required that one was a *bona fide* member of the Church of England.
10. N. Sykes, *Church and State in England in the eighteenth century* (Cambridge: Cambridge University Press, 1934) p. 381.
11. *See* J. Gascoigne, *Cambridge in the Age of the Enlightenment: Science, Religion and Politics from the Restoration to the French Revolution* (Cambridge: Cambridge University Press, 1989) pp. 190–5. Grafton wrote and published anonymously *Hints submitted to the serious attention of the Clergy, Nobility*

and Gentry by a Layman (1789) and *Serious Reflections of a Rational Dissenter from 1788 to 1797* (1797).

12. J. Jebb, *Letters on the Subject of Subscription to the Liturgy and Articles of the Church of England...* (1770), republished by J. Disney in *Works of John Jebb with Memoirs of the Life of the Author*, 3 vols (Cadell, 1787) I pp. 171–5.
13. F. Blackburne, *Proposals for an Application to Parliament for Relief in the Matter of Subscription to the Liturgy and Thirty-nine Articles of the Church of England, humbly submitted to the Consideration of the Learned and Conscientious Clergy* (1770). For the petition *see Autobiography and Political Correspondence of Augustus Henry, third Duke of Grafton* ed. Sir William Anson (1898), p. 267.
14. For the USPKS *see* Chapter 10; for Disney at Essex Street *see* Chapters 4, 6 and 10.
15. McLachan, *Letters of Lindsey* [Intro. 24] p. 44. Gascoigne (p. 195) thinks McLachlan misread Jesus for Queens'; Sykes (p. 381) says Peterhouse.
16. PH XVII p. 256.
17. PH XVII p. 266. Priestley would later censure the English universities for requiring of their students 'absolute subscription to complex articles of faith, which it is impossible they can have studied, and which it is not generally supposed that they have ever read'. *See* his *Proper Objects of education in the present State of the World*, 2nd edn (Johnson, 1791) in Rutt, XV p. 430.
18. PH XVII pp. 272–4.
19. PH XVII pp. 288–9.
20. The University Tests were abolished in 1871.
21. *Correspondence of King George the third with Lord North from 1768 to 1783*, ed. W. B. Downe (1867), pp. 101–2. For George III's attitude to the campaign against subscription *see* A. Valentine, *Lord North*, 2 vols (University of Oklahoma Press, 1967), I p. 244.
22. PH XVII pp. 435–7.
23. Priestley to Lindsey, 2 March 1772 in Rutt, I. 1. pp. 160–2.
24. Priestley to Lindsey, 3 April 1772 in Rutt, I. 1. p. 164.
25. PH XVII pp. 768–9.
26. Lindsey to Turner, 23 October 1772 in McLachlan, *Letters* p. 48.
27. R. Garnham, *Examination of a Sermon preached in the Cathedral-Church of St Paul's before the Right Honourable the Lord Mayor, the Judges, Aldermen and Sheriffs...* (Johnson, 1789). For the text of Garnham's Cambridge sermon *see* Rutt, XV pp. 578–81.
28. W. Frend, *Address to the Inhabitants of Cambridge...* (St Ives, 1788). The second edition entitled, *Address to the Members of the Church of England, and to Protestant Trinitarians in general, exhorting them to turn from the worship of Three Persons, to the Worship of the One True God* (Johnson, 1788) was reviewed in CR 67 (Feb. 1789) p. 153. For *Peace and Union see* Chapter 9; for Frend's trial, and the atmosphere in Cambridge at the time, *see* N. Roe, *Wordsworth and Coleridge: the Radical Years* (Oxford: Clarendon Press, 1988).
29. Gascoigne, p. 227.
30. H. Gunning, *Reminiscences of the University, Town and County of Cambridge, from the Year 1780*, 2 vols (Bell, 1854) I p. 303.
31. M. Milner, *Life of Isaac Milner* (1842) p. 162.
32. In 1789 Dyer published *Enquiry into the Nature of Subscription to the Thirty-nine Articles* (2nd edn, Johnson, 1792).

33. T. Whelan, 'Coleridge and Robert Hall of Cambridge', *Wordsworth Circle* (Winter 2000) p. 38. On Robinson *see* G. Hughes, *With Freedom Fired: the Story of Robert Robinson, Cambridge Non-Conformist* (Carey Kingsgate, 1955).
34. R. Robinson, *Political Catechism intended to convey in a familiar manner, just ideas of good civil government, and the British Constitution*, 3rd edn (Cambridge: Leppard 1784), pp. 63, 68, 98.
35. Rutt, XV p. 417n.
36. J. Disney, *Letter to the Most Reverend Lord Archbishop of Canterbury on the Present Opposition to any Further reformation* (1774) p. 15.
37. J. Toulmin, *Two Letters on the Late Application to Parliament by the Protestant Dissenting Ministers* (1774) pp. 8–10, Toulmin would found the Western Unitarian Society in 1792. *See also* Chapter 12.
38. *Memoirs of Priestley* in Rutt, I.1. p. 153. *See* J. Toulmin, *Memoirs of the Life, Character, Sentiments and Writings of Faustus Socinus* (Johnson, 1777).

3 Predicting the Millennium

1. Priestley to Lindsey, 23 August 1771 in Rutt, I. 1. p. 146. On the continuity of British millennialist thought, and the importance of Hartley's contribution, *see* J. Fruchtman, 'The Apocalyptic Politics of Richard Price and Joseph Priestley' in *Transactions of the American Philosophical Society*, 73 Part 4 (1983) pp. 11–20.
2. J. Priestley, *The Present State of Europe compared with Antient Prophecies; a Sermon preached at the Gravel-pit Meeting in Hackney, 28 February 1794, being the Day appointed for a General Fast; with a Preface containing the Reasons for the Author's leaving England* (Johnson, 1794) in Rutt, XV.
3. Rutt, XV pp. 534–5.
4. Rutt, XV pp. 536–7.
5. Rutt, XV p. 538.
6. Rutt, XV pp. 539–40.
7. J. Priestley, *Sermon preached at the Gravel-Pit Meeting, in Hackney, 19 April 1793. Being the Day appointed for a general Fast* (Johnson, 1793) in Rutt, XV p. 504.
8. *Present State of Europe* in Rutt, XV p. 551.
9. 1793 Fast Sermon in Rutt, XV p. 513.
10. J. Barrell, *Imagining the King's Death: Figurative treason, fantasies of regicide, 1793–1796* (Oxford: Oxford University Press, 2000) pp. 504–26. Brothers was not released until after Pitt's death, when Erskine became Lord Chancellor.
11. *The French Revolution foreseen in 1639. Extracts from an Exposition of the Revolution by an eminent Divine of both Universities, in the beginning of the last Century* (Johnson, 1791) in AR XI (Sep. 1791) p. 85. *See also* C. Garrett, *Respectable Folly: Millenarians and the French Revolution in France and England* (Baltimore and London: Johns Hopkins University Press, 1975); and J. F. C. Harrison, *The Second Coming: Popular Millenarianism* (New Brunswick: Rutgers University Press, 1979), who reserves 'millennialism' for non-popular forms.
12. For details of these publications, and of the reviewers' reactions to them, *see* S. Andrews, *The British Periodical Press and the French Revolution, 1789–99* (Palgrave, 2000) Chapter 14; for the millenarianism of other minor sects in Priestley's day, *see* E. P. Thompson, *Witness against the Beast: William Blake and the Moral Law* (Cambridge: Cambridge University Press, 1993).

13. Thompson, p. 60.
14. S. T. Coleridge, *Poems* ed. J. Beer (London and Vermont: Dent Everyman, 1993) pp. 88–9. For Priestley's millennialism as a 'religion of the oppressed' *see* W. H. Oliver, *Prophets and Millenialists: The Uses of Biblical Prophecy in England from the 1790s to the 1840s* (Auckland University Press and Oxford University Press, 1978), Chapter 3.
15. Priestley to Lindsey, 12 November 1794 in Rutt, I. 2. p. 280.
16. Priestley to Lindsey, 20 December 1794 in Rutt, I. 2. p. 284. J. Bicheno, *Signs of the Times; or the Overthrow of the Papal Tyranny in France, the Prelude to the Destruction to Popery and Despotism, but of Peace to Mankind* (Parsons, 1793) in AR XVI (July 1793) p. 342. In the 1780s, Robert Garnham published articles entitled 'Observations on Isaiah' and 'An Enquiry into the Time at which the Kingdom of Heaven will commence' in TRep V (1785) and VI (1787). In 1794 he published *Outline of a Commentary on Revelations xi 1–14*, to which Priestley refers; *see also* Chapter 9.
17. T. Belsham, *Memoirs of the late Theophilus Lindsey MA including a brief analysis of his works; together with Anecdotes and Letters of Eminent Persons, his Friends and Correspondents; also a general view of the progress of Unitarian Doctrine in England and America*, centenary edn (Williams & Norgate, 1873) p. 248n.
18. Priestley to Lindsey, 12 February 1796 in Rutt, I.2. p. 331
19. Priestley to Lindsey, 13 January 1797 in Rutt, I.2. p. 370. The Unitarian minister, Joseph Lomas Towers, was son of Dr Joseph Towers, one of the anti-Burke pamphleteers. *See* Chapter 8.
20. *Authorised Daily Prayer Book of the United Hebrew Congregations of the British Commonwealth of Nations* (Eyre & Spottiswoode, 1962) p. 338.
21. Priestley to Lindsey, 16 June 1798 in Rutt, I.2. pp. 403–4.
22. Priestley to Belsham, 25 October 1798 in Rutt, I.2. p. 409.
23. Priestley to Belsham, 30 March 1800 in Rutt, I.2. p. 430.
24. *Notes on Old Testament* [1.38] in Rutt, XII pp. 305–7.
25. Rutt, XII p. 463.
26. Rutt, XII pp. 484–6.
27. GM 68 (May 1798) p. 405.
28. *Appeal to the Public* [Intro. 26] and J. Barlow, *Advice to the Privileged Orders in the European States of Europe, resulting from the Necessity and Propriety of a General revolution in the Principles of Government* (Johnson, 1792) in AR XII (Apr. 1792) pp. 434–5, 452–61.
29. MR VII (Mar. 1792) p. 314.
30. J. Barlow, *Conspiracy of Kings; a Poem: addressed to the Inhabitants of Europe from another Quarter of the World* (Johnson, 1792) pp. 7, 18 in AR XIII (May 1792) 62.
31. *See* R. H. Bloch, *Visionary Republic: Millennial Themes in American thought, 1756–1800* (Cambridge: Cambridge University Press, 1985) pp. 85–93.
32. MR VIII (July 1792) p. 336. For a discussion of Priestley's millennialism, and how it differed from secular versions, *see* M. Fitzpatrick, 'Joseph Priestley and the Millennium', in R. G. W. Anderson and C. Lawrence (eds), *Science, Medicine and Dissent: Joseph Priestley (1733–1804)* (Wellcome Trust/Science Museum, 1987) pp. 29–37. *See also* Fruchtman pp. 46–62 on the 'republican millennialism' of Price and Priestley.

4 Essex Street: Lindsey, Disney, Belsham

1. T. Lindsey, *Farewell Address to the Parishioners of Catterick* (Johnson, 1774) pp. 7–8.
2. *Farewell Address*, pp. 9–10. Liverpool's Octagon Chapel had experimented with a reformed liturgy in the 1760s. William Turner Jr records that the congregation comprised seceders from other Dissenting chapels and 'malcontents within the pale of the Establishment'. *See* MRep VIII (1813) p. 626.
3. *Farewell Address*, pp. 10–11.
4. *Apology of Theophilus Lindsey, MA, on resigning the Vicarage of Catterick, Yorkshire*, 2nd edn (Johnson, 1774) pp. 211–12.
5. N. Lardner, *Credibility of the Gospel History*, 14 vols (1727–55); *see* extract in *Apology*, pp. 169–71.
6. *Apology*, pp. 185–92.
7. J. Priestley, *Letter to a Layman on the Subject of the Rev. Mr Lindsey's Proposal for a Reformed English Church upon the Plan of the late Dr Samuel Clarke* (1774) pp. 36–7, 39.
8. T. Belsham, *Memoirs of Lindsey* (1873) [3.17] p. 70n.
9. Cited in G. M. Ditchfield, 'Some Aspects of Unitarianism and Radicalism, 1760–1810' (University of Cambridge PhD thesis 1968) pp. 96–7. Ditchfield traces Essex Street's links with Dissenting MPs, devoting 60 pp. to John Lee. *See also* J. Seed, 'Rational Dissent and Political Opposition, 1770–90' in K. Haakonssen, *Enlightenment and religion: Rational Dissent in eighteenth-century Britain* (Cambridge: Cambridge University Press, 1996) pp. 142–68.
10. T. Lindsey, *Sermons with Appropriate Prayers Annexed*, 2 vols (Johnson, 1810) I p. 175; II pp. 194, 395, 527, 535.
11. *See* A. M. C. Waterman, 'The nexus between theology and political doctrine in Church and Dissent' in Haakonssen pp. 194–216.
12. [T. Lindsey] *The Polish Partition Illustrated in Seven Dramatic Dialogues or Conversation Pieces between Remarkable Personages, published from the Mouths and Actions of the Interlocutors* . . . (Elmsly, 1773). A French edition appeared in 1775.
13. Ditchfield, pp. 19, 22.
14. For evidence of the USPCK's political outreach from Essex Street *see* Chapter 10.
15. *See* J. Graham, *The Nation, the Law and the King, Reform Politics in England, 1789–1799*, 2 vols (Lanham, New York, Oxford: University Press of America, 2000) I p. 138n.
16. J. Disney, *Reasons for resigning the Rectory of Panton and Vicarage of Swinderby in Lincolnshire; and quitting the Church of England* (Johnson, 1782) pp. 5–6.
17. *Reasons*, p. 7.
18. *Reasons*, pp. 15–16.
19. *Reasons*, p. 19.
20. [J. Disney] *Friendly Dialogue between a common Unitarian Christian and an Athanasian . . . or, an Attempt to Restore Scripture forms of Worship* . . . 2nd edn (1787) pp. 32–5.
21. *Works of Jebb* [2.12] pp. iii, vi.
22. J. Disney, *Arranged Catalogue of the Several Publications which have appeared relating to the Enlargement of the toleration of Protestant-Dissenting-Ministers, and the Repeal of the Corporation and Test Acts* . . . (Johnson, 1790) pp. 21, 23n.

23. J. Disney, *Address to the Bishops upon the Subject of a late Letter from one of their Lordships to certain Clergy in his Diocese with the letter prefixed* (Kearsley, 1790) p. 1. *See also* Chapter 7.
24. *Address to the Bishops*, pp. 3–4.
25. *Address to the Bishops*, pp. 5, 7–8.
26. *Address to the Bishops*, p. 14.
27. J. Disney, *Sermons in Two Volumes* (Johnson, 1793) p. iii. Two more volumes were published, but not until 1816. Later sermons cited in this and successive chapters are among the half-dozen that were published separately in the year they were delivered.
28. J. Disney, *Reciprocal Duty of a Christian Minister and a Christian Congregation. Preached in the Chapel in Essex St, London; on Sunday 21 July 1793, on undertaking the pastoral Office of that Place* (Johnson, 1793) p. 8.
29. For Belsham's conversion at Daventry *see Memoirs of the late Reverend Thomas Belsham including a brief Notice of his published Works and copious Extracts from his Diary, together with letters to and from his Friends and Correspondents* ed. J. Williams (published by editor, 1835) pp. 14, 24.
30. Belsham to Palmer, 24 December 1783 in *Memoirs* p. 247.
31. *Memoirs*, pp. 235, 240.
32. On Priestley's Daventry *see* Schofield [1.23]. For the respective importance of Warrington and Daventry *see* D. L. Wykes, 'The contribution of the Dissenting Academy to the Emergence of Rational Dissent' in Haakonssen pp. 133–7, for example his judgement that 'Daventry may not have matched Warrington in the teaching of languages and the sciences, but in theology, metaphysics and ethics it was superior'.
33. Belsham to Rev. Thomas Reader, 2 October 1787 in *Memoirs*, p. 328.
34. *Memoirs*, 351. *See* also *Character and Writings of the Rev. Thomas Belsham extracted from the Monthly Repository*... (Unitarian Association, 1830) pp. 9–11.
35. *Memoirs*, pp. 360–1.
36. *Memoirs*, p. 391.
37. Among three Daventry students who followed Belsham to Hackney was John Kentish, future afternoon preacher at the Gravel Pit, and (from 1803) minister of the New Meeting, Birmingham.
38. *Memoirs*, pp. 300–2.
39. Belsham to Samuel Shore, 22 April 1805 in *Memoirs*, p. 545.
40. *Character and Writings*, pp. 35, 39, 78–9. For Madge at Norwich *see* Chapter 12.
41. T. Belsham, *Discourse occasioned by the Death of the Right Hon. Charles James Fox*... *12 October 1806* (Johnson, 1806) pp. 4–7.
42. *Death of Fox*, pp. 13–17.
43. *Character and Writings*, p. 41.
44. T. Belsham, *Discourse delivered at Hackney, 8 April 1804 on Occasion of the Death of the Rev. Joseph Priestley, LLD, FRS, &c*... (Johnson, 1804) pp. 6–7.
45. T. Belsham, *Rights of Conscience asserted and defined in Reference to the modern Interpretation of the Toleration Act in a Discourse at Essex Street Chapel, 5 February 1812. Being the Day appointed for a General Fast* (Johnson, 1812) pp. 3–4; *see also* Chapter 15.
46. T. Belsham, *Sufferings of Unitarians in former Times, urged as a Ground for Thankfulness for their restored Liberties, a Discourse preached at Essex Street Chapel,*

25 July 1813. Being the first Sunday after 'the Act to relieve Persons who impugn the Doctrine of the Trinity' had received the royal Assent (Johnson, 1813) p. 4.

5 Old Jewry and Gravel Pit

1. For Godwin at Hoxton *see* P. H. Marshall, *William Godwin* (Newhaven: Yale University Press, 1984) pp. 32–45. *See* A. Kippis, *Vindication of the Protestant Dissenting Ministers with regard to their late application to parliament* (Robinsons, 1772), p. 63: 'The magistrate hath no right to interpose in religious matters, so as to lay any restraint upon, or prescribe any test to those who behave as peaceful subjects.'
2. *Minutes of the General Body of Protestant Dissenting Ministers*, II p. 214 in Barlow [Intro. 7] p. 209. For Kippis's role in the General Body *see* Chapter 10.
3. A. Kippis, *Sermon preached at the Old Jewry on the Fourth of November, 1788, before the Society for Commemorating the Glorious Revolution...* (Robinsons, 1788) pp. 2–3, 4.
4. *Sermon*, pp. 13–14.
5. *Sermon*, pp. 26–8.
6. *Sermon*, pp. 28–9.
7. *Sermon*, pp. 46–7.
8. A. Kippis, *Address at the Interment of the late Rev. Dr Richard Price on the Twenty-sixth of April 1791* (Cadell, Johnson, 1791) pp. 14–15.
9. *Address*, p. 17.
10. R. Price, *Discourse on the Love of our Country delivered on 4 November 1789 at the Meeting-house in the Old Jewry to the Society for Commemorating the Revolution in Great Britain with an Appendix*, 5th edn (1790) p. 49.
11. *Love of our Country*, Appendix pp. 11–13.
12. *Love of our Country*, pp. 11, 5, 49, 51.
13. MR I (Jan. 1790) pp. 114–17.
14. J. Priestley, *Letters to the Rev. Dr Price* Part I (Birmingham, 1787) in Rutt, XV p. 416. For Priestley's comparison of Arianism and Socinianism *see* Chapter 1.
15. Priestley to Lindsey, 29 November 1789 in Rutt, I.2. p. 47.
16. Priestley to Lindsey, 10 December 1789 in Rutt, I.2. p. 49.
17. R. Price, *Observations on the Nature of Civil Liberty, the Principles of Government and the Justice and Policy of the War with America*, 8th edn (Cadell, 1778) in *Richard Price and the Ethical Foundations of the American Revolution* ed. B. Peach (Durham, N. Carolina: Duke University Press, 1979) pp. 69, 74.
18. R. Price *Sermon delivered to a Congregation of Protestant Dissenters at Hackney on 10 February 1779* in Peach, p. 278.
19. Peach, pp. 115, 116, 118.
20. *Journal of John Wesley* ed. N. Curnock, 8 vols (Epworth Press, 1938) VI p. 100.
21. R. Price *Additional Observations on the Nature and Value of Civil Liberty and the War with America* (Cadell, 1777) in Peach, p. 139n.
22. R. Price, *General Introduction and Supplement to the Two Tracts on Civil Liberty, the War with America and the Finances of the Kingdom*, 2nd edn (Cadell, 1778) in Peach, pp. 54–5.
23. R. Price, *Observations on the Importance of the American Revolution, and the Means of Making it a benefit to the World...* 2nd edn (Cadell, 1785) in Peach pp. 182–3.

24. *See* Peach, pp. 14 and 312n; and R. Price, *Observations on Reversionary Payments; on schemes for providing annuities for widows ... and on the National Debt* (Cadell, 1771).
25. Price to Franklin, 26 September 1787 in Peach, p. 341.
26. For Price's linking of the three revolutions *see* S. Andrews, *Rediscovery of America: transatlantic crosscurrents in an age of revolution* (Macmillan, 1998) Chapter 6.
27. R. Price, *Evidence for a future period of Improvement in the State of Mankind, with the Means and Duty of Promoting it represented in a Discourse delivered on Wednesday the 25th April 1787, at the Meeting-house in the Old Jewry London to the Supporters of a new academical Institution among Protestant Dissenters* (Cadell, 1787) p. 4.
28. *Evidence*, p. 12.
29. *Evidence*, p. 18.
30. *Evidence*, pp. 21–2n.
31. *Evidence*, pp. 30–1.
32. *Evidence*, p. 31n.
33. *Evidence*, p. 32.
34. *Evidence*, pp. 39–40.
35. Peach, p. 275.
36. Peach, p. 284.
37. *Address*, pp. 17–18.
38. *Address*, p. 18. For Kippis and NANR *see* Chapter 14.
39. J. Priestley, *Discourse on the Occasion of the Death of Dr Price; delivered at Hackney, on Sunday, 1 May 1791* (1791) in Rutt, XV p. 444.
40. Rutt, XV pp. 444, 447.
41. GM 61 (April 1791) p. 389.
42. *Autobiography* [1.6] p. 130.
43. J. Priestley, *Objects of Education* [2.17] pp. 422–4. On Hartley *see* Chapter 1.
44. *Autobiography*, p. 130.
45. J. Priestley, *Letters to the Philosophers and Politicians of France on the Subject of Religion* (1793) in Rutt, XXI pp. 87–8.
46. *Memoirs of Lindsey* (1812) [1.41] pp. 282–3. Belsham adds that tutorial authority was undermined by the trustees' insistence that 'a superintending committee should always be at hand to watch over the conduct of the students'.
47. AJR V (Jan. 1800) pp. 99–100.
48. T. Belsham, *Reflections and Exhortations adapted to the State of the Times: A Sermon preached to the Congregation at Hackney, 1 June 1802, being the Day appointed by Proclamation for a General Thanksgiving to Almighty God for putting an End to the late bloody, extended and extensive War* (Johnson, 1802) pp. 3–4. Belsham was presumably thinking of the departure of Pitt, Grenville and Castlereagh.

6 Fasts and Thanksgivings

1. *Journal of John Wesley* [5.20] for example IV p. 112, VI p. 49. For Priestley's Fast Sermons *see* Chapter 3; for Price on providential effects of the American war *see* Chapter 5.
2. T. Belsham, *Rights of Conscience asserted* [4.45] pp. 21, 35–7.

3. T. Belsham, *Prospect of Perpetual and Universal Peace. A Thanksgiving Sermon for the Conclusion of Peace with France preached at Essex Street Chapel 3 July 1814* (Johnson, 1814) p. 4.
4. *Thanksgiving Sermon*, p. 6.
5. *Thanksgiving Sermon*, pp. 7–8.
6. *Thanksgiving Sermon*, p. 13.
7. *Thanksgiving Sermon*, p. 17.
8. R. Price, *Discourse addressed to a Congregation of Protestant Dissenters at Hackney on 21 February 1781. Being the Day appointed for a Public Fast* (Cadell, 1781) pp. 2–3.
9. *Discourse*, p. 4.
10. *Discourse*, p. 11.
11. *Discourse*, p. 19.
12. *Discourse*, pp. 19–20.
13. *Discourse*, pp. 24–5.
14. *Discourse*, p. 26.
15. *Discourse*, p. 32.
16. J. Disney, *Trust and Confidence and the Universal and Sovereign Government, and Constant providence of God. Preached on Wednesday 19 October 1803, being the day appointed for a general fast* (1803) pp. 73–4.
17. *Trust and Confidence*, pp. 75–6.
18. *Trust and Confidence*, p. 83.
19. *Trust and Confidence*, p. 85.
20. *Trust and Confidence*, pp. 85–6.
21. *Trust and Confidence*, pp. 87–8.
22. *Trust and Confidence*, pp. 88–9.
23. J. Disney, *Progressive Improvement of Civil Liberty. A Sermon preached in the Unitarian Chapel in Essex-Street; on Sunday November IV. MDCCXCIII being the Anniversary of the Revolution of 1688* (Johnson, 1793) p. 13.
24. *Progressive Improvement*, p. 14.
25. *Progressive Improvement*, p. 15.
26. *Progressive Improvement*, p. 17.
27. *Progressive Improvement*, pp. 19–20.
28. T. Belsham, *Year of Jubilee considered in a Discourse delivered at the Unitarian Chapel in Essex Street on Sunday, 22 October 1809* (Johnson, 1809) pp. 35–6.
29. *Year of Jubilee*, p. 28.
30. *Year of Jubilee*, p. 32–3.
31. T. Belsham, *Reflections and Exhortations adapted to the State of the Times* [5.48] pp. 14–15.
32. *Reflections and Exhortations*, p. 17.
33. *Reflections and Exhortations*, p. 32.

7 Censuring Pitt

1. W. Belsham, *Remarks on a late Publication styled the History of the politics of Great Britain and France* (Robinsons, 1800). For a longer version of the extract *see* J. E. Cookson, *Friends of Peace* (Cambridge and New York: Cambridge University Press, 1982) pp. 16–17; for a hostile review of Belsham's *Remarks see* AJR IX (May 1801) pp. 39–47.

2. J. Priestley, *Letter to the Right Hon. William Pitt . . . on the Subjects of Toleration and Church Establishments, occasioned by his Speech against the Repeal of the Test and Corporation Acts on Wednesday, the 28th of March 1787* (Johnson, 1787) in Rutt, XIX p. 113. Gascoigne [2.11] claims that George Pretyman, Pitt's Cambridge tutor, 'largely pulled the strings on the ecclesiatical stage' from 1787 to Pitt's death (p. 220).
3. Rutt, XIX pp. 114–15.
4. Rutt, XIX p. 117.
5. Rutt, XIX p. 117.
6. Rutt, XIX p. 118. Priestley's footnote refers us to 29 Car. II c. 9 'An Act for taking away the writ *De Haeretico Comburendo*'.
7. Rutt, XIX pp. 118–19.
8. Rutt, XIX p. 119.
9. Rutt, XIX p. 121.
10. Rutt, XIX p. 121.
11. Rutt, XIX pp. 122–3.
12. Rutt, XIX p.127.
13. Rutt, XIX p. 128. For the Cambridge campaign against subscription *see* Chapter 2.
14. Rutt, XIX pp. 131–2.
15. Rutt, p. 134.
16. *Appeal* [Intro. 26] in Rutt, XIX p. 368.
17. Rutt, XIX p. 369.
18. For the 1789 and 1790 parliamentary debates *see* introductory chapter.
19. GM 60 (May 1790) p. 425.
20. *Free Inquiry* [Intro. 36] pp. 40–1.
21. *Debate* [Intro. 14] p. 58.
22. J. Priestley, *Letters to the Rev. Edward Burn, of St Mary's Chapel, Birmingham, in Answer to his Letters on the Infallibility of the Apostolic Testimony concerning the Person of Christ* (Birmingham, 1790) in Rutt, XIX p. 311.
23. *Appeal*, in Rutt, XIX p. 357.
24. Rutt, XIX pp. 356–7n.
25. T. Sherlock, *Vindication of the Corporation and Test Acts . . .* (1732), reissued 1787 as *Bishop Sherlock's Arguments against a repeal of the Corporation and Test Acts . . .*
26. *See* [4.23].
27. G. Walker, *The Dissenter's Plea; or the Appeal of the Dissenters to the Justice, Honour and Religion of the Kingdom* (Birmingham, 1790) p. 3.
28. G. Wakefield, *Memoirs of the Life of Gilbert Wakefield*, 2 vols (1804) I pp. 227–8.
29. *Arranged Catalogue* [4.22].
30. *Sermon before the Lord Mayor* [2.27] p. 55.
31. J. Gifford, *History of the Political Life of the Right Honourable William Pitt including some Account of the Times in which he lived*, 3 vols (Cadell & Davies, 1809) II p. 95.
32. Gifford, II p. 83.
33. Gifford, II pp. 637–8.
34. Gifford, II pp. 91–2.
35. Gifford, II pp. 41, 43.
36. Gifford, II p. 98.

37. AJR V (Jan. 1800) pp. 3–4.
38. Archbishop Moore to Pitt, 19 January 1792 in J. Mori, *William Pitt and the French Revolution 1785–1795* (Keele University Press, 1997) p. 38. Mori argues that Pitt 'at heart, had no real objections to test repeal'.
39. M. Fitzpatrick, 'The Enlightenment, politics and providence: some Scottish and English Comparisons' in Haakonssen [4.9] p. 86.
40. Enfield's preface to *Exercises in elocution; selected from various authors and arranged under proper heads: intended as a sequel to a work entitled The Speaker* (Johnson, 1787). The work went through 25 editions in various forms between 1774 and 1814. For Enfield and the French Revolution *see* Chapter 14.

8 Challenging Burke

1. AR IX (Jan. 1791) pp. 73–6; MR n.s. IV (Apr. 1791) p. 425.
2. J. Priestley, *Letters to the Right Hon, Edmund Burke, occasioned by his Reflections on the Revolution in France...* (Birmingham, 1791) in Rutt, XXII p. 147.
3. For Burke on the 1688 Revolution *see* his *Reflections on the Revolution in France, and on the Proceedings in certain Societies in London relative to that event...* (Dent Everyman, 1910) pp. 14–32. Burke's executors claimed that he had been consistent in his principles since the 1750s. *See* J. C. D. Clark's critical edition of *Reflections* [Intro. 41] p. 29.
4. *Letters to Burke* in Rutt, XXII p. 149.
5. Rutt, XXII pp. 152–3.
6. Rutt, XXII pp. 156–7.
7. Rutt, XXII pp. 159–60.
8. Rutt, XXII p. 162.
9. Rutt, XXII p. 168.
10. Rutt, XXII pp. 168–9.
11. Rutt, XXII p. 169. The third of Price's fundamental rights, stated in his *Discourse on the Love of our Country* [5.10] had been: 'The right to choose our own governors, to cashier them for misconduct; and to form a government for ourselves.'
12. Rutt, XXII p. 171.
13. Rutt, XXII p. 181.
14. *Appeal* [Intro. 26] in Rutt XIX p. 388.
15. Priestley, *Fast Sermon* (1793) [3.7] in Rutt, XV p. 497
16. J. Priestley, *Essay on the First Principles of Government and on the Nature of political, civil and religious Liberty* (1768; 2nd edn 1771) in Rutt, XXII p. 11.
17. Rutt, XXII p. 18.
18. Rutt, XXII p. 16.
19. Rutt, XXII pp. 23, 25.
20. Rutt, XXII p. 26. Adams in his *Defence of the Constitutions of Government of the United States of America against the attack of M. Turgot in his Letter to Dr Price...* 3 vols (1794) wrote (I p. 208): 'The constitution of England is in truth a republic, and has ever been so considered by foreigners, and by the most learned and Enlightened Englishmen.'
21. Rutt, XXII pp. 26–8.
22. Rutt, XXII p. 30.

23. Rutt, XXII p. 34.
24. Rutt, XXII p. 37.
25. Rutt, XXII p. 55.
26. Rutt, XXII p. 60.
27. Rutt, XXII p. 62.
28. *Letters to Burke* in Rutt XXII p. 147.
29. Rutt, XXII pp. 186–7.
30. Rutt, XXII p. 190.
31. Rutt, XXII p. 193.
32. Rutt, XXII p. 224.
33. Rutt, XXII p. 229.
34. Rutt, XXII p. 230.
35. Rutt, XXII pp. 231–2.
36. Rutt, XXII p. 236.
37. Rutt, XXII p. 237.
38. Wollstonecraft agreed with Christie that the constitution of the *ancient regime* was beyond repair. *See Vindication of the Rights of Men in a Letter to the Right Honourable Edmund Burke* (Johnson, 1790) p. 94.
39. C. Lofft, *Remarks on the Letter of the Right Hon. Edmund Burke, concerning the Revolution in France* ... (Johnson, 1790) in CR 70 (Dec. 1790) pp. 685–6.
40. MR IV (Mar. 1791) p. 266.
41. MR IV (Mar. 1791) pp. 267–8n.
42. MR IV (Mar. 1791) p. 272.
43. MR IV (Mar. 1791) p. 346.
44. J. Towers, *Thoughts on the Commencement of a New Parliament, with an Appendix, containing Remarks on the Letter of the Rt Hon. Mr Burke on the Revolution in France* (Dilly, 1790) in AR VIII (Dec. 1790) p. 430.
45. *Thoughts* in Rutt, XXII p. 196n.
46. *Thoughts* in AR VIII (Dec. 1790) p. 430.
47. *Thoughts* in *Political Writings of the 1790s* ed. G. Claeys, 8 vols (Pickering & Chatto,1995) I p. 115.
48. Claeys, I p. 88.
49. [A. L. Barbauld *nee* Aikin], *Address to the Opposers of the Repeal of the Corporation and Test Acts* (Johnson, 1790) in L. Barbauld, *Works of Anna Laetitia Barbauld, with a Memoir,* 2 vols (Longman etc., 1825) p. 362. The *Address* was directed against the bishops rather than against Burke, but the concluding paragraphs give a resounding endorsement of the French Revolution (pp. 374–7). For Barbauld's Unitariansim as reflected in her poetry *see* Jonathan Wordsworth's introduction to her *Poems* (Oxford and New York: Woodstock Books, 1993).

9 Campaigning for Peace

1. W. Frend, *Peace and Union recommended to the Associated Bodies of Republicans and Anti-republicans* (St Ives, 1793) republished in facsimile with introduction by Jonathan Wordsworth (Oxford and New York: Woodstock Books, 1991) p. 49.
2. *Peace and Union,* p. 48.

3. *Peace and Union,* p. 49.
4. *Peace and Union,* p. 45.
5. *Peace and Union,* pp. 45–6.
6. *Peace and Union,* pp. 1–2.
7. *Peace and Union,* pp. 3–5.
8. *Peace and Union,* pp. 6–11.
9. *Peace and Union,* pp. 15–16.
10. *Peace and Union,* pp. 16–23.
11. *Peace and Union,* pp. 26–7.
12. *Peace and Union,* pp. 36, 40.
13. *Account of the Proceedings in the University of Cambridge against William Frend, MA* (Cambridge, 1793) p. x.
14. MR n.s. XII (Nov. 1793) pp. 353–4.
15. A. L. Barbauld, *Sins of Government, Sins of the Nation; or A Discourse for the Fast appointed on 19 April 1793* (Johnson, 1793) in *Works* [8.49] II p. 389.
16. *Works,* II pp. 410–11.
17. *Works,* II p. 386.
18. *Works,* II pp. 400–1.
19. *Works,* II pp. 401–2.
20. *Works,* II pp. 397–8.
21. *Works,* II pp. 403–5.
22. [B. Vaughan], *Letters on the Subject of the Concert of Princes, and the Dismemberment of Poland and France, by a Calm Observer* (Robinsons, 1793).
23. MR XII (Sep. 1793) p. 78.
24. MR XII (Sep. 1793) pp. 79–81.
25. *Concert of Princes,* p. 203.
26. Jasper Wilson [J. Currie], *Letter, commercial and political, Addressed to the Right Hon. William Pitt; in which the real Interests of Britain in the present Crisis are considered, and some Observations are offered on the general State of Europe* (Robinsons, 1793). *See* AR XVI (July 1793) p. 323.
27. W (17 March 1796) in *Collected Works* [see abbreviations] II pp. 108–9 and in MP (9 March 1796).
28. W (1 March 1796) in *Collected Works* II pp. 16–22.
29. S. T. Coleridge, *Conciones ad populum. Or Addresses to the People* (1795) in J. Morrow, *Coleridge's Writings on Politics and Society* (Princeton: Princeton University Press, 1991) p. 37. For Coleridge's Bristol lectures *see* Chapter 12, and S. Andrews 'Coleridge, Bristol and Revolution' in *Coleridge Bulletin* 7 (Spring 1996) pp. 2–29.
30. W (9 Mar. 1796) in *Collected Works* II pp. 52–3.
31. *Isaiah* 53 in *Collected Works* II p. 55.
32. *See* Andrews [3.12] Chapter 7.
33. G. Dyer, *Complaints of the Poor People of England . . .* (Ridgway, 1793) p. iv.
34. MR XIII (Jan. 1794) p. 75.
35. *Complaints of the Poor* in MR XIII pp. 75–6.
36. *Complaints,* p. 5.
37. MR XIII p. 77.
38. *Complaints,* p. 101.
39. *Complaints,* pp. 131–5, 114, 118, 129–30.
40. S. T. Coleridge, *Religious Musings* [3.14].

41. *Catalogue of Books distributed by the Unitarian Society, for Promoting Christian Knowledge and Virtue,* bound in Bristol Reference Library's *Letters and Sermons* containing T. Belsham's, *Letters addressed to the Right Reverend the Lord Bishop of London in Vindication of the Unitarians* (Rowland Hunter, 1815).
42. R. Garnham, *Outline of a Commentary on Revelations XI: 1–14* (Johnson, 1794) pp. 11, 11n.

10 National Networks

1. W. Frend, *Peace and Union* [9.1] pp. 31–2.
2. Priestley to Turner 19 February 1774 in Rutt, I. 1. p. 224.
3. *See* J. E. Bradley, 'Anti-catholicism as Anglican anticlericalism: Nonconformity and the ideological origins of radical disaffection' in *Anticlericalism in Britain* eds N. Aston and M. Cragoe (Stroud: Sutton, 2000).
4. P. Furneaux, *Letters to the Honourable Mr Justice Blackstone concerning his Exposition of the Act of Toleration* (Cadell, 1770) p. 54.
5. 10 June 1772 in *Minute Books of the General Body of Ministers of the Three Denominations in and about the Cities of London and Westminster* II pp. 154–5.
6. *Candid Thoughts on the late Application of Some Dissenting Ministers to Parliament... by an Orthodox Dissenter* (1772) in Barlow [Intro. 7] p. 183.
7. *Vindication* [5.1] pp. 16, 63.
8. *See* Barlow [Intro. 7] p. 208n.
9. *See* Barlow, pp. 221–2.
10. *Life of Pitt* [7.31] I p. 548.
11. *Life of Pitt,* I p. 551.
12. T. Jervis, *Sermon, occasioned by the Death of Joseph Towers, LLD delivered at Newington-Green, June 2nd 1799* (Johnson, 1799) p. 35.
13. J.Towers, *Observations on Mr Hume's History of England* (Robinsons, 1778), pp. 74–5, 84.
14. *Observations,* pp. 91–2.
15. J. Tucker, *Treatise Concerning Civil Government* (1781) p. 30; J. Towers, *Vindication of the Political Principles of Mr Locke in Answer to the Objections of the Revd Dr Tucker, Dean of Gloucester* (1782) p. 96. *See also* Graham [4.15] I pp. 27–9.
16. Henriques [Intro. 6] pp. 63–4.
17. E. Jeffries, DWL MS.
18. *See* Barlow, pp. 281–2.
19. Ditchfield [4.9] pp. 259–60.
20. Tayleur to Lindsey, 26 February 1784 in Ditchfield, p. 261.
21. Ditchfield, p. 263.
22. Lindsey to Tayleur, 24 December 1790 in Ditchfield, p. 264.
23. *Catalogue* [9.41].
24. Lindsey to Tayleur, 9 February 1791 in Ditchfield p. 267.
25. Ditchfield, pp. 270–6.
26. *Reflections* [8.3] p. 3.
27. AR VIII (Dec. 1790) p. 429.
28. Ditchfield [4.9] p. 332.
29. *Appeal* [Intro. 26] in Rutt, XIX p. 437.

30. Lindsey to Tayleur, 27 June 1791 in McLachlan [Intro. 19] p. 16.
31. *Reflections* [Intro. 41] p. 56.
32. *See* J. C. D. Clark, *English Society 1688–1832: Religion, ideology and politics during the ancien regime* (Cambridge: Cambridge University Press, 1985).
33. J. Disney, *Memoirs of Thomas Brand Hollis Esq. FRS and SA* (Gillet, 1808) p. 14.
34. Towers to Wyvill, 2 August 1794 in Graham, II p. 638.
35. Graham [4.15] II p. 638.
36. A. Wharam, *The Treason Trials, 1794* (Leicester and London: Leicester University Press, 1992) p. 227.
37. M. R. Watts, *The Dissenters II: The Expansion of Evangelical Nonconformity* (Oxford: Clarendon Press, 1995), p. 350.
38. R. Hall, *Apology for the Freedom of the Press, and for General Liberty* (Robinsons, 1793) pp. 105–6.
39. Whelan [2.33] p. 44. For Hall, and other examples of retreat from political radicalism *see* Watts, II pp. 356–7. For combined Dissenting opposition to Sidmouth's Bill of 1811 *see* Chapter 15.
40. Watts, II pp. 397–8.
41. McLachlan, p. 18.
42. Ditchfield, pp. 287–9.

11 Midlands and the North

1. Coleridge to Josiah Wade, [18] January 1796 in *Collected Letters of Samuel Taylor Coleridge* ed. E. L. Griggs, 6 vols (Oxford: Oxford University Press, 1956) I p. 176; J. Edwards, *Discourse on Friday 19 April 1793* (1793) pp. iv–v.
2. P. Magnuson, 'Coleridge and the *Watchman* Subscribers' in *Coleridge Bulletin* n.s. XII (Winter, 1999).
3. Coleridge to Wade, [2 February] 1796 and to Edwards, [29 January 1796] in *Collected Letters*, I pp. 179–80.
4. Bradley [2.4] p. 189. For Bradley on Walker *see* pp. 131–3.
5. G. Walker, *Duty and Character of a National Soldier* in G. W., *Sermons on Various Subjects* 4 vols (Johnson, 1808) II p. 431.
6. *Dissenters' Plea* [7.27], p. 3.
7. *Dissenters' Plea*, p. 23.
8. *See* M. I. Thomis, *Old Nottingham* (Newton Abbot: David & Charles, 1968) pp. 103–4.
9. The petition was rejected on the grounds that it contained expressions disrespectful to the House and irreverent to the constitution. *See* E. C. Black, *The Association: British ExtraParliamentary Political Organization 1769–1793* (Harvard University Press, 1963) p. 256.
10. J. Bowles, *Thoughts on the Late General Election as demonstrative of the Progress of Jacobinism* (Rivington, 1802). For an account of the 1802 election in Nottingham *see* Thomis Chapter 6.
11. For resolutions *see* appendix to S. Madan, *Principal claims of the Dissenters considered, in a Sermon preached in Birmingham, on the 14th of February 1790*... (Birmingham, 1790).
12. *See* Wyvill to Shore, 28 May 1792 in Graham [4.15] I p. 86; and Lindsey to Tayleur, 15 February 1792 in McLachlan [Intro. 24], p. 132.

13. SR 28 December 1792. For the abridged Locke *see* MR XVIII (Sep. 1795) p. 104.
14. SR 28 December 1792.
15. SR 4 January 1793.
16. Graham, I pp. 451–2.
17. *Patriot* I (20 Mar. 1792) p. 10.
18. Graham, II p. 596.
19. SR 27 June 1794.
20. B. Naylor, *Right and Duty of Defensive War. A sermon preached . . . on the 19th October, 1803, being a day recommended by Government for a national fast. To which is added, An Appendix, containing some observations on the French preparations for invasion* (Sheffield [1803]).
21. Kenrick to Wodrow, 28 June 1794 and 18 October 1794 in Graham, II pp. 583, 635.
22. In 1796, 1807 and 1812. Darwin's daughter-in-law (Charles Darwin's mother) was a Unitarian.
23. *See* Graham (Appendix) for full text of Derby Address.
24. *Derby Mercury* (3 December 1795).
25. Coleridge to Wade, 27 January 1796 in *Collected Letters* I p. 99.
26. Coleridge to Thelwall, 6 February 1797 in *Collected Letters* I p. 176.
27. 'Address to Dr Priestley. Agreed upon at a Meeting of the Philosophical Society at Derby Sept. 3, 1791' in *Letters of Erasmus Darwin* ed. D. King-Hele (Cambridge: Cambridge University Press, 1981) p. 216.
28. Priestley to Lindsey, 12 March 1790 in Rutt, I.2. p. 52.
29. Priestley to Lindsey, 23 February 1791 in Rutt, I.2. p. 103.
30. Priestley to Russell, 29 July 1791 in Rutt, I.2. p. 125.
31. Rutt, XIX pp. 545–8. Russell noted 'three elegant emblematic pieces of sculpture' in the room: 'The central piece was a finely executed medallion of His Majesty, encircled with a glory, on each side of which was an alabaster obelisk; the one exhibiting Gallic liberty breaking the bonds of despotism, and the other representing British liberty in its present enjoyment.'
32. Priestley to J. Toulmin, 7 October 1791 in Rutt, I.2. p. 164.
33. Rutt, I.2. p. 130; Rutt cites other letters of condolence; pp. 133–49, 151–60, 179–80.
34. Priestley to Lindsey, 30 August 1791 in Rutt, I.2. p. 149.
35. J. Money, 'Birmingham and the West Midlands 1760–1793: politics and regional identity in the English provinces in the later eighteenth century' in ed. P. Borsay, *The Eighteenth Century Town: A Reader in English Urban History, 1688–1820* (London and New York, 1990) p. 224.
36. Money, p. 268.
37. Graham, II p. 724.
38. Other intended recipients were: Cambridge (400), Canterbury (150), Exeter (200), Glasgow (400), Great Yarmouth (250), Norwich (1200), Portsmouth (100), Royston (200), Taunton (100). In addition, Joyce was to receive 100 and Johnson 700 for general distribution. *See* Graham, I p. 325n. Of nine individually identified recipients, six were Unitarians or their close associates.
39. *Memoirs* [1.7] II p. 354. *See* D. Malone, *Public Life of Thomas Cooper, 1783–1839* (Newhaven: Yale University press, 1926) p. 14. For echoes of Priestley's

materialistic and Socinian theology *see* T. Cooper, *Tracts, Ethical, Theological and Political* (1789).

40. T. Cooper, *Reply to Mr Burke's invective against Mr Cooper and Mr Watt, in the House of Commons on the 30th April, 1792* (Manchester, 1792) pp. 97–8.
41. *Reply to Burke*, pp. 9–11.
42. T. Cooper, *Letters on the Slave Trade* (Manchester, 1787). Brissot founded *Les Amis des Noirs* in 1788.
43. PH XXVIII (2 Mar. 1790) pp. 437–8.
44. T. Walker, *Review of Some Political Events which have occurred in Manchester during the last Five Years* (1794) p. 126.
45. *See* Graham, I pp. 150–3
46. Claeys [8.47] III pp. 403–4. *See also* Graham, I pp. 422–6.
47. *Manchester Herald* (15 Sep. 1792).
48. *Political Events*, p. 55.
49. For full text of Address dated 10 December 1792 *see* Graham, II pp. 937–40.
50. Cooper to Watt Jr, 18 July 1794 in Graham, II p. 603. For the trial *see* Malone p. 69 and Wharam, pp. 123–5.
51. On O'Coigly and United Englishmen *see* Graham, II pp. 813–17, 821–6, 876; on wearing of cockades *see also* Malone, pp. 29–30.
52. Coleridge to George Coleridge [March 1798] in Samuel Taylor Coleridge: Selected Letters ed. H. J. Jackson (Oxford and New York: Oxford University Press, 1988) pp. 69–70

12 Norwich, Bristol and the South West

1. *Journal of John Wesley* [5.20] III p. 315.
2. W. James, *Memoir of Thomas Madge, late Minister of Essex Street Chapel, London* (Longman, 1871) pp. 41–2.
3. W. Turner Jr, *Lives of Eminent Unitarians; with a Notice of Dissenting Academies*, 2 vols (Unitarian Association, 1840) I p. 308.
4. *Eminent Unitarians*, I pp. 320–1.
5. *Dr Rigby's Letters from France* ed. Lady Elizabeth Eastlake (Longman, 1880) p. 28.
6. MRep XXI (Aug. 1826) p. 486.
7. R. Dinmore, *Exposition of the principles of the English Jacobins; with Strictures on the political Conduct of Charles James Fox, William Pitt, and Edmund Burke; including Remarks on the Resignation of George Washington* (Norwich and London, 1796) in AR XXV (Jan. 1797) pp. 85–6.
8. J. W. Robberds, *Memoir of the Life and Writings of the late William Taylor*, 2 vols (Murray, 1843) I pp. 67–8.
9. C. B. Jewson, *Jacobin City: a Portrait of Norwich in its Reaction to the French Revolution, 1788–1802* (Glasgow, 1975) p. 56.
10. For frequent contributions by William Taylor Jr to MR (from 1793) and MMG (from 1796) *see* Chapter 14.
11. Jewson, p. 64.
12. Jewson, pp. 68–9.
13. Bradley [2.4], p. 392.
14. Sir Thomas Baker, *Memorials of a Dissenting Chapel, its Foundation and worthies* (London and Manchester, 1884) pp. 41–2.

15. W. Enfield, *Principles and Duty of Protestant Dissenters considered in a Sermon preached at the Ordination of the Rev. John Prior Estlin, at Lewin's Mead, Bristol, 5 August 1778* (Dilly, 1778) p. 1.
16. *Principles and Duty*, p. 8.
17. W. Enfield, *Sermon on the Centennial Commemoration of the Revolution, preached at Norwich, 5 November 1788* (Johnson, 1788) pp. 9–10.
18. Enfield to Roscoe, 1 January 1793, lamenting that the 'cause of freedom' is 'everywhere in discredit'. *See* Graham [4.15] I p. 460. For Enfield's contributions to MR *see* Chapter 14.
19. Jewson, p. 107.
20. John Hookham Frere, friend of Canning, had assisted with AJW in 1797–8. For Fellowes *see* AJR XI (Feb. and Apr. 1802) pp. 220–2, 434.
21. Richard Champion to Burke, 14 January 1775. *See* P. Underdown, 'Bristol and Burke' in *Bristol in the Eighteenth Century* ed. P. McGrath (Newton Abbot: David and Charles, 1972) p. 54.
22. McGrath, pp. 55–9.
23. P. Marshall, 'The Anti-Slave Trade Movement in Bristol' in McGrath pp. 188–94.
24. A. L. Barbauld, 'Memoir of the late J. P. Estlin, LL. D.' prefixed to J. P. Estlin, *Familiar Lectures on Moral Philosophy*, 2 vols (Longman, 1818) p. xxx.
25. *Memoir*, p. xix. *See also* Estlin, *Evidences of Revealed religion and particularly Christianity Stated with reference to a Pamphlet entitled The Age of Reason; in a Discourse delivered at the Chapel in Lewin's-Mead Bristol, 25 December 1795, and, with Omissions, in Essex-Street, London, 17 January 1796* (Bristol, Cottle; London, Johnson; both 1796); *Apology for the Sabbath* (Bristol 1801) and *Nature and Causes of Atheism pointed out in a Discourse delivered at the Chapel in Lewin's Mead . . .* (Bristol and London, 1797).
26. *Familiar Lectures*, I pp. viii, 1.
27. *Familiar Lectures*, II pp. 3–5.
28. *Familiar Lectures*, II pp. 321–2.
29. *Familiar Lectures*, II pp. 316–17.
30. Priestley to Estlin, 18 February 1792 in Rutt, I.2. pp. 181–2.
31. *List of the Members of the Society of Unitarian Christians in the West of England* (Bridport [1805]). As early as 1774 Thomas Belsham wrote to his mother that at Bridport 'they have introduced a kind of Anti-Test, for no man is admitted a member of the Corporation who is not a Dissenter'. For Bridport's first Unitarian minister *see* B. Short, *Respectable Society: Bridport 1593–1835* (Bradford-on-Avon, 1976).
32. *See* T. Whelan, 'Joseph Cottle the Baptist' in *Charles Lamb Bulletin* 111 (July 2000).
33. J. Cottle, *Early Recollections of Samuel Taylor Coleridge*, 2 vols (Longman etc., 1837–8) I p. 277. On the financing of Coleridge's Bristol lectures *see* Coleridge, *Collected Works* [see abbreviations] I p. xxv.
34. Reprinted in *600 Years of Bristol Poetry* ed. R. E. Morris (Bristol, 1973).
35. Coleridge to Estlin [16 Jan. 1798] in *Collected Letters* I p. 372. *See also* [11.52].
36. Bradley [2.4] p. 359.
37. J. Toulmin, *History of Taunton. A new edition greatly enlarged and brought down to the present time by James Savage* (Taunton and London, 1822) p. 555,

quoting Sir Brooke Boothby, *Letter to the Right Hon. Edmund Burke* (Debrett, 1791). Toulmin's 1791 edition is entitled *History of the Town of Taunton in the County of Somerset.*
38. J. Toulmin, *Memoirs of the life, character, sentiments and worship of Faustus Socinus* (1777). For Priestley's encouragement of the project *see* p. 30.
39. J. Toulmin, *Conduct of the First Converts to Christianity Considered and Applied in a Sermon preached at Bridport on the 10th July, 1788* . . . (Bridport, Exeter and London, 1788).
40. Brand Hollis to Adams, 18 February 1793 in Graham, II p. 503.
41. London Revolution Society Minutes (10 July 1790).
42. Graham, I pp. 325–6n.
43. *Application to Parliament* [2.37] p. 8; *Considerations on the Present State of the Church of England* (1779) p. 46. *See also* Toulmin, *Letter to the Bishops on the application . . . for a repeal of the Corporation and Test Acts* . . . (Johnson, 1789).
44. J. Toulmin, *The American War lamented. A Sermon preached at Taunton, February 18th and 25th 1776* (Johnson, 1776) pp. 3–8.
45. *See* Bradley, pp. 351–5.
46. *American War*, p. 19.
47. *Record of Unitarian Worthies* [1876] p. 44.

13 Scottish Convict, Irish Exile

1. *Autobiography of Archibald Hamilton Rowan* ed. W. H. Drummond (Dublin, 1840) in facsimile edition with introduction by R. B. McDowell (Shannon: Irish University Press, 1972) p. 180.
2. W. Turner [Jr], *Lives of Eminent Unitarians; with a Notice of Dissenting Academies*, 2 vols (Unitarian Association, 1840) II pp. 218–19.
3. Turner, II p. 215n.
4. *Unitarian Worthies* [12.47] pp. 232–3.
5. Turner, II p. 220.
6. Ditchfield [4.9] p. 348.
7. Millar to Lindsey, January 1804, DWL MS.
8. Millar to Lindsey, 4 December 1790, DWL MS.
9. Ditchfield, p. 353.
10. T. F. Palmer, *Narrative of the Sufferings of T. F. Palmer and W. Skirving during a voyage to New South Wales, 1794, on board the Surprise Transport* 2nd edn (Cambridge etc. and London, 1797).
11. Millar to Lindsey, 18 June 1791, DWL MS.
12. TRep V p. 180.
13. TRep VI p. 105.
14. *Complete Collection of State Trials* ed. T. B. and T. J. Howell 30 vols (1809–28) XXIII p. 325.
15. Turner, II p. 226.
16. *Trial of the Rev. Thomas Fyshe Palmer before the Circuit Court of Justiciary held at Perth on the 12th and 13th September 1793* . . . (Edinburgh etc. and London, 1793) p. 5.
17. *Trial of Palmer*, pp. 7–9.
18. *See* Graham [4.15] II pp. 546–7.

19. Turner, II p. 228. *Cambridge Intelligencer* (28 September 1793) printed Palmer's speech before sentence.
20. *Trial of Palmer*, p. 160.
21. Lindsey to Millar, 13 January 1794, DWL MS.
22. Turner, II p. 232.
23. Palmer, *Narrative*, p. xi.
24. Millar to Lindsey, January 1804, DWL MS.
25. Turner, II p. 237.
26. Turner, II p. 238.
27. MRep VI (1811) p. 121.
28. Rowan, *Autobiography*, pp. 16–17.
29. *Bible Christian* (Apr. 1834) in *Autobiography*, p. 444.
30. *Bible Christian* (Dec. 1834) in *Autobiography*, p. 451.
31. *See* Rowan, *Autobiography*, p. 45 and *Unitarian Worthies*, p. 45.
32. Jebb to Rowan, 5 March 1785 in *Autobiography* pp. 127–9. *See also* pp. 129–33. Cartwright campaigned for annual parliaments, universal manhood suffrage and equal electoral districts.
33. *Autobiography*, p. 113.
34. *Autobiography*, pp. 117–18.
35. *Autobiography*, p. 148.
36. *Autobiography*, p. 149.
37. The National Guard seems to have enrolled only '200 select men' instead of its target figure of 6000–10 000. *See* N. J. Curtin, *The United Irishmen: popular politics in Ulster and Dublin, 1791–1798* (Oxford: Clarendon Press, 1994) p. 52.
38. *Autobiography*, p. 156.
39. *Autobiography*, p. 157.
40. *Autobiography*, p. 159.
41. R. Musgrave, *Memoirs of the different Rebellions in Ireland, from the Arrival of the English: also a particular Detail of that which broke out the 23rd May, 1798; with the History of the Conspiracy which preceded it* (London, Stockdale; Dublin, Milliken; both 1801). *See also* M. Elliott, *Partners in revolution: the United Irishmen and France* (Newhaven: Yale University Press, 1982).
42. *Full Report of the Trial of... A. H. Rowan... for having published a Seditious Libel* (Perth, 1794) pp. 8–12.
43. Rowan to Sarah Anne Rowan, 10 January 1799, and to Hamilton, January 1799 in *Autobiography*, p. 340.
44. *Autobiography*, pp. 193–5.
45. But *see* Curtin (n. 38) and K. Whelan, *Tree of Liberty: Radicalism, Catholicism and the Construction of Irish Identity 1760–1830* (Cork: Cork University Press, 1996).
46. *Autobiography*, pp. 202–3.
47. *Autobiography*, p. 248.
48. *Autobiography*, p. 354.
49. Rowan to Sarah Anne Rowan, 28 October 1795 in *Autobiography*, p. 290.
50. *Autobiography*, p. 279.
51. Curtin, pp. 285–6.
52. Lord Camden to Portland, 17 June 1796 in K. Whelan, p. 113.
53. *Autobiography*, p. 382.

14 'Jacobin' Journalism

1. AJR I (July–Dec. 1798) pp. 2–3.
2. T. Christie, *Miscellanies, Philosophical, Medical and Moral* (Johnson, 1789).
3. T. Christie, *Letters on the Revolution in France . . . occasioned by the Publications of the Right Honourable Edmund Burke, MP* and Alexandre de Calonne . . . Part I (Johnson, 1791).
4. CR XXXVII (1774) p. 49. For Lindsey's *Apology see* Chapter 4.
5. T. Belsham, *Memoirs of Lindsey* [3.17] pp. 108–9.
6. *Arranged Catalogue* [4.22] in AR VII (July 1790) pp. 337–9.
7. *See* G. P. Tyson, *Joseph Johnson: A Liberal Publisher* (Iowa City: University of Iowa Press, 1979) pp. 35–7.
8. G. Wakefield, *Translation of the Gospel of Matthew, with copious Notes, critical, philological and explanatory* (Warrington, 1782).
9. G. Wakefield, *Translation of the New Testament,* 3 vols (Deighton, 1791) and *Memoirs of the Life of Gilbert Wakefield. Written by Himself* (Deighton, 1792).
10. G. Wakefield, *The Spirit of Christianity compared with the Spirit of the Times in Great Britain,* 3rd edn (Kearsley, 1794) p. 39.
11. *Spirit of Christianity,* p. 10.
12. *Spirit of Christianity,* p. 25.
13. *Spirit of Christianity,* pp. 26–7.
14. *Spirit of Christianity,* p. 28.
15. *Spirit of Christianity,* p. 11n.
16. *Spirit of Christianity,* p. iii.
17. G. Wakefield, *Reply to some Parts of the Bishop of Llandaff's Address to the People of Great Britain* (Cuthell, 1798) p. 6.
18. *Reply,* p. 7.
19. *Reply,* pp. 21–3.
20. *Reply,* p. 35.
21. MR XXV (Mar. 1798) p. 315.
22. W. Turner, *Eminent Unitarians* [13.2] II p. 273.
23. *Memoirs of the Life of Gilbert Wakefield,* 2 vols (Johnson, 1804) II p. 325.
24. Tyson, pp. 159–61. *See also* P. Magnuson, *Reading Public Romanticism* (Princeton: Princeton University Press, 1998) p. 68.
25. GM 79 (1809) p. 1167.
26. *Sheffield Register* (25 January 1793).
27. AJR I (Aug. 1798) pp. 198–200. *See* Hall [10.38]. For the government's deliberate targeting of booksellers and editors in the mid-1790s *see* Graham [4.15] especially II pp. 654–7.
28. *Cambridge Intelligencer* (20 July 1793).
29. Priestley to Lindsey, 20 December 1794 in Rutt, I.2. p. 285.
30. *Cambridge Intelligencer* (25 June 1796).
31. W X (3 May 1796) in *Collected Works,* II p. 374.
32. AJW XXVI (7 May 1798) p. 264.
33. AJR III (July 1799) p. 341.
34. AR XXVI (Oct. 1797) pp. 380–2.
35. AR XIII (June 1792) p. 192.
36. [T. Atkinson], *Oblique View of the Grand Conspiracy against the Social Order* (1798) in Roper, *Reviewing before the Edinburgh, 1788–1802* (Methuen, 1978) p. 181.

37. Roper, pp. 254–60. For Hazlitt'e tribute to Taylor as precursor of the critical style of the *Edinburgh Review see* Robberds [12.8] I p. 127n.
38. MR XXV (Mar. and Apr. 1798); Robberds II pp. 171–2.
39. Griffiths to Taylor, 21 June 1798 in Robberds II pp. 192–3.
40. AJR III (May–Aug. 1799) p. viii.
41. AJR V (Jan. 1800) pp. 71–2. Rogers was nevertheless offered the poet laureateship when Wordsworth died, though he declined it on grounds of age.
42. AJR VIII (Jan. 1801) p. 77.
43. J. Stillingfleet, *National Gratitude enforced in a Sermon, preached in the Cathedral Church of Worcester, on Thursday, 29 November 1798, the Day appointed for a General Thanksgiving* (1798) in CR XXVI (Aug. 1799) p. 468, and AJR IV (Sep. 1799) pp. 112–13.
44. AJR V (Jan. 1800) p. 58.
45. AJR VI (May 1800) p. 89.
46. NANR 1792 (Robinsons, 1793) p. 208.
47. AJR III (Aug. 1799) pp. 462, 467.
48. AJR IV (Sep. 1799) pp. 106–7.
49. AJR V (Jan. 1800) p. 100. From 1801 NANR would side with the government.

15 Confronting Napoleon

1. AJR XI (Jan. 1802) pp. 77–8. For the numerical decline of Unitarians in early nineteenth century *see* Seed [4.9] p. 142n.
2. AJR VIII (Sep. 1800) p. 80.
3. J. Edwards, *Sermon occasioned by the Death of the late Rev. Dr Joseph Priestley, delivered in the dissenting Chapel in Moinkwell-street on Sunday Evening, 15 April 1804* (1804) in AJR XXI (May 1805) pp. 61–5.
4. AJR XXVI (Feb. 1807) p. 179.
5. *Guilt of Democratic Scheming fully proved against the Dissenters. At the particular request of Mr Parsons, Dissenting Minister, of Leeds. By the Inquirer.* (Hurst, 1802) in AJR XIII (Sep. 1802) p. 68. *See also* AJR XI (Dec. 1801) pp. 428–9.
6. B. Flower, *Reflections on the Preliminary Peace between Great Britain and the French Republic*, 3rd edn [1802] p. vii.
7. Flower, pp. 18–19.
8. Flower, pp. 24–5.
9. Flower, pp. 28–9.
10. AJR XIII (Nov. 1802) p. 328; MMG XIV (Nov. 1802) pp. 350–1.
11. MMG XV (Apr. 1803) p. 271.
12. MMG XVI (Aug. 1803) p. 72. But *see* Cookson, [7.1] pp. 248–9 for MMG's part in peace campaign of 1812–13.
13. NANR 1803 (published 1804) pp. 257, 279.
14. AJR XIX (Oct. 1804) pp. 216–17.
15. B. Naylor, *Right and Duty of Defensive War; a Sermon preached before a Society of Unitarian Dissenters at Sheffield, on the 19th October 1803, being a Day recommended by Government for a National Fast...* (Sheffield, Gales; London, Johnson; both 1803) in AJR XIX (Nov. 1804) p. 312.
16. W. Roscoe, *Considerations on the Causes, Objects and Consequences of the present War, and on the Expediency or the Danger of Peace with France* 2nd edn

(Cadell & Davies, 1808) in AJR XXIX (Feb. 1808) pp. 175, 179. AJR has 'dogstar' for 'daystar'. Roscoe's *Life and Pontificate of Leo the Tenth* was published in 1805.

17. CR XIII (Mar. 1808) pp. 274–9.
18. For a full list of contributors to the first volume *see* R. B. Aspland, *Memoirs of the Life, Works and Correspondence of the Rev. Robert Aspland of Hackney* (Whitfield, 1831) pp. 190–1. Aspland had attracted public notice by his Fast Sermon preached on 19 October 1803, when minister of the Arian congregation at Newport, Isle of Wight.
19. F. Mineka, *Dissidence of Dissent: The Monthly Repository 1806–38. Under the editorship of Robert Aspland, W. J. Fox, R. H. Horne and Leigh Hunt, with a Chapter on Religious Periodicals, 1700–1825* (Chapel Hill: University of North Carolina Press, 1944) p. 103.
20. MRep I (1806) p. vii.
21. MRep I (Jan. 1806) pp. 42–4.
22. MRep I (Mar. 1806) p. 129.
23. MRep III (Feb. 1808) p. 110. The regular 'Monthly Retrospect' was compiled by William Frend.
24. MRep I (July 1806) p. 344.
25. MRep I (Sep. 1806) p. 479.
26. MRep II (Sep. 1807) pp. 502–3.
27. F. D. Kirwan, *Translations of the Parisian Sanhedrin and Causes and Consequences of the French Emperor's Conduct towards the Jews* (Jones 1807) in MRep II (Dec. 1807) pp. 651–2.
28. 'Monthly Retrospect' in MRep III (May 1808) p. 274.
29. MRep III (Oct. 1808) p. 567.
30. *Letter from Mr Whitbread to Lord Holland on the present Situation of Spain* (Ridgway, 1808) in CR XIV (July 1808) pp. 311–12.
31. *Inquiry into the Causes and Consequences of Continental Alienation, written as a Sequel to the Inquiry into the State of the Nation* (Symonds, 1808) in CR XIV (May 1808) p. 41.
32. W. Roscoe, *Remarks on the Proposals made to Great Britain for opening Negotiations for Peace in the Year 1807* (Cadell & Davies, 1808) in CR XIV (July 1808) p. 283.
33. A. Baring, *Inquiry into the Causes and Consequences of the Orders in Council; and an Examination of the Conduct of Great Britain towards the Neutral Commerce of America* in CR XIII (Mar. 1808) pp. 302–3. Lord Sheffield, defending the Orders in Council, designated Baring and Whitbread 'the advocates of American pretensions'.
34. Rathbone to Roscoe [8 Mar. 1808] in Cookson [7.1] p. 223. Cookson observes that the liberal opposition in Liverpool 'was centred on the Unitarian chapels no less than on the American Chamber', and suggests that 'the Liverpool liberals were readier than most to articulate the values and beliefs of their rational Christianity'.
35. The *Athenaeum* tribute is printed in MRep V (Apr. 1809) p. 233.
36. MRep VI (Sep. 1811) p. 527. For AJR's reaction to the Lords defeat of Sidmouth's Bill *see* preface to XXXVIII (1811). For Belsham's interview with Sidmouth *see Memoirs* [4.29] p. 630.
37. Watts [10.37] pp. 369–72.

38. Jervis to Wyvill, 26 February 1812 in Cookson p. 227. For Baines *see* Watts pp. 382–3.
39. PH XXI (1812) 1162–3; *Life and Times of Henry Lord Brougham*, 3 vols (Edinburgh, 1871).
40. H. Roscoe, *Life of William Roscoe*, 2 vols (Edinburgh: Blackwood, 1853) II pp. 26–7. For text of Roscoe's address see *Liverpool Mercury* (20 Mar. 1812).
41. *Liverpool Mercury* (15 May 1812).
42. AJR XXXIX (May 1811) p. 453.
43. AJR XLI (Jan. 1812) p. 196. *See also* pp. 78–81.
44. T. Belsham, *Elements of the Philosophy of the Mind, and of Moral Philosophy. To which is prefixed a Compendium of Logic* (1801) and W. Belsham, *Memoirs of the Reign of George III to the Session of Parliament ending in A.D. 1793*, 4 vols (Robinsons, 1795–1801).
45. AJR XXXIV (Dec. 1809) p. 340.
46. 'Reviewers Reviewed' in AJR XXXII (Feb. 1809) p. 195.
47. AJR XXXI (Sep. 1808) p. 61.
48. AJR XXXV (Mar. 1810) p. 327, and *Dangers of the Edinburgh Review; or a brief exposure of its principles in Religion, Morals and Politics*... (Rivingtons, 1811) in AJR XXXVIII (Feb. 1811) p. 136.
49. MRep VII (Jan. 1812) pp. 32–6.
50. Roper [14.39] p. 24; *Memoir of Aspland* p. 234. AR in its closing years had a circulation of 1500.
51. MRep VII (Aug. 1812) p. 502. For text of Amending Act *see* VII (Sep. 1812) pp. 577–82; and for Dissenters' resolutions expressing gratitude *see* VII (Sep. and Dec. 1812) pp. 654, 753.
52. MRep VIII (July 1813) p. 485. For text of 'An Act to relieve Persons who impugn the Doctrine of the Trinity from certain Penalties' *see* MRep VIII (Aug. 1813) pp. 543–5.
53. AJR XLI (Apr. 1812) p. 358.
54. MRep VII (Apr. 1812) pp. 230–1.
55. MRep VIII (Feb. 1813) pp. 137–8
56. AJR XLV (Nov. 1813) pp. 462, 468.
57. MRep VIII (Jan. 1813) p. 64. For peace petitions of 1812–13 *see* Cookson Chapter 10.

Epilogue: Transatlantic Perspectives

1. J. Currie to J. Currie, 12 July 1793 in W. W. Currie, *Memoir of the Life and Correspondence of James Currie*, 2 vols (1831) II p. 38: and on Pitt, I p. 322.
2. For pamphlets of Price and Priestley defending the colonists *see* Chapter 5; for Unitarian contribution to pro-American protest in the 1770s *see* Seed [4.9].
3. MRep V (1810) p. 306.
4. GM 64 (Supplement) p. 1171.
5. *See* [12.40 and 44].
6. For Priestley's ecstatic reception in New York, the political background to pantisocracy, and Cooper's promotion of emigration *see* Andrews [5.26].

7. Priestley to Belsham, 27 August 1794 in Rutt, I.2. pp. 270–1.
8. Priestley to Belsham, 14 December 1794 in Rutt, I.2. p. 283.
9. Belsham [3.17] p. 388.
10. London, 18 March 1794 in Rutt, I.2. p. 213.
11. Dublin, 28 March 1794 in Rutt, I.2. pp. 218–21.
12. GM 64 (Apr. 1794) pp. 344, 354; *see also* GM 64 (May 1794) pp. 428–30, (Sep. 1794) p. 850 and (Supplement) p. 1171.
13. W. Cobbett, *Observations on the emigration of Dr J. Priestley and on the several addresses delivered to him on his arrival at New York* (Philadelphia and London, 1794), pp. 4, 23, 29; for the New York congratulatory addresses and Priestley's replies *see* H. Wansey, *Journal of an excursion to the United States of North America in the summer of 1794* (Salisbury and London, 1796).
14. Priestley to Lindsey, 30 April 1797 in Rutt, I.2. p. 378.
15. Priestley to Lindsey, 5 July 1794 in Rutt, I.2. p. 270.
16. Priestley to Belsham, 27 August 1794 in Rutt, I.2. p. 272.
17. Priestley to Belsham, 30 August 1795 in Rutt, I.2. p. 316.
18. Priestley to Lindsey, 15 February 1796 in Rutt I.2. p. 332.
19. *Unitarianism explained and defended in a Discourse delivered in the Church of the Universalists at Philadelphia 1796* in Rutt, XVI p. 473.
20. Wansey, 2nd edn (1798) p. 203 in Rutt, XVI p. 3n.
21. Priestley to W. Russell, 22 March 1798 in Rutt I.2. p. 399.
22. S. H. Jeyes, *The Russells of Birmingham in the French Revolution and in America, 1791–1814* (George Allen, 1911) p. 198.
23. Priestley to Lindsey, 12 June 1796 in Rutt I.2. p. 346.
24. Priestley to Lindsey, 6 June 1795, 3 December 1796 and 8 March 1798 in Rutt, I.2. pp. 325, 363, 396.
25. Priestley to Dyer, 4 October 1796 in Rutt, I.2. p. 356.
26. *See* Rutt, XVII p. 8.
27. W. S. Sprague, *Annals of the American Unitarian Pulpit*... (New York, 1865) p. xi.
28. Jeyes, p. 184.
29. Sprague, p. x; Belsham [3.17], p. 153. *See also* MRep VII (March 1812) p. 200.
30. MRep VI (Mar. 1811), pp. 126–38.
31. Jeyes, p. 211.
32. *See* Vaughan [9.22]. He has long entries in both DNB and DAB.
33. Jeyes, pp. 272–5.
34. Jeyes, p. 282.
35. A. H. Rowan to Sarah Rowan, 20 February 1796 in *Autobiography* [13.1], p. 290.
36. A. H. Rowan to Sarah Rowan, 5 November 1797 in *Autobiography*, p. 319.
37. *See Autobiography*, pp. 327–83.
38. A. H. Rowan to Sarah Rowan, 15 March 1799 in *Autobiography*, pp. 341–2.
39. *Autobiography*, pp. 358–9.
40. Editorial note in *Autobiography*, p. 366. For Rowan's return to Ireland *see* Chapter 13.
41. Priestley to Lindsey, 1 January 1803 in Rutt I.2. p. 501, and to G. Logan, in Philadelphia *Aurora* 2 March 1804.

42. Jefferson to J. Smith, 8 December 1822 in *Life and Selected Writings of Thomas Jefferson* ed. A. Koch and W. Peden (New York, 1944) pp. 703–4.
43. Malone [11.39] p. 261.
44. Cited in *Record of Unitarian Worthies* [1876] p. 19.
45. W. E. Channing, *Sermon preached in Boston (America) 5 April 1810, the day of a Public Fast* (Boston and London, 1811) in AJR XL (Nov. 1811), p. 307.

Bibliography

The following titles, though not cited in the text, are recommended for further reading.

Aikin, J. (1790) *Spirit of the Constitution and that of the Church of England Compared.*

Aikin, L. (1823) *Memoir of John Aikin M. D.*, 2 vols.

Bartel, R. (1955) 'The story of public fast days in England', *Anglican Theological Review*, 38.

Belsham, T. (1822) 'A list of students educated at the academy at Daventry', *Monthly Repository*, XVII.

Belsham, T. (1813) *A Plea for the Catholic Claims.*

Belsham, T. (1799) *A Review of Mr Wilberforce's Treatise.*

Belsham, T. (1807) *The Providence of God, Overruling the Issues of War and Conquest. A Sermon Preached at the Chapel in Essex Street,* 25 February, 1807.

Bogue, D. and Bennett, J. (1812–13) *History of the Dissenters from the Revolution in 1688 to the Year 1808*, 4 vols.

Bonwick, C. (1977) *English Radicals and the American Revolution.*

Cartwright, F. D. (ed.) (1826) *Life and Correspondence of Major Cartwright,* 2 vols.

Chandler, G. (1953) *William Roscoe of Liverpool.*

Clive, J. (1957) *Scotch Reviewers: the 'Edinburgh Review' 1802–1815.*

Courtney, J. (1790) *Philosophical Reflections on the Late Revolution in France and the Conduct of the Dissenters in England.*

Coxe, W. (1790) *Letter to the Revd Richard Price.*

Creasy, J. (1966) 'Some Dissenting attitudes towards the French Revolution', *Transactions of the Unitarian Historical Society,* XIII.

Davis, R. W. (1971) *Dissent in Politics, 1780–1830: The Political Life of William Smith M.P.*

Dinwiddy, J. R. (1971) *Christopher Wyvill and Reform 1790–1820* (York, 1971).

Ditchfield, G. M. (1991) 'Anti-Trinitarianism and toleration in eighteenth-century British politics: the Unitarian Petition of 1792' in *Journal of Ecclesiastical History.*

Dyer, G. (1796) *Memoirs of the Life and Writings of Robert Robinson.*

Emsley, C. (1979) *British Society and the French wars 1793–1815.*

Enfield, W. (1785) *Institutes of Natural Philosophy.*

Frend, W. (1804) *Patriotism; or the Love of our Country: an Essay Illustrated by Examples from Ancient and Modern History.*

Frend, W. (1804) *Principles of Taxation: or Contribution According to Means.*

Frend, W. (1795) *Scarcity of Bread. A Plan for Reducing the High Price of this Article. . . .*

Frend, W. (1801) *Effect of Paper Money on the Price of Provisions. . . .*

Frend, W. (1793) *Thoughts on Subscription to Religious Tests, in a Letter to Rev. H. W. Coulthurst.*

Goodwin, A. (1979) *Friends of Liberty: the English Democratic Movement in the Age of the French Revolution.*

Gow, H. (1928) *The Unitarians.*

Graham, J. (1989) 'Revolutionary philosopher: the political ideas of Joseph Priestley (1733–1804)' in *Enlightenment and Dissent*, 8.

Hall, R. (1802) *Reflections on War. A Sermon Preached at the Baptist Meeting, Cambridge on Tuesday 1 June 1802 being the Day of Thanksgiving for a General Peace.*

Holt, R. V. (1938) *Unitarian Contribution to Social Progress in England.*

Horsley, S. (1790) *Review of the 'Case of the Protestant Dissenters'.*

Jardine, D. (1794) *Seasonable Reflexions on Religious Fasts, in a Discourse Delivered April 13, 1794 in the Chapel, Frog Lane, Bath.*

Joyce, J. (1803) *Courage and Union in a Time of National Danger. A Sermon Preached October 19, 1803 at the Unitarian Chapel, Essex Street.*

Knight, F. (1971) *University Rebel: The Life of William Frend.*

Le Breton, A. L. (1874) *Memoir of Mrs Barbauld.* (1808) *Letter to William Roscoe, Containing Strictures on his late Publication Entitled 'Considerations on the Causes, Objects and Consequences of the Present War'.*

Lindsey, T. (1783) *Historical View of the State of the Unitarian Doctrine and Worship.*

Lofft, C. (1790) *History of the Corporation and Test Acts.*

Lofft, C. (1783) *Observations on a Dialogue on the Actual State of Parliament.*

MacEvoy, J. E. and McGuire, J. E. (1975) 'Priestley's way of Rational Dissent' in *Historical Studies in the Physical Sciences*, 5.

McLachlan, H. (1931) *English Education Under the Test Acts.*

McLachlan, H. (1934) *Unitarian Movement in the Religious Life of England.*

Moss, D. J. (1976) 'Birmingham and the campaigns against the Orders-in-Council and East India Company charter 1812–1813', *Canadian Journal of History* XI.

Murphy, M. J. (1977) *Cambridge Newspapers and Opinion, 1780–1830.*

Paine, T. (1794) *Age of Reason*; (1795) *Part II.*

Paley, W. (1774) *Considerations on the Propriety of Requiring a Subscription to Articles of Faith.*

Parker, I. (1914) *Dissenting Academies in England.*

Pearce, S. (1790) *The Oppressive, Unjust and Profane Nature and Tendency of the Corporation and Test Acts.*

[Percival, T.] (1807) *Works, Literary, Moral and Medical of Thomas Percival, M. D.*

[Price, R.] (1983) *Correspondence of Richard Price*, ed. D. O. Thomas and B. Peach.

Rathbone, E. F. (1908) *William Rathbone, a memoir.*

Rees, A. (1790) *Two Sermons Preached at Cambridge on Occasion of the Death of the Reverend Robert Robinson.*

Roscoe, W. (1811) *Letter to Henry Brougham, esq. M. P. on the Subject of Reform in the Representation of the People in Parliament.*

Roscoe, W. (1800) *Occasional Tracts Relative to the War Between Great Britain and France, Written and Published at Different Periods, from the year 1793.*

Sellers, I. (1968) 'William Roscoe, the Roscoe circle and radical politics in Liverpool, 1787–1807', *Transactions of the Historic Society of Lancashire and Cheshire*, 120.

Smith, J. W. A. (1972) *Birth of Modern Education: The Contribution of the Dissenting Academies, 1660–1800.*

Toulmin, J. (1797) *Injustice of Classing Unitarians with Deists and Infidels.*

Toulmin, J. (1802) *Prospect of Future Universal Peace Considered in a Sermon Preached in the Baptist chapel at Taunton.*

Towers, J. (1772) *Dialogue Between two Gentlemen Concerning the late Application to Parliament for Relief in the Matter of Subscription.*

Towers, J. (1769) *Observations on Public Liberty, Patriotism, Ministerial Despotism, and National Grievances.*

Towers, J. (1797) *Thoughts on National Insanity.*

Vaughan, B. (1790) *Collection of Testimonies in Favour of Religious Liberty.*

[Wakefield, G.] (1799) *Address to the Judges on being called up for Judgement, May 30, 1799.*

[Wakefield, G.] (1799) *Defence of Gilbert Wakefield on an Official Information from the Attorney-General for a Reply to the Bishop of Llandaff's Address to the People of Great Britain, on February 21, 1799.*

Wakefield, G. (1794) *Remarks on the General Orders of the Duke of York to his Army on June 7, 1794.*

Ward, W. R. (1972) *Religion and Society in England 1790–1850.*

Wellbeloved, C. (1800) *Principles of Roman Catholics and Unitarians contrasted . . .*

Wesley, J. (1770) *Preservative against unsettled Notions in Religion.*

Wilberforce, W. (1797) *Practical View of the Prevailing System of Professed Christians . . . Contrasted with Real Christianity.*

[Wyvill, C.] (1796) *Correspondence of the Rev. C. W. with the Rt Hon. William Pitt.*

Wyvill, C. (1793) *Defence of Dr Price and the Reformers of England.*

Wyvill, C. (1771) *Thoughts on our Articles of Religion with respect to their Utility to the State.*

Index

Published works (with abbreviated title and date of publication) appear under author's name, *except that*, where there is only a single reference to the author, an asterisk indicates that the title appears in the corresponding endnote. Other exceptions are newspapers, periodicals and anonymous works: these titles appear in alphabetical order of first significant word. Where the page reference is in square brackets, the title or author's name does not appear in the text, but only in the endnote. Only surnames are used in sub-headings, except where confusion might otherwise arise. In addition to abbreviations used in the text, and already listed, the following abbreviations appear in the index: *Unitarian Society for Promoting Knowledge of the Scriptures* (1783) USPKS and *Unitarian Society for Promoting Christian Knowledge and Virtue* (1791) USPCK.